Turn the Dream Into A Reality!

Have you always harbored a dream of working in a foreign country, of adding something special to your career by gaining exposure to new cultures, new ideas, and new people? If so, the time for dreaming is past—it's time to start your international career!

Arthur Bell's *International Careers* gives you a six step method for finding international employment. The system works for seasoned employees considering a job change, those between jobs, and recent graduates looking for a first position. The book's excellent reference section also offers detailed information on:

- U.S. firms that employ internationally

- Foreign employers

- Foreign embassies in the U.S.

- Temporary overseas employment opportunities

- State and Commerce Department assistance

international careers

international careers

Arthur H. Bell, Ph.D.

BOB ADAMS, INC.
PUBLISHERS

Published by Bob Adams, Inc.
260 Center Street Holbrook, MA 02343

ISBN: 1-55850-944-5

Printed in the United States of America.

10   9   8   7   6   5   4   3   2   1

The inclusion of an employer in the listings section in this book does not imply that the employer in question is currently recruiting for any specific position, or that there is any recommendation or endorsement of pursuing employment with that organization.

Contents

Acknowledgements

My sincere thanks to the many international managers, personnel directors, employment recruiters, students and academic colleagues who gave generously of their experience and advice for this book. I am especially grateful for the expert work of my editor, Brandon Toropov, and his associates at Bob Adams, Inc.

Dedication

With love to Louis and Anita Smith.

Chapter One

Taking Aim at the International Workplace

You know where you'd like to be—managing that chic restaurant in Italy . . . learning the London version of investment banking . . . serving as an import/export representative in Tokyo . . . or in Paris, if only for the summer, if only to sweep sidewalks.

But how do you get there?

This book offers a six-step method for finding international employment. These steps apply to seasoned employees considering a job change, those between jobs, and recent graduates looking for a first position.

As you thumb through the book, you'll immediately notice that hundreds of pages are devoted to company, government and association names, addresses, and telephone numbers. These are actual sources you can begin contacting today about international employment. Also listed are commonly available library resources that can speed your search for the right job in the right company in the right country.

But First a Word of Caution

Given the inevitable excitement of the international job search, there's a tendency for authors and readers to fall prey to hype. It's tempting to view the international employment picture as an endless line of benevolent employers, all bidding for your services. Think again: You'll find opportunity abroad, but also some closed doors. It may be tempting to think that each and every address in this book will lead to a warm, interested response and on-the-spot job offer. Not so. You must fit your talents to an international company's needs and often beat the bushes a bit in the process. In short, finding international employment requires the same kind of hard work on your part as finding employment within this country.

How Can This Book Help?

We can save you time, frustration, and a few dead ends by providing you with

- an effective plan for figuring out what kind of international work to seek

- people and agencies who can help you understand the business and social life of other countries—for no cost

- hundreds of names and addresses in dozens of countries for your use in the job application process

- names, addresses, and phone numbers for some of the best language schools in the world

- lists of American companies with foreign branches and, conversely, foreign companies with American branches. It may be possible to apply in person for an international job without leaving your hometown

- step-by-step instructions for developing your international resume and application letter

- a guide to the international interview process—your last and most important hurdle before the job offer. You'll learn the most common questions employers ask and how you can answer effectively.

- a wealth of information on business directories, organization listings, world trade center locations, commercial officers, employment agencies, and cultural information

Why Think International?

Let's begin at the beginning. What gave you the notion to seek employment in Singapore instead of Cincinnati? I asked that question of four U.S. citizens now working abroad—one in Japan, two in Europe, and one in Brazil. I promised them anonymity on the condition that they "tell it like it is." Here are the reasons—some of them quite personal—why they chose international careers:

Phyllis

"I'm designing microcomputers for a major Japanese company in Kyoto. I left a job in Silicon Valley in 1986 when a major contract was canceled and, frankly, after a painful divorce. The career possibilities over here intrigued me. In my industry, the Japanese tend to plan in a more thorough and long-term way. After three years here, I feel that I'm on a true career path instead of a roller-coaster."

It's a theme you'll hear often when talking to international business people: stability. Many of these men and women have left behind the ups and downs of positions in U.S. "go-go" companies to associate themselves with international corporate giants. Phyllis, our Japanese transplant, says she feels like she really belongs—that she won't be squeezed out or overlooked in corporate restructuring. (I'm not asserting that all international positions are more stable and secure than all U.S. positions. It is true, however, that many employees have found the kind of long-term career environment they were seeking in international employment.)

David

"I'm working in England because of all the nonwork advantages. My family and I walk to famous museums, art galleries, and theatres. We can take the train on a Saturday morning to the countryside or seashore. On even a short vacation—say, an three- or four-day weekend—we pop across the Channel to France, Germany, or the Netherlands. My children are receiving superb public educations. I wouldn't trade this stage in my career for a huge raise and promotion stateside. Besides, I'm making quite decent money here."

This is a second common theme for international workers: the sheer fun and personal enrichment of intercultural experience. But again, the response is deeply personal and individual. For every employee thrilled with the excitement of a new culture there's at least one who misses McDonald's and can't wait to return stateside.

Paul

"I manage an airline office for a major air carrier in France. I'm here instead of my former home, Denver, because of career advancement. Given the seniority system within my company, several very healthy senior managers in the Denver area would have had to die or quit before I would get my turn as manager. I just didn't want to commit several years of my life to the waiting game. Here I'm doing the job I do best, as top manager. It puts me in a good position for administrative promotions in the U.S. when openings occur."

An employee in an American company with foreign branches often finds that an international position can offer career advancement. Instead of being just one more face in the Chicago office, he or she is "our Paris representative." In many industries, there's less competition for advancement in international offices and agencies. And often there's considerable freedom. Many international managers find it easier to run the kind of operation that gets one noticed by top management.

Lillith

"I'm employed as a sales/marketing agent for a food producer here in Brazil. While I don't want to talk exact numbers, I'll admit that I'm here strictly for the money. In the U.S., commissioned sales people are often held back by an elaborate quota system—the idea is to keep them from making more than their office-bound, salaried bosses. But in Latin America, the sky is still the limit for someone who can put deals together. We call it the 'wild, wild West.' I probably made fifty percent more last year here in Brazil than in my previous year as a food broker in the U.S. Many of my major accounts are in the U.S., so I get home to California several times each year."

The Money

As U.S. manufacturers reach out to international sources for materials, fabrication, and affordable labor, the potential for English-speaking entrepreneurs (whether inside or outside the company) is unlimited.

But Phyllis, Dave, Paul, and Lillith suggest only a few of the reasons for seeking international employment. What are your reasons? Perhaps you haven't spelled them out, or even thought them through in a conscious way. There's no time like the present. On a separate sheet of paper, list your top three reasons for wanting an international work experience. (Fight the impulse to skip on with your reading. Actually writing down your reasons for seeking international employment will set you on your way to determining what you want to do and where you want to do it.)

The Right Idea at the Right Time

We can't peek over your shoulder, of course, to kibbitz on whether an international career is the right move for you. But we can tell you that many U.S. organizations, companies, and business-related academic and professional programs are now looking to Europe, Asia, Africa, Latin America, and elsewhere for business relations. In 1989, more than one-fifth of all agricultural products and manufactured goods produced in the U.S. were exported abroad. And we imported even more than we exported, for a import-export total of $600 billion. That number is a headline—Jobs Here!—for someone seeking international employment.

Business schools in the U.S. were among those to read the headline. Harvard, Georgetown, Stanford, Wharton, Virginia and others are now gearing up for what *Fortune* (July 17, 1989) called a global vision: "Students will have to master a foreign language and culture as well as the usual tough material on marketing and finance." Schools offering bonafide degrees in international management, such as Arizona's American Graduate School of International Management have rocketed in prestige, with dozens of major corporations coming each year to court their graduates.

Congressional and corporate leaders have found the scent as well. In 1989, a broad-based group of top politicians and CEOs published "An Action Agenda for American Competitiveness," which called for a strengthening of "international studies courses— language, cultural, political, and economic." These government and business leaders have glimpsed the "Sold War" that will replace the "Cold War"—the European Economic Community closing its ranks, the Pacific Rim looming larger (if that's possible) as a trading force, and Russia and China getting down to fighting weight. The 1990s and certainly the twenty-first century will be the era of the international worker.

But you didn't need a college bulletin or a Congressional mailing to remind you that international careers were opening up. You've probably seen the new international emphasis in your newspaper classified section.

So International Employment Is Right for Me— What Do I Do?

Somewhere out there, an international employer wants to hire you. You want to be hired by an international employer. How do we bring the two of your together?

That process can be divided into six steps. Each takes a bit of time and effort—your investment in a successful job application. We will list the six steps now, and explain them with plenty of examples and illustrations in subsequent chapters.

Step One

Look Internally before Internationally—Who Are You and What Can You Do?

Step Two

Settle upon One or More Career Possibilities That Fit You and Your Goals

Step Three

Find Companies/Organizations and Countries for Application

Step Four

Strengthen What You Have to Offer in Your Resume and Employment Application

Step Five

Assemble a Professional Application Package

Step Six

Market Your Application Package and Follow Up

What's so special about these steps? They may seem to be common sense for any job application. But common sense isn't enough.

These steps are special because, when they are followed diligently, they work. We're reminded of the elderly preacher who gave a sermon one Sunday on the importance of brotherly love. The next week he gave exactly the same sermon, and the week after, again the same sermon. One of the deacons of the congregation approached the minister after the service: "Reverend, do you realize that you've given the same sermon for three weeks in a row?" "Of course," the minister replied. "I'm waiting for you to do it."

The same holds true with the search process. In matters of employment, we all have a tendency to rush to the resume preparation stage, then mail off a snowstorm of letters in hopes of attracting interest somewhere by someone. That lottery approach to job applications simply doesn't work—and can often harm our chances. When we send a half-baked, ill-considered application to a company abroad, we spoil our chances of applying in a more thorough, specific, and targeted way in the future.

Take time to work through each of the six application steps. Your effort will be rewarded by more prompt and favorable responses from potential international employers.

Burying a Few Myths

Wrong assumptions about international employment often lead to career mistakes. We can avoid some of the traditional potholes on the road to application success by discussing and discrediting several myths about international employment:

* *Myth: To be considered for employment, you must speak a foreign language as well as natives in the country of your intended career.*

Some foreign language ability is advantageous for most international employment applications and interviews. But employers rarely expect native speaking ability. At Japan's Fujitsu Corporation, the company's current efforts to attract non-Japanese engineers, programmers, technical writers, and others would be stifled if the company considered only those who spoke flawless Japanese.

* *Myth: There's a single book that contains, country by country, the job openings that are currently available to Americans.*

No book, including the dozens listed for your reference in our book, can claim to list actual job openings available for your application. Most international openings are not advertised in the traditional American way. Many are known only to the company itself and to employment agencies. So please save your time at the book racks and spend it on the six application steps suggested in this chapter.

* *Myth: To get an international position, you have to know someone.*

There's no denying that many people get jobs through friends, relatives, acquaintances, and friends of friends. Some books assert (without empirical data) that eighty-five percent of international hiring happens through such personal contacts. This figure is grossly exaggerated, especially for the hundreds of American firms hiring for their foreign branches. Most companies are constrained by federal and state guidelines in their hiring practices, and can't afford to hire simply on the basis of personal contacts.

If your friends and relatives can't deliver names and addresses of potential international employers, don't despair. With a polished and well-written application and personal contact, you'll definitely be in the running for consideration.

* *Myth: International employers don't care about your education; they just want to know about your work experience.*

Nothing could be further from the truth for the great majority of career positions in international companies. Respect for education is greater in most countries than it is in the U.S. Your training certificates, college degree(s), and other marks of educational accomplishment will be definitely be a key asset in your application.

International employers, like U.S. employers, do want to see a pattern of experience and practical responsibility in addition to education. Your application resume and letter should portray a balance.

* *Myth: You should take any job, even menial work, to get your foot in the door of a foreign company. You'll quickly be moved up to where you belong.*

Turning janitors to generals isn't common in any corporation, domestic or foreign. As a rule, international corporations don't want a cadre of Ph.D.'s sweeping the floors. (The result is dirty floors!) Don't seek out a position substantially beneath your training and expertise. This is not to say that you can't get by in London by washing dishes—just don't expect to climb from dishwasher to business manager within the same company. It's an unusual career path at best.

* *Myth: Once you've taken an international position, you've burned your bridges for comparable positions within the U.S. You're "out of the loop."*

As demonstrated by the movement of managers within such international corporations as Heinz, IBM, and Nestle, a stint as an international manager or employee usually adds to a worker's attractiveness for the company. Thanks to FAX machines, electronic mail, teleconferencing, and other communication technologies, the loop between employees is electronic, not physical. You can't have coffee with the gang in Chicago as you sit in your office in Bombay, but you can still communicate with them (daily, if necessary), attend their meetings by teleconference, and fly on short notice to their conventions. The company need not forget you while you're abroad. And you'll be the resident expert when the company prepares to meet the global trading challenges of the 1990s.

* *Myth: For the employee, most foreign employment situations are cultural successes but financial disasters.*

Those who believe this myth haven't checked on the latest monetary rates for Germany, Switzerland, France, Great Britain, Japan, and other trading nations. Your international salary often compares quite favorably to your U.S. numbers. Employees from the U.S. are often pleasantly surprised when they add up their housing allowance, travel funds, salary, tax advantages, and other aspects of compensation. But for your own sake, don't trust anyone's estimate or general arithmetic. Find out what your living expenses and other costs will be before accepting a particular salary.

Chapter Two

Look Internally Before Internationally: Who Are You and What Can You Do?

In Chapter 1, you jotted down your reasons for seeking an international career. Let's assume that you're satisfied with those reasons and they make sense to you, although your mother still thinks you should be a dentist in St. Paul. Your reasons seem to be compelling enough to carry you through the interesting, but difficult work of locating appropriate positions and applying for them.

The hard work begins not by investigating companies or countries but investigating yourself. Only by knowing yourself well can you plan effectively for successful job applications.

Viewed as concentric circles, your search comprises three areas. The largest, What You Can Do, includes all those skills, abilities, and competencies that you've learned. On a separate sheep of paper, make your list of what you can do. Put down not only tasks you've performed at work ("handled payroll") but also those skills and abilities you've demonstrated in organizations and civic life ("very organized," "a good public speaker"). Orient your list toward items a potential employer will value.

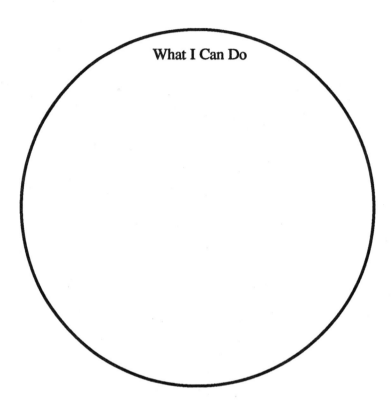

What I Can Do

Unhappy employees are often those people doing what they know they can do, but they dislike doing it. In the inner circle, therefore, consider What I Like to Do. These items will be drawn from your previous list. Set down those career-related skills, activities, and competencies that give you pleasure, satisfaction, or a feeling of accomplishment. Let's say, for example, that you're good at public speaking, but hate, hate, hate to do it. Leave it in the outer circle.

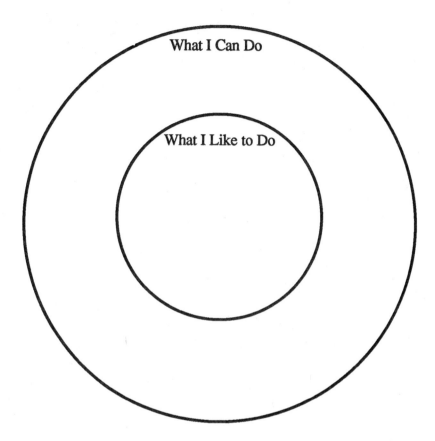

In this inner circle, you've defined the "heart" of what you have to offer to an employer—those things that you'll do with energy, enthusiasm, and caring. These are the items that make work seem like a form of "serious play." At the end of a day you've had more pleasure than pain, and at the end of a career more satisfaction than disappointment. Perhaps, as Thoreau said, "the mass of men lead lives of quiet desperation." But not you.

Now for the difficult—and humbling—part. Review your second list to locate those items that you not only like to do, but also have proven your skill in. Write those "proof experiences" in the blanks. For example, if you mentioned in your second list that you "like to work with people," you should now put down an actual example (e.g., "sales clerk of the month") of your skill. As much as possible, these examples should come from real-world work situations.

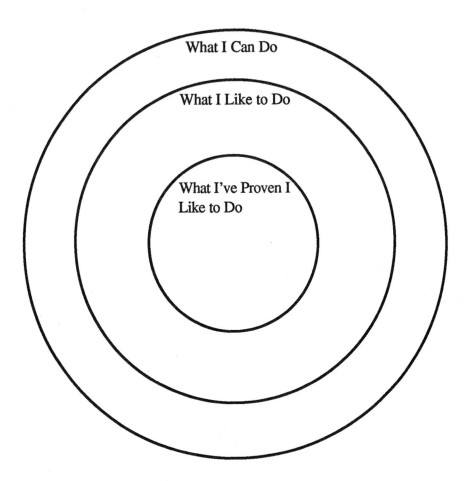

In preparation for a winning resume and for great interview responses, we shall now expand a bit on each of your proven skills listed above. Use your own paper as necessary to fill in these blanks for each of your proven abilities:

Proven Ability: _____

Past Proof: _____

Present Proof: _____

Future Proof: _____

Here are some quick definitions that may make your job easier: Past Proof (something from the past that demonstrates the ability), Present Proof (something you're now doing that demonstrates the ability), and a Future Proof (something you plan to do that will require the ability).

In making your list, consider both paid and unpaid experiences. At this stage in your analysis, don't ignore seemingly marginal or insignificant activities, positions, or associations. Consider not only your present occupation, but also avocations, memberships, volunteer work, church and charity associations, civic involvement, and academic interests.

In completing your Future Proof, send yourself back to the future for a moment. Consider those short-term and long-term plans that will prove your abilities in the future. It may be a somewhat strange thought at first to contemplate how future events will prove your abilities. Perhaps the analogy of a fruit tree can help: How will the seeds you're planting in the present bear fruit? What will you be doing six months from now, a year from now, two years from now that will prove particular abilities? For example, how will your participation in an upcoming convention or trade-show demonstrate your professionalism? How will your promotion to a supervisory position demonstrate your leadership skills? How will your attainment of a certificate, license, or degree demonstrate your competence? In drawing up this list, let your imagination go. Your future employer, after all, is hiring you for what lies ahead, not behind, in your productive life. The act of drawing up this list gives you a chance to face that future—and shape it to your advantage.

The Hand You Hold for International Employment

In assembling your past, present, and future proven abilities, you're looking at the hand that you bring to the table of employment application. On the basis of this hand, you can make quite accurate estimates of what kind of jobs to apply for, how to approach employers, and what to expect in your international career path.

Choosing a Career Field

There's no better time than now to contemplate exactly what you want to do than with your past, present, and future proven abilities laid out before you. You may have already made up your mind—an accountant, an engineer, a sales person, and so forth. But, for the international employment arena, you may want to throw a wider net in considering related occupations you would also qualify for. Many jobseekers within the U.S. and abroad have come up empty in their search only because they confined their search too narrowly.

To help you throw open the gates of imagination, read through the following job titles. The list, of course, isn't complete by any means. But it does include many emerging careers named by the New York *Times* as "the best opportunities of tomorrow." You may want to investigate several of these careers to determine if they make use of your abilities. For detailed descriptions of each, see the *American Almanac of Jobs and Salaries*, 1988 edition (Avon) and *The New York Times Career Planner* (Times, 1988).

Accountant
Accounting Firm Manager
Actuary
Agricultural Economist
Architect
Banker
Bank Examiner
Biotechnologist
Breathing Therapist
Broker
Business Realtor
Ceramics Technician
Chemist
City Planner
Civil Engineer
College Administrator
College Housing Manager
College Real Estate
   Manager
Convention Center
   Manager
Company Fitness
   Program Manager
Computer Programmer
Corporate Aide
Coporate Attorney
Crisis Manager
Dental Technician
Direct-Mail Marketer
Earthquake Engineer
Economist
Entrepreneur
Financial Planner
Fire Safety Expert

Food Marketer
Georgrapher
Gerontologist
Grievance Handler
High-Rise Expert
Horticulturalist
Hospital Manager
Hotel/Club Manager
Human Factors Specialist
Industrial Hygenist
Investment Analyst
Investment Banker
Investor Relations
   Specialist
Journalist
Language Expert
Management Consultant
Management Information
   Systems (MIS)
   Specialist
Manufacturing Engineer
Manufacturing
   Representative
Marketing Specialist
Meteorologist

Mining Engineer
Musician
Overseas Political Analyst
Paralegal
Pharmacist
Public Relations Specialist
Purchasing Agent
Radiation Therapist
Real Estate Appraiser
Real Estate Manager
Retailer
Security Manager
Securities Analyst
Software Engineer
Sports Manager
Stockbroker
Stragic Planner
Teacher
Textile Worker/Manager
Traffic Manager
Veterinarian
Water Expert
Welding Engineer
Zoologist

Take an afternoon or evening at your public library to browse through the career section in search of possible career areas that fit your skills and interests.

Strengthening the Hand You Hold for International Employment

Before we begin to play your hand for high stakes in the international job market, let's see if we can strengthen it in key areas.

Languages

Put yourself in your employer's position. If you were doing the hiring for a sales position, let's say, within the United States, would you require fluency in English? Of course. Your new hire would be paralyzed without such ability.

Which leads to the question that discourages many people interested in international careers: How's your foreign language ability? Put another way, can you read and speak with ease in the language of the country where you want to work?

That question can't be answered by school transcripts: "Well, I had French in high school and for two semesters in college." Many of us (your author included) have good grades in school language classes, but heaven help us if we had to speak and write in all those languages on the job tomorrow. And "tomorrow" is just the point: When you mail off a job application to Germany, let's say, you may well receive a phone interview the next week—*auf Deutsch*! Your language skills should be at their peak when you mail off your application.

But let's be practical. Most of us probably aren't going to speak or write superb German, French, Spanish or another foreign language as a prerequisite for seeking international employment. We're going to learn what we can, then hope our prospective employer gives us time to play catch-up in the first few months of the job. Many jobs in Europe, Asia, and Latin America require only social language skills at the beginning—the ability to lunch with a client, keep up with small group conversation, and answer the telephone.

Unfortunately, those are precisely the skills that American language instruction often fails to address during high school and college. A Washington, D.C., executive complained to me recently that "I have a minor in Spanish. I can translate Borges. But take me to a Chicano neighborhood and I'm tongue-tied. I can't even ask directions without getting flustered."

Begin to strengthen your hand for international employment, therefore, by enrolling in the kind of language instruction that will give you quick, solid results in terms of practical, day-to-day language ability. You may be lucky enough to have such a program at a local university or community college. Check particularly with extended or continuing education programs, many of which meet in evening hours.

If you can't find a suitable college class, bite the bullet and pay for an intensive language course through a commercial school. The organizations listed below are famous for their ability to turn a sheepish grin—"Uh, I don't speak any French"—to a confident fluency.

But brace yourself: The instruction is far from cheap. You may want to attend a class or two on a trial basis before signing on as a contracted student. And don't waste your money, by the way, on those omnipresent cassette tapes promising to "teach Italian in six easy lessons." For meaningful competence, you need face-to-face instruction with a trained teacher.

Here are U.S. offices and phone numbers for some of the most prominent and reputable language schools. All have programs and schedules geared to fit your business or academic day. When you call, be sure to describe in detail the kinds of positions you'll be seeking abroad. You don't want to get stuck in a tourist-language class ("Would the beautiful lady care to dance?") when you need a battery of business phrases.

(By calling or writing these offices, you can find a language school in your location.)

Berlitz Language Centers
1050 Connecticut Ave.
Washington, DC 20008
(202) 331-1160

Inlingua Schools of Languages
1030 15th St. NW Suite 828
Washington, DC 20005
(202) 289-8666

Linguex
1255 23rd St.
Suite 285
Washington, DC 20005
(202) 296-1112

International Center for Language Studies
727 15th St. NW
Suite 400
Washington, DC 20005
(202) 639-8800

As your language instructor will probably recommend, surround yourself with foreign language materials—magazines on your coffee table, a novel by your bed, a foreign language videotape in your VCR. Try as much as possible to "live" in the foreign language of your choice when you're home. Talk yourself through the names of household items when you cook or clean. Talk out loud in the car if you drive to work: to yourself, give directions and point out sights in the foreign language. Most of all, try to find someone among your acquaintances who speaks the language well. Talk his or her ear off several times a week.

By using this type of language immersion, you'll be amazed how quickly you can become comfortable and confident in speaking (and, later, writing) your newly acquired language. As the old joke goes, foreign languages must be easy—even two-year-olds learn them overseas.

You'll have to be the judge of when and how to use your foreign language ability in applying for an international position. As a general rule, do not write your application letter in a foreign language unless 1) you can be absolutely sure that your letter is correct in grammar, style, form, and mechanics, and 2) you can reflect the same level of language competence in speaking. Many international employers have received flawless, native-language letters from job applicants only to discover later (usually in the first telephone interview) the letters were written by hired language instructors.

If your first contact with your prospective employer is in person or by phone, it is courteous to greet the person in his or her native language, then to move as graciously as possible to a mutually comfortable language. (Many French employers, for example, prefer to conduct interviews somewhat haltingly in English rather than in the applicant's bad French.)

It may help to remind yourself that employers abroad are probably not expecting you to speak like a native your first day on the job. They will expect, however, that you are taking steps to master the language and are willing to use it, albeit tentatively, in social and business situations.

Your Growing Network

Strengthen your employment hand next by broadening your network of contacts and associations. It often costs little more than a postage stamp to receive publications and membership information (and sometimes membership itself) in international and regional commerce associations and trade groups. The mention of one or two of these contacts on your resume may be just the touch that sets you apart from other, less "connected" applicants.

One of the best ways to learn about such associations in your chosen country is to use a service your tax dollars pay for—the Foreign Commercial Service of the U.S. Department of Commerce. Most U.S. embassies abroad include a Commercial Officer, whose job it is to assist American citizens attempting to enter the international market. Commercial officers are not employment agents, and you should not expect a list of job openings when they reply to your inquiry. Their mission is to assist in the development of new trade relations with foreign countries. These individuals can provide a wealth of general and specific information about the current business climate of the country, its future growth areas, and its business problems. In many cases, they will know a great deal about the company or agency you are contacting for employment, and can make practical suggestions about the kind of associations and homework you should undertake. (See the appendices for more information on contacting Commercial Officers.)

The Foreign Commercial Service maintains district offices within the United States where you may be able to pick up useful printed materials. According to John Havasy, Commercial Officer in Athens, Greece, "the FCS can supply available country background and sector analyses." Depending upon the applicant's level of expertise, the FCS "can identify contacts and provide a list of prospective marketing agents for the businessperson to meet with when he/she visits the market countries."

This extremely valuable resource is often under-utilized by Americans hoping to find international employment. But the resource should be approached persuasively—again, the FCS is not an employment agency. Often a phone call to your nearest district office can establish the person-to-person spirit of helpfulness that leads to specific names and addresses you can contact in the country of your interest. Or you might want to write a letter, perhaps after the following model:

```
Nov. 30, 1989


Ms. Linda Forest
Commerce Officer
U.S. Embassy
Frankfurt, West Germany


Dear Ms. Forest:

    As a recent graduate in Marketing from the
University of Illinois, I'm very interested
in learning more about the wholesale clothing
industry in West Germany.
    Specifically, can you point me towards the
kind of people, companies, or trade associa-
tions that are seeking American markets? I'd
like to write to these sources directly to
get information on their product lines and
possible need for American intermediaries.
```

I certainly appreciate your help. On June 8-9, 1991, I plan to visit Frankfurt for a company tour. If your schedule allows, perhaps I could stop by for a few minutes to say hello and discuss mutual interests. I look forward to hearing from you.

Sincerely,

Robert R. Evans

Note what was and wasn't said in this letter. The letter did specify that the writer wanted information on the clothing industry with an eye toward possible participation in some way. The letter did not say that the writer was seeking a job in the German clothing industry. Commercial officers are understandably unwilling to share their contacts with every jobseeker who knocks at the door.

If you fail to receive the material and contacts you need from a Commercial Officer, consider writing to companies directly. Your local librarian will be able to direct you to the proper reference sources.

Your Growing Work Experience

A third way to build your international employment profile is to create some kind of business or quasi-business experience, however slight, in your intended career area. For example, an Iowa elementary school teacher wanted to teach for a year in England. While on summer vacation there, she took time to visit two schools and was invited to participate in classes. On her eventual application, she was able to state truthfully that she had "enjoyed helping to teach classes during visits to public schools at Manchester and Leeds." That sentence stood out like a beacon on her successful application.

Or take four other quick examples to give you the idea.

1. An Accounting major volunteers time for a semester to help keep association books for the Mexican American Business League (thus strengthening his resume for Latin American positions).

2. A computer programmer puts together a short tutorial in German on social customs a German manager needs to know when visiting America. For $80 he markets it, with moderate success, through a couple of classified ads in German newspapers. But his real "score" comes when he includes this entrepreneurial activity on his application for a systems analyst position in Germany—and gets the job.

3. An advertising major makes a hobby for several months of clipping interesting print advertisements out of French magazines. In an interview for an advertising job in Paris, the candidate can talk about actual French ads and is head and shoulders above her competition.

4. An assistant manager in a grocery store sets up a "Foods of Italy" display in the deli section of his store. This item becomes one small but telling bit of evidence on his application to be an import broker for a major Italian food distributor.

The point: You too can take steps now to position yourself well for international employment. A sound guide to your efforts is simply to put yourself in the place of your potential employer: What kinds of experiences and interests would you be pleased to find in an application? These activities and involvements shouldn't be phony, of course, or merely drummed up for the sake of the resume. But there is every reason to shape your choice of activities toward your goal of international employment.

You've now strengthened your international employment profile by brushing up (or acquiring) language skills, developing contacts and associations, and creating business-related experiences that will attract the eye of an international employer. We're ready to commit those strengths to writing, in your resume and application letter.

Chapter Three

Assembling Your Application Package

In this chapter, we'll walk through the application process step by step, giving examples of all forms of communication—resumes, letters, interviews, and phone calls—used in that process. Applications differ somewhat, however, depending on whether your response involves a blind advertisement, a "full disclosure" ad, a cold call, or a personal recommendation. We'll term these various approaches Paths A, B, C, and D.

The Application Package

No matter what path of application you are pursuing, you will be sending your "application package" to potential employers. This package is made up of the following items:

1. A cover letter expressing your interest in a position, highlighting your education and experience, and setting the stage for an interview, even if only by telephone.

2. A resume setting forth your career goals, education, experience, special skills, personal background, and references.

3. Optional letters of recommendation and samples of your work.

We'll see examples of this package customized to each of the application paths.

Path A: **Responding to a Blind Ad**

You open the classified pages of the New York *Times* and spot the following "blind" ad ("blind" because it doesn't let you see the name of the company or its representative):

> Opportunities in Europe
> for creative individuals
> with business experience
> and/or business degrees.
> Top salaries, benefits,
> travel allowances. Send
> resume, Box 293, New
> York Times.

Your imagination works overtime as you contemplate your ideal position—blind ads encourage such flights of fancy. But you gradually come down to earth as you begin to wonder why a reputable company would hide its name, the nature of its business, and even its address and country from you.

Blind ads make up about one-fifth of all classified job advertising. Sometimes a company chooses the "blind" approach for sound reasons. Perhaps it doesn't want to expose specific personnel needs, as in the case of a hospital desperately seeking qualified nurses. (An ad specifying that need would be bad advertising for the hospital.) Or a company may want to find "fresh blood" without letting its present employees know that it is trying to fill vacancies. A company may want to limit the number of inquiries it receives to a single box or telephone number instead of clogging company mail and telephone channels.

Just as often, however, "blind" ads are written in an effort to deceive the job applicant. You respond in good faith with your resume only to discover that the company behind the ad has little to offer you.

Let's pursue the blind ad above, although it includes no name, company, or specific position information. We'll then see if it turns out to be our ticket abroad or just another con-job.

Here is the type of letter you might write in response to a blind advertisement. Note that we haven't lowered the tone or reduced the amount of detail in the letter or accompanying resume. Just because you're responding to a blind ad doesn't mean that decision-makers in major corporations may not be reading your application package.

```
7432 W. 45th St.
Washington, DC 29953


Nov. 29, 1989


Personnel Director
Box 293
New York Times


Dear Director:
    I'm interested in the career opportunities
you advertised in the New York Times, Nov.
28, 1989, and would appreciate receiving more
information.
    I graduated from the University of Maryland
in 1988 as a Marketing major. Since that time
I have been employed as an assistant manager
in charge of wholesale accounts at Revex, a
large Maryland pharmaceutical chain. In that
capacity, I supervise eight employees and
manage an administrative budget of $540,000.
I enjoy working closely with clients on a day-
to-day basis and encourage good communication
skills among my employees.
```

> It has long been my goal to apply my busi-
> ness training to an international position
> involving retail or wholesale marketing. I'm
> willing to undertake intensive language
> training if required by the positions you
> offer.
>
> I look forward to hearing more from you
> regarding these opportunities. Thank you for
> considering my qualifications and strong in-
> terest.
>
> Sincerely,
>
> Rebecca R. Johnson

Rebecca mails this letter along with her resume. (She could have included general letters of reference, but decides to hold these back until she finds out what kind of positions are available.) She has gone to the trouble of sending a full letter and resume rather than just a note. ("Yes, I'm interested. Please send details.") She reasons that the employer will respond first to expressions of serious interest—and her time and effort in writing a detailed letter will demonstrate that level of interest.

Four days pass and then the phone rings. Here's what Rebecca hears: "This is Ted Conway, vice president at Trans-Atlantic Associates. We represent several large European corporations who are about to open up new managerial positions in Paris, Amsterdam, Rome, and London. I'm calling to thank you, Rebecca, for your response to our New York *Times* advertisement. Your credentials certainly are impressive, and we'd like to pursue the possibilities of employment with you." (Pause.)

Rebecca can't quite "read" the conflicting messages she's receiving. What companies are hiring? For what positions? When? She decides to find out: "I'd like that too, Mr. Conway."

He continues: "As you probably realize, Rebecca, it takes many skills to participate effectively in the international business community." And as his voice drones on, Rebecca's hopes fade. It turns out that "Trans-Atlantic Associates" is nothing more than a school trying to sell language tapes and correspondence courses in intercultural relations. Following successful completion of their courses, Rebecca would be given access to the company's "private data base" of current openings throughout Europe and Asia. She would be "virtually assured" of receiving a position abroad.

Rebecca indicates that she's not interested and hangs up. She feels she has wasted considerable effort in responding to this blind ad.

Up to half of all blind ads turn out to be smokescreens for people who are selling something, not hiring you. But don't let that fact discourage you from exploring very real career opportunities that may be available through such ads. Just listen carefully for the first hints of monetary "investment" on your part as a requisite to the hiring process. That's usually your key that you're not dealing with a bonafide company wanting to hire you.

Some employment agencies routinely run blind ads, but honestly set forth the terms under which they do business. In some cases, the company will require an advance fee for services it renders in finding you an international position.

Path B: Responding to a "Full Disclosure" Advertisement

In this case, you know the name of the company, the person to whom you're writing, and many of the details of the position offered. This information will allow you to adapt and personalize somewhat the previous model letter reproduced in Path A. Obviously, the more convincingly you can target your skills and accomplishments to the needs identified in the ad, the greater your chances for success.

Path C: Making a Cold Call

The great majority of job openings at all levels never get advertised, or perhaps are advertised in newspapers and magazines you don't see. The key to finding such positions is the cold call—the unsolicited call or letter expressing your interest in exploring career possibilities with a particular company.

It's not a matter of asking "Are you hiring?" Few companies are willing to send lists of open positions to anyone. Instead, use your letter of inquiry (as in the example below) to sell yourself. Positions have a way of becoming available when the right person comes along—and you want to be that right person.

In the following letter, Andrea Wu pays a "cold call" on NVK Microcomputer Systems of Taiwan. She has found the name of the company's personnel director and the address of company headquarters in *Asia's Top 7500 Companies*, one of the directories available at her library. Andrea begins her letter by showing that she's interested in recent company developments, then goes on to show how she can be useful to the firm. A growing company in need of skilled employees will find it hard to resist Andrea's logic and enthusiasm:

```
Dec. 2, 1989
300 Levett St.
Alexandria, VA 22304


Mr. Zhou Chang
Director of Personnel
NVK Microcomputer Systems
687-A South Extension
Taipei, Taiwan NW8923


Dear Mr. Chang:
    In the Nov. 27, 1989, Wall Street Journal,
I read with great interest of your success in
developing a prototype 386 laptop computer in
the U.S. $1000 price range. As the first
manufacturer in this market, surely you will
enjoy strong sales, no doubt with the need
for an expanded staff.
```

I would like to join NVK as a systems architect and United States marketing specialist. My resume (enclosed) sums up my academic training in Electrical Engineering and Business as well as my experience as a systems designer for NCR Corporation. You may be particularly interested in my design for a CAD software package at NCR—the kind of development software that you may be contemplating for production of your new laptop.

Thank you for reviewing my qualifications and for considering my interest in a career at NVK. I would welcome a telephone call or letter from you. I'm eager to learn more about NVK and to answer your questions about my background and skills.

Sincerely,

Andrea Wu

In her resume, Andrea identifies the location of her colleges and workplaces. International employers may not be as familiar as domestic employers with, say, Rice University. But they may well know of Houston, and associate the college favorably with that business center.

Nor does Andrea presume that an international employer will know intuitively what a computer programmer/analyst at NCR Corporation does. She breaks out a thorough description of her tasks and accomplishments there in hopes that one or more of these items will strike the interest of the employer. She uses both spelled- out and abbreviated forms of some key terms—"printed circuit board" (PCB)—to make sure the reader understands. She wisely chooses not to spell out well-known computer terms (CAD, etc.) so as not to seem naive or inexperienced to those evaluating her resume.

Under "Volunteer Work" Andrea includes material that also could have been grouped under "Personal Background" or a similar category. Knowing that NVK will need skilled English speakers and writers to sell its laptop to the United States market, she makes a point of mentioning her work as an English tutor for Asian refugees.

ANDREA K. WU
1509 N. Jackson Avenue, #24
Alexandria, VA 22304
(703) 555-9293

EDUCATION

Capital University, Washington, D.C.
M.B.A., expected May 1991.
- Member, Graduate Marketing Association and American Marketing Association.
- Member, Production and Operations Management Club.

RICE UNIVERSITY, Houston, TX.
B.S. Electrical Engineering, May 1987.
Area of Concentration: Computer Engineering.

WORK EXPERIENCE

NCR CORP., Wichita, Kansas.
Computer Programmer/Analyst, VLSI CAD/CAE group. June 1987-July 1989.
- Developed a new release of a CAD software package used extensively company-wide for both in-house and customer cnip design analysis.
- Provided on-going maintenance and support for existing in-house CAD software.
- Transported software written for VAX hardware to the Mentor workstation environment.
- Wrote and updated software documentation.
- Participated in planning printed circuit board (PCB) simulation strategy and prepared current databases and tools for simulation.
- Studies process flow of engineering bill of materials creation to target areas for automation.
- Implemented an automated backup system for PCB symbol libraries and menus on the Mentor workstation platform.

RICE UNIVERSITY, Houston, Texas.
Lab/Teaching Assistant, Electrical Engineering Dept. August 1986-May 1987.
- Conducted a digital logic design lab class.
- Graded lab reports and exams.
- Maintained lab equipment.

NCR CORP., Wichita, Kansas.
Summer Intern, VLSI CAD/CAE group. May-August 1986.
- Developed a menu-based interface for a CAD software tool.

VOLUNTEER WORK

Rape Crisis Hotline Counselor. Houston Women's Center, Houston, Texas.

English as a Second Language Tutor (Specifically, for Southeast Asian Refugees). Houston Community College, Houston, Texas.

COMPUTER SKILLS

Excellent command of Lotus 1-2-3, WordPerfect, Microsoft Word, Flowcharting II+, MS-DOS and UNIX operating systems. Functional knowledge of C, Pascal, Modula-2, and Basic programming languages.

REFERENCES   Available upon request.

To highlight the skills that will matter most to NVK, she creates a special category, "Computer Skills." Here she recaps many of the skills that were implicit from her list of job tasks and experiences. She knows that such skills should not be suggested only implicitly, and so spotlights them explicitly to end her resume with power.

For a different employment opportunity—one, perhaps, utilizing her business skills more than her computer skills—Andrea would have drawn up an entirely different resume highlighting her M.B.A. studies and supervisory experience at NCR.

So: what happened as a result of all this? Within two weeks, Andrea received a thick packet of employment information from NVK, along with a warm letter of interest from Mr. Chang. He referred to the inevitable obstacles of interviewing Andrea at such a great distance, but went on to ask if she would be willing to travel to New York to meet with the company's senior United States trade representative. Andrea's cold call had worked like a charm.

How many such inquiries can you make at once? Thanks to the resources of word processing, you can make as many contacts by letter as you wish. Be careful, however, not to blanket the world with a standard, catch-all resume that speaks to no one because it tries to speak to everyone. Employers have a right to expect that you have tailored your application materials to their needs and type of business.

In general, you will have much more success targeting a dozen or so businesses or organizations for a customized, personalized application than in mailing a standard letter and resume to a hundred or more companies. It's still a "people" world where real individuals read your letters and decide whether to respond. Employment directors around the world get reams of "junk mail" from applicants each year. Make your application the one that distinguishes itself by a personal touch, a sincere interest in the company, and a customized description of your background and skills.

Mail Merge to the Rescue

The task of creating such tailored communications need not be arduous. Virtually all popular word processing systems now allow you to create a relatively standard letter text with interspersed "field markers" where you can put customized material (including company information, names, and so forth).

Your resume, similarly, can be customized to include the name of your prospective employer in your statement of your career objective ("To begin as a systems architect with NVK; with experience, to assume responsibility for technical product adjustments to the United States market.") Personnel directors, like the rest of us, love to see their names and/or the company name mentioned in your letter. Whenever possible, find out the name of the personnel director before writing your letter. (Often this involves just a quick phone call to the company's receptionist— at most a $3-$4 expense.)

Making the Cold Call by Telephone

Using the directories listed in the appendix, you can find the main telephone number for virtually any major company in the world. And given the recent lowering of international telephone rates, you can talk to just about any location on earth for less than $10 for 3 minutes. But here's the question: How are your nerves? Making an international cold call for employment brings a cold sweat to many applicants, especially those whose foreign language skills aren't up to par. Probably the best advice in the matter of telephone cold calls is to follow your own intuitions. If you feel that you have the personal charisma, gung-ho spirit, and financial resources to win a personnel director's attention by an initial call, dial away.

If your "nerves show," however, on such occasions and you forget every bit of your foreign language under pressure, send a letter. For many countries, letters will be the expected means of communication. In France, Germany, Latin America, and large parts of Asia, a personnel director will be surprised (sometimes unpleasantly so) to receive an out-of-the-blue phone call from a United States job applicant. The effect for these cultures is not unlike the feeling you may have when a salesperson comes uninvited to knock at the door of your residence. In England, Australia, New Zealand, and above all in the United

States itself, personnel directors are more used to applicants who come on strong in an initial contact over the phone.

Path D: Using a Personal Contact in Your Application

Often your route to a job application has been greased for you by the supportive words of a mutual acquaintance—perhaps a friend of an executive in the company, an employee in the company, or an academic or professional big-wig known to you and the company. Every survey of how people actually get jobs underlines the importance of these personal contacts. People get jobs through people more often than through paper.

The trick is to use personal contacts without abusing them. Notice in the following job application letter how Blair Fallows gets maximum mileage out of his personal contact without appearing to "ride on the coattails" of his reference.

```
389 Western St.
Toronto, Canada SW893


Dec. 4, 1989


Ms. Virginia Walsch
Director, Optical Scanning Laboratory
Forbst Optical Systems
Berlin, West Germany
Dar Ms. Walsch:


    Professor Samuel Owens, who directed my
senior thesis at the University of Waterloo,
suggested that I write to you regarding pos-
sible career opportunities at Forbst in laser
optics or allied fields. Professor Owens men-
tioned how much he enjoyed meeting you at the
recent Laser Optics convention in Paris, and
hearing of your exciting research in micro-
laser applications.
```

As my enclosed resume suggests, I have been active in the development of new laser optical systems since 1986 for PRA International and Waterloo Scientific, Inc. You may have stopped by the Waterloo Scientific booth at the Laser Optics convention; our representatives were unveiling there the company's new laser microscope (written up in the September, 1989, issue of *Optics*). You may be particularly interested in my computer training, a background more and more necessary in developing sophisticated laser applications.

To work effectively in Germany, I recognize that I'll require an intensive course in written and spoken German. Such a course is available through Waterloo University, in partnership with Berlitz, and I am certainly ready to enroll in it if an employment opportunity arises with Forbst.

I'm eager to learn more about current lines of research at Forbst and your staffing needs. Thank you for reviewing my resume and considering my desire to join your optics team.

Sincerely,

Blair Fallows

Here's what actually took place between Professor Owens and Virginia Walsch at the Laser Optics convention in Paris. Professor Owens delivered a paper, after which Virginia Walsch introduced herself and expressed interest in Owens' topics. They chatted briefly and exchanged business cards. The whole social transaction took no more than five minutes.

But that five minutes proves crucial to Blair Fallows' job search. When Professor Owens gives Blair permission to use his name in a letter to Virginia Walsch, he gives Blair access to the German firm on a higher level than off-the-street candidates. In receiving Blair's letter of inquiry, Virginia Walsch associates this applicant with the brilliant paper she has just heard in Paris. She's interested in hiring Blair partly for his own merits but also partly because it helps to create an ongoing link between Forbst and Professor Owens.

Blair would have ruined the usefulness of mentioning Professor Owens by stating it too baldly: "Professor Owens said you were hiring . . ." or "I studied under the world-famous Professor Samuel Owens, whom you approached at. . . ." Be careful not to undo the power of personal contacts by overkill.

Blair received a letter from Virginia Walsch indicating that Forbst was in the midst of a temporary hiring freeze. He was invited, however, to participate in a company-sponsored symposium on optics, to be held in Switzerland the following summer. At that time, Ms. Walsch suggested, there would be time to explore career possibilities more seriously. Blair wrote a gracious letter of acceptance in which he again expressed his interest in joining the company. This time he included a letter of recommendation written for him by Professor Owens. At the Switzerland symposium Virginia Walsch offered Blair an attractive position with the company.

BLAIR FALLOWS

P.O. Box 4621, Capital University
Washington, DC
(202) 555-1117

EDUCATION

University of Waterloo, Waterloo, Canada
BSc (Co-op) Honours Applied Physics, Management Studies minor, April 1989.
• Received **Mike Moser Award** for Academics, Athletics, and Activities, 1989.
• Received **Alexander Rutherford Scholarship,** 1984.

WORK EXPERIENCE

University of Waterloo, Waterloo, Canada
Department of Science
Teaching Assistant   • Assisted teaching a technical writing and speaking course.
Sept 1988-April 1989   • Tutored students in the use of microcomputer networks and word processors.
     • Experienced in technical report writing.

Waterloo Scientific Inc., Waterloo, Canada
Scanning Laser Microscopes
Project Assistant   • Led project involving the development of a Scanning Photoluminescence Microscope.
May 1988-August 1988   • Coordinated software and hardware design modifications.

Research Assistant   • Performed outside contract research with prototype Laser Microscope.
Sept 1987-Dec 1987   • Author, Contract Research study, 1987.

PRA International, Inc., London, Canada
Optical Scientific Equipment
Technician/Demonstrator   • Explained uses and applications for spectrometers and lasers at International
Sept 1986-April 1987   and Canadian conferences.
     • Conducted application experience on a new type of spectrometer.
     • Contributing Author, *Pittsburgh Conference (Spec) paper 621, 1987.*

Esso Resources, Calgary, Canada
Quirk Creek Sour Gas Plant
Operator   • Controlled all process functions and detected Hydrogen Sulphide leaks.
Jan 1986-May 1986   • Assumed Fire Control officer and Safety Officer duties.

Physical Metallurgy Labs, Ottawa, Canada
Metals/Mining Research Group
Software Developer   • Wrote software in FORTRAN and Assembler to control x-ray diffractometer.
April 1985-Aug 1985   • Executed various research experiments.

INTERESTS/ACTIVITIES

• Reporter, University of Waterloo "Imprint," 1988-1989.
• Athletic Dept. Mascot, "The Warrior," 1988-1989.
• Don, Village I student residence, 1987.
• President, University Residents' Council, 1986.
• Varsity Rugby, Waterloo, 1984-1989; elected Captain,, 1987; Vice Captain, Treasurer, 1988.
     • Organized West Coast Tour, April 1989; toured United Kingdom, 1987; Eastern U.S., 1985.
• Some spoken and written French.

Those Pesky Application Forms

Because job applicants often fail to include necessary information in their resumes and cover letters, more and more companies are using lengthy job application forms. These forms frustrate applicants by requiring large answers in small spaces, or in asking obtuse and ambiguous questions. As a result, the forms are often dispatched quickly and carelessly by many applicants—especially those who don't get the jobs.

Take the preparation of an application form as seriously as you take the preparation of your resume. Attach an extra page where space doesn't allow for a complete answer. Type whenever possible. Above all, write well in response to questions asking for your written opinion. Spelling, grammar, and mechanics should be flawless—and no less so if you are writing in a foreign language.

Neat, complete, typed answers convey an impression of the applicant as professional, skilled, and interested in the company.

What to Do When a Response Comes

Make it a practice always to have the last word in any application process. For example, let's say that you have sent your application package to the TWA office in Cannes. You receive a short letter from the director of the office there, M. Oberge, informing you that no positions are open. He thanks you for your interest and wishes you well in your job search.

Ninety-five percent of job applicants would leave the matter there. But you're part of that distinctive five percent that always try to turn "no" to "maybe." You respond with a brief personal note:

Dec. 10, 1989

M. Pierre Oberge
Director, TWA District Office
Cannes, France OA7898

Dear Mssr. Oberge:

Thank you for taking time to consider my application for employment and for responding so promptly.

I'd like to check with you again this summer to see if openings are available. In the meantime, I'm participating in TWA's domestic internship program for management trainees through my university and polishing my French.

Thanks for keeping me in mind as career opportunities arise in your office.

With best regards,

Michele Covington

Though Michele didn't find the opening she wanted, she has put herself in a good position for further correspondence and contact with this international employer. In short, she hasn't just let things drop. She's left a final, positive impression that may turn out to help her with the company at a later date.

Having the last word to a positive reply to your application is easy: Say thank you, repeat the jist of the letter or call you've received, and indicate what action you are taking.

Dec. 10, 1989

M. Pierre Oberge
Director, TWA District Office
Cannes, France OA7898

Dear M. Oberge:
I am delighted to accept your offer for a summer, 1990, position in your office. I understand that I will be assisting you in implementation of a computer scheduling system for area travel agents. You also mentioned that TWA would provide transportation to and from Cannes.

I look forward to making final arrangements for what I hope will be an on-going association with TWA. Feel free to call me at home (389) 987-7987 or send messages via FAX (389) 389-3892.

With best wishes,

Michele Covington

What about FAX?

International letters still can take ten days or more to reach their destination in Europe or Asia, and often longer for parts of Africa. Can't you speed the job application process by FAXing your cover letter and resume?

It depends. In many company cultures, the use of the FAX machine is reserved for high-priority matters—the kind of thing that used to require courier or express mail. When an applicant's cover letter and resume arrive on this sacrosanct machine, the company may react adversely. "The medium is the message," as McLuhan claimed, and the medium (FAX) can undo the message (your application) in such companies.

Other firms have embraced the future and use FAX for all kinds of communications, including employment matters. But how do you know when to FAX and when not to?

Probably the safest course is to send your initial inquiry via traditional mail, but then to invite the employer's response to you by FAX. You say you don't own a FAX machine and don't foresee an extra $1000 to buy one? Not to worry. In virtually every city, town, and hamlet in the United States are "mail stop" shops offering public FAX availability. For a dollar or so per page, these shops will receive your FAX message for you and telephone you to report that the message has arrived. Simply call a mail-stop or other FAX merchant in your town and make arrangements to refer to the shop's FAX number in your letters to employers (as in Michele's letter above).

Keys to an Effective International Resume

As suggested in the resumes that appear earlier in this chapter, international resumes differ from domestic resumes in at least five ways:

1. Names of companies, colleges, and organizations should not be referred to in abbreviated form alone (USC, YMCA, etc.). International decision-makers may not recognize the abbreviated form. After spelling out the term at least once in your letter or resume, you may refer to it by abbreviations thereafter, so long as the reference is clear.

2. Places of study and employment should be specified (George Mason University, Fairfax, Virginia). International employers are used to reviewing resumes from applicants who have worked and studied in a half dozen countries or more. Only American resumes seem to presume that everyone knows where Colgate is located, and so forth. By specifying location, you gain the additional advantage of "gilt by association"—that is, favorable associations based on location. An international employer who has never heard

of Macy's may nonetheless be impressed that you worked in its Washington, D.C., or New York City locations.

3. College studies and job responsibilities should be spelled out in more detail on international resumes. Typical American college majors such as economics or management may leave international employers wondering precisely what you studied and what you can do. You may want to list five or six of your major courses, by title, to suggest the nature of your academic training. Job responsibilities, similarly, should be defined thoroughly: What projects you supervised, why the results were important for the company, how many people you oversaw, where your products were distributed, and so forth. To avoid heavy paragraphs of prose, use bullets to break out these responsibilities beneath the name and location of the company and your job title.

4. While references may be available upon request, many international employers prefer that recommendation letters simply be sent along with the application package. Then all materials necessary for decision-making are at hand, without waiting (sometimes for weeks) for recommendation letters to arrive. To assemble your recommendation letters, simply inform your reference sources that you will be photocopying their letters and sending them to several companies. Your resume can then offer "Additional References Available Upon Request" for those companies that desire confidential or personalized reference letters.

5. Consider providing personal background about yourself and a professionally appropriate photograph. Employers within the United States prefer not to see your picture along with your resume simply because they are constrained by law not to consider race, age, or sex in hiring decisions. International employers, as a rule, are not so constrained, and often welcome the chance to get an impression of you as a person. For personal data, you might consider describing your outside interests, sports involvement, volunteer work, hobbies, civic involvement, and family life. (You must be the

judge of when such information will be an apropriate and advantageous addition to your resume. For some positions— international finance, for example—a more austere and impersonal resume may be desirable.)

An Example of a Personal Background
Statement at the End of a Resume

```
     PERSONAL BACKGROUND I'm a 24-year-old
entrepreneur who enjoys working closely with
people to actualize new ideas. As a member of
Rotary International since 1981, I've led
seminars on intercultural management and now
serve as chapter president for the Toledo,
Ohio, club. I maintain an active physical
life through jogging, swimming, and skiing.
My avocations include computers, HAM radio,
and volunteer work at a local hospital.
```

What about Desktop Publishing?

Desktop published resumes, like those included at the end of this chapter, have become the standard for international resumes. Others done in ordinary ribbon-type look amateurish by comparison.

If you don't have desktop publishing equipment, check with a university computing center or commercial photocopy center for the use of software such as Page Maker (Apple) or Ventura (IBM) to use in connection with a laser printer. Photocopy centers usually rent time on their computers (perhaps Macintosh) for desktop publishing. You'll want to have your resume and cover letter composed before renting such time—at $8 to $10 per hour, "writer's block" can be expensive!

Many resume and secretarial services offer desktop-published resumes from either your paper draft or word-processing disk. There are advantages, however, from undertaking the somewhat painful process of learning to use desktop publishing yourself. You will find it possible to make customized changes in your resume according to the company you're sending it to. Those kinds of changes are usually not possible or impractical when you're relying on (and paying for) a resume service for alterations.

Sample International Resumes

The following resumes are presented not as perfect models but as various approaches to the crisp, clear communication of business and personal information.

Maureen Connell
435-F South Lark Road
Arlington, Virginia 22206
(703) 555-2233

EDUCATION

Georgetown University, Washington, DC 1989-1991. Master of Business Administration candidate
Emphasis: International Business

St. Joseph's University, Philadelphia, PA 1978-1982. Bachelor of Arts in Political Science

University of Paris, La Sorbonne, Paris, France 1981. Foreign Exchange program, spring semester

EXPERIENCE

U.S. House of Representatives, Washington, DC Office of the Republican Leader   Fall, 1989
Intern.
Worked with leadership staff of Representative Robert H. Michel on budget reconciliation and
Congressional redistricting.

Republican Research Committee   1987-1989
Senior Research Analyst for House Leadership Committee.
Worked with Republican Members and Committee staff. Directed 9 task forces for the development,
introduction and implementation of specific legislation and of general policy initiatives. Participated
in strategy sessions and briefings between Members, White House personnel, and Administration
officials. Worked with national political party organization and special interest groups.

Budget Committee, Minority Staff   1986-1987
Policy analyst.
Tracked legislation, wrote staff reports and legislative summaries. Analyzed budget proposals, worked
with other Congressional staff, House and Senate committees, and federal agencies. Coordinated
Congressional activities with the Office of Management and Budget.

Children, Youth, & Families Committee, Minority Staff   1984-1986
Staff Assistant.
Assisted with committee projects, Congressional and constituent inquiries, drafted correspondence.
Organized local and national hearings. Acted as committee liaison to Republican Congressional
Offices and to outside organizations.

Fund For a Conservative Majority, Washington, DC   1983-1984
Receptionist for Political Action Committee.
Assisted staff in preparation of direct mail campaigns, preparation of Federal Committee Reports.

ACTIVITIES

Georgetown International Business Forum, Georgetown M.B.A. Yearbook, Georgetown M.B.A.
"Annual Report" student review.

OTHER

Proficient in Wordperfect, Lotus 123. Conversational French.

William Gorka
1724 Downey Lane, N.W. Washington, D.C. 20007
(202) 555-9125

EDUCATION

LAW: Georgetown University Law Center J.D., May 1992; G.P.A. — 8.5 (B/B-) (Honors in Legal Research & Writing)

BUSINESS: Georgetown University School of Business Administration M.B.A., May 1992

ENGINEERING: University of California, Los Angeles Ph.D. Mechanical Engineering, June 1992 (anticipated); G.P.A.—4.0(A) M.S. Mechanical Engineering, June 1988; G.P.A.—4.0(A) B.S. Mechanical Engineering, June 1988, cum laude; G.P.A.—3.7(A-)

PROFESSIONAL EXPERIENCE

Lyon & Lyon, Los Angeles, California　　　**May 1989 to August 1989**
Summer Associate
Researched and drafted legal memoranda; conducted patent disclosures; drafted patent application; composed patent amendment and restriction requirement.

CADAM INC, Burbank, California　　　**June 1985 to August 1988**
Product Analyst
Supported intellectual property copyright litigation; managed specialized marketing and development projects; conducted legal, marketing, and technical research; provided marketing competive analyses; developed research-oriented software in FORTRAN; conducted dealer training and trade show demonstrations (both demestically and in South America).

Jet Propulsion Laboratory, Pasadena, California　　　**June 1983 to June 1985**
Technical Aide B
Designed and built various scientific and technical apparatuses; operated machine shop equipment; conducted laboratory experiments.

ORGANIZATIONS

Georgetown University Law Center, American Criminal Law Review, Georgetown Law & Business Society (Chairman—High Tech Committee), The James Brown Scott Society of International Law.

University of California, Los Angeles, Tau Beta Pi (Engineering Honor Society), Phi Eta Sigma (Freshman Honor Society), Engineering Society of the University of California, Bruin Christian Fellowship, Golden Key National Honor Society Order of the Engineer.

Professional American Bar Association (ABA), Society of Manufacturing Engineers (SME), Computer Automated Systems Association (CASA), National Society of Professional Enineers (NSPE), California Society of Professional Engineers (CSPE), American Society of Mechanical Engineers (ASME), Christian Legal Society (CLS).

HONORS AND SCHOLARSHIPS

University of California, Los Angeles, UCLA Alumni Scholarhsip, UCLA Chancellor's Scholarship, Departmental Scholar American Society of Cost Engineers Scholarship, National Dean's List (1987-1988), Fourragere Bearer (Top 15% of graduating class).

Meet Twenty People Who Did It

Often the best information about the methods used in an international job search comes from Americans who have worked abroad. We interviewed twenty such people and asked them two questions: How did you get your international job? How do you recommend that others go about getting a similar job?

Brad Eberhart, a broker for Pacific Sun Financial:
"I worked in London as a researcher for an investment banking firm. I got the job simply by responding to an ad in the New York Times. A friend of mine also obtained a position as an exporter for Izod in Paris by applying directly to company. My advice to others? Get your application package in top shape and stick it out there."

Matthew Meyer, a bond broker for Gintelco, Inc.:
"It may sound like a typical story, but I got my job as a corporate bond broker in London through my Uncle Vincent. He knew the managing director of the London office and put in a good word for me. I would advise jobseekers to scan their relatives and acquaintances carefully to look for people who have international contacts. The inside track really helps."

Bob Foster, a systems analyst for TRW:
   "I was hired by the Mitsubishi Corporation in the United States, and was then sent to Japan for a year of training. It was an incredible year, filled with wave after wave of new learning experiences. I would recommend that anyone seeking work in Japan try to make connections first through a United States branch of the company."

Andrea Liu, a computer programmer/analyst for NCR Corporation:
   "I'm now seeking an international position in the Far East, so I can't speak from actual experience yet. But I have a good friend who got a job in Switzerland under an internship program for programmers. The process of finding that international job wasn't hard at all: He simply watched for foreign company who were recruiting at his school, the University of Colorado. I think your college recruitment office is one of your best tickets abroad."

Brenton R. Babcock, a product analyst for CADAM, Inc.:
   "Our parent company, Lockheed, has offices throughout the world. I accepted foreign assignment to Santiago, Chile, as a product analyst and trainer. One of the highlights of my stay was participation in an international trade show there. Talk about contacts! You meet people in your industry from all over the world. I was passing out and collecting business cards like mad. I guess my advice to others would be to link up with a company that offers the possibility of international assignment."

Maureen Mingey, a policy analyst for the State Department:
   "It doesn't always appear on my resume, but I worked as a nanny for a year while attending school in Germany. In my case, the job was arranged through the college placement office. But it provided me with an opportunity to get to know a prominent family and their friends. I learned about a lot of career opportunities that never appeared in the want ads. My roommate, however, didn't need personal contacts at all to get

her first international position. She saw an ad in the Wall Street *Journal*, sent in her resume and cover letter, and three weeks later was on her way to Europe for a career in sales and marketing. So I would advise others to try several channels of application—at the same time, if possible."

Michael J. Farrand, Senior Associate, ICF Corporation International:

"I worked as an English instructor in Rome, and got my job the old-fashioned way: by knocking on doors of private language schools there. Needless to say, my moderate competency in Italian was absolutely necessary to getting an interview. The instructors all spoke English, of course, but they only wanted to hire people who could communicate with clients. My advice to international jobseekers is to go to the country you're interested in, then try to make social and business connections. Often you can get your foot in the door by sending letters of inquiry in advance of your visit. Even though they may not offer you a job on the basis of your letter, they may invite you to stop by their place of business. That can lead to contacts, information, and eventually a job. Be aware of work permit regulations in the country you're visiting. Sometimes your employer can get you the necessary permits or can invent creative ways around them."

Richard Larson, a history professor in California:

"Four of my college friends and I saw an ad in the Los Angeles *Times* from an employment agency looking for teachers of English to send to a company school in Japan. On a lark, we all sent our resumes in, not expecting much. To our surprise, all five of us were interviewed by a company manager within a week and had offers of employment in Japan within two weeks. Only two of us accepted, but I was amazed at how streamlined the hiring process can be for jobs 10,000 miles away. Based on our experience, I would recommend that jobseekers watch the classified ads in major city newspapers and contact employment agencies that specialize in foreign positions."

Jennifer McCullough, a registered representative for Drexel Burnham Lambert, Inc.:

"Through relatives, I heard that positions were often open at United States embassies abroad. I applied to our Belgian embassy, and landed a job as Assistant Immigrant Visa Counselor. My advice to others would be to send your resume along with a dynamite cover letter to as many embassies as possible. But be prepared to move quickly if a job offer comes. The embassy jobs tend to be here today, gone tomorrow."

Cynthia North , a tax accountant with Price Waterhouse:

"Just out of college I accepted an entry-level accounting position with a "Big 8" firm with branch offices in Canada. I flew up on assignment for a week, and eventually ended up there for several years. I suppose I trace my international employment experience back to one question I asked in my initial job interview: 'Does your company do work outside the United States?' I made my selection of employers on that basis."

Craig Walker, a sales representative for Lanier:

"I had the time of my life as a claims broker for Lloyd's of London (in London) for six months. It may sound like boring work, but my cases brought me in contact with all kinds of people and situations. I think I learned more about international business in those six months than in any other period of my life. I got the job through a friend of my family. He knew of the opening, and made a phone call for me. But, once there, I worked with a lot of non-British employees who had simply applied for their positions without personal contacts. Those seeking international jobs shouldn't despair if they don't have influential family members or friends to help them out."

Joan Stein, a software consultant for American Management Systems:

"It wasn't the most lucrative job of my career, of course, but I wouldn't have traded the experience for anything: my months working on a communal farm—a *kibbutz*—in Israel. I made a few calls in Tel-Aviv and located the Central Office where assignments were made to such jobs. It was one of those situations, however, where I had to 'be there.' The process couldn't have taken place very well by mail. On the other end of the financial spectrum, I might mention a friend who got a marketing position for Avon in Japan. He had taken a series of intensive Japanese courses and applied through Avon's home office in the United States. Knowing a language well really sets you apart from the competition."

Sprague Simonds, a research analyst for Citibank:

"In one of the wildest years of my life, I was a white water river leader in a job that took me to several continents. I had always wanted to turn my avocation into an occupation. So I watched travel ads in the newspaper and magazines for agencies that were putting trips together. I went in person to see if they needed a trained leader, and got the job. Even though the resume is important, I would recommend that jobseekers get up the nerve to simply show up and shake some hands in the application process."

Bob Karig, operations officer, United States Army:

"I took the ads seriously about 'Join the Army and see the world.' I accepted assignment as executive officer for a United States Army Aviation battalion in Germany. Without sounding like a recruiter, I want to tell those looking for international positions not to ignore the many, many opportunities in the armed services. It's hard to think of a business or technical field that isn't represented in some form within the military."

Becky Bleich, a corporate assistant with Alex Brown & Sons, Inc.:
"My sister has all the luck. She worked as a marketing researcher at Interior Selections, a fabric-making and interior
design firm in London. The job came about when the general
manager of the firm mentioned to my parents that he needed
help with a marketing project. I would advise those seeking international jobs to tell parents, aunts, uncles, grandparents, and
extended family to keep their eyes and ears open for job possibilities. Many times these people have built up terrific contacts over the years."

Deborah Rich, new products supervisor, Cornnuts, Inc.:
"I literally walked into my international position. I was visiting
the University of Madrid, and wondered what kind of positions
were posted on the 'Employment Available' board for students
there. One posting advertised a position for an English
teacher—which turned out to be me. I would advise jobseekers
to turn a vacation into a job search. Find an area you really like,
then spend time around the university or town center finding
job leads and making personal contacts. If you're in college in
the United States now, consider asking some of your professors
for contacts abroad. Often they have colleagues who need research assistants or teaching aides."

Finally, we asked several nationals in major trading regions to
offer their advice to United States citizens seeking international
employment.

*Kazuto Wakatsuki, Staff Member, International Planning
Department, The Saitama Bank, Ltd., Japan:*
"Americans are generally unaware how aggressively Japanese
banks, insurance companies, security firms, and others are
recruiting foreign employees. In most cases, Japanese firms are
more interested in your academic preparation than in your work
experience. They are especially interested in finance and

economics majors. You can locate such firms by watching for their advertisements in the Wall Street *Journal*, New York *Times*, Washington *Post*, and other papers. Or you can make direct contact with Japanese companies by consulting the directories in your college careers office.

"Don't be discouraged if you don't speak or write flawless Japanese. Few Americans do. Japanese companies will appreciate it if you have taken a intensive course to give you the basics of the language, but all job interviews and initial job assignments will be in English, not Japanese.

"One word of advice, however: Do study Japanese management techniques and Japanese culture. Foreign employees are hired in part on their likelihood of 'fitting in' to the company and country. You can help your application by knowing how the Japanese relate at work and in their social lives."

Jean-Michel Beghin, software engineer, Hewlett-Packard, France:
"It is very difficult for a noncitizen to get a work permit for a career position in France without the assistance of a company or trade association. It makes best sense, therefore, to contact French companies that have branch offices here in the United States. For instance, 'Societe Generale' is a large French bank that has offices in New York City. These branch offices will know of hiring opportunities in France, and will be able to provide the kind of introduction and assistance for you that will avoid permit problems.

"Especially when seeking employment in France, know the language well. Your usefulness to a French company will be very limited if you cannot speak French with a high level of competency."

Barbara Thwaites, Consultant, Rehabilitation Services:
"In the Caribbean, newspapers are filled with job ads but hiring usually takes place through personal references and contacts. If you have a friend in Jamaica, for example, ask him or her to

find out about potential jobs for you. Once you have entre to the company, send a complete resume and follow-up, if possible, by a visit to the company. Latin cultures pay much more heed to your personal presence (an expression of sincere interest) than to the fanciest of resumes or application letters."

Amit Pande, Chartered Accountant, Mohinder Puri & Co., Chartered Accountants:

"The private sector in India is exploding with business opportunities, and the need for American liaisons and joint ventures has never been greater. Indian business leaders will take your paperwork very seriously, and often hire on the basis of it. Spend time putting together a flawless, complete application package. You may not get a second chance to add material later. Language competence is helpful, but most Indian firms will be looking primarily for your business or technical skills. Emphasize what you can do in your resume. At some point in the job application process, you will have to meet with your prospective employee or his representative in the United States. You may want to read about Indian culture prior to this meeting to understand customs, religion, diet, and so forth."

Mohammed Shanshal, Construction Manager:

"In Canada, the first step in your job search should be to apply through the Immigration Service for a work permit. Few career opportunities will be open to you without this necessary legal step. Thereafter, the application process is very similar to that in the United States. In French-speaking portions of Canada, you will want to demonstrate not only your language ability but also your respect for things French. Canadians dislike American applicants who 'have all the answers'—United States answers—from the beginning; better to show sincere interest in the Canadian approach to things."

Luis Edvardo Bravo, Financial Analyst, Central Bank of Chile:

"Latin American companies put great stock in formal introductions. It would be best if one of their trusted branch managers or trade representatives in this country wrote a letter (or made a call) of introduction to the home office prior to the arrival of your job application. Once you've been introduced, the company will probably follow up with a brief letter of interest inviting you to apply. You'll then have the name and direct address of one or more decision-makers in the company.

"Business documents, including applications, run somewhat longer in Chile and other Latin American countries than in the United States. A short, snappy resume, therefore, may do you more harm than good. Take time—and several pages, if necessary—to explain your education, your experience, your special skills, and your career goals. Your Latin American reader will take this volume of language as a sign of sincere interest and respect. Your cover letter should be similarly courteous and fulsome. If you do not speak Spanish, take the kind of course that will give you basic business and social phrases. Latin American companies resist interviewing or hiring applicants who have made no effort to learn Spanish."

Chapter Five

Finding the Right Country

Face it. The world isn't getting smaller. As more and more opportunities open up for each of us throughout the world, this planet is growing exponentially. It was Dorothy in *The Wizard of Oz* who inhabited the small world of yesterday—"right here in our own backyard." In sheer variety of possible experiences and involvements, our world is getting larger for each us by the minute.

The question is where you'll set down your stake and say, with Brigham Young, "This is the spot." If you've traveled at all, you know that for every international oasis there are a dozen hideous spots where you couldn't live or work with any satisfaction. How do you get to know a country's economy, customs, geography, recreations, attitudes, and religions?

Some applicants play the mental equivalent of darts with their international career futures—"Let's see, where shall I work?" The mind darts to a country on the map. "Hmm, New Zealand sounds interesting. I'll apply there." But New Zealand may not be at all your cup of tea. Your year or two of work there proves to be just an expensive and time-wasting detour on your eventual career path.

How can you prevent unintentional detours of this sort?

For most of us, it isn't a simple matter of Picking the Country, Picking the Company, Picking the Job, in that order. Sometimes we'll take our second or third choice of a country if the company or job is right. The process of evaluating our opinions is like juggling: One must keep as many balls in the air at once as we look them over and rearrange them.

This chapter suggests a four-part plan to help you settle upon a select list of countries, companies, and jobs for your application. The plan asks you to invest a total of twelve hours (in any installments you wish) to the task and pleasure of exploring your options.

Step One

Take a walking tour of international business by reading one or more of the following books:

The Global Marketplace: 102 of the Most Influential Companies Outside America, by Milton Moskowitz (Macmillan, 1987) [for everyone]

Work Your Way Around the World, by Susan Griffith (Writer's Digest, 1989) [especially for those who want short-term international work]

Going to Work, by Lisa Birnbach (Villard, 1988) [for internationals who are thinking about finding work in the United States]

As you read, make notes for yourself on 3 x 5 cards divided as follows:

Attractive country: _____

Attractive company: _____

Attractive job: _____

You don't have to fill in the entire card as you read. Sometimes you'll run across a particularly stimulating job idea—jot it down, even if no particular company or country is mentioned. Or you may run across a company and a country that interest you, but no job category may leap to mind. The goal is to jot down one or more of the three items.

At the conclusion of this first stage of reading, you'll probably have a dozen or more cards partially filled in with countries, companies, or positions you might be interested in. The process of using the cards has helped you keep many options open and growing without premature dismissals: "Naw, can't consider Spain because the book doesn't mention a furniture company there."

Step Two

Fill out the missing portions of each card. Consult one or more of the following directories to locate major corporations throughout the world, their principal activities, and addresses for information and application.

A key to your eventual success is to build wherever possible your career search around American companies with branch offices abroad or foreign companies with branch offices in the United States. Remember, the difficulties of obtaining work permits are formidable in many countries. You can save time and make money by working through some corporate base within the United States.

To identify companies and countries, see the *Directory of American Firms Operating in Foreign Countries*. Volume one lists in alphabetical order American firms which have operations overseas. Each entry contains the company's United States address and telephone number; the names of the president, CEO, and foreign officer in charge of overseas operations, and personnel director. Also listed are the company's principal products or services, number of employees, and the countries in which the company operates.

Volumes two and three contain listings by country—from Afghanistan to Zimbabwe—of the American firms' foreign operations. Each country listing includes alphabetically the name and United

States address of the parent firm, the name and address of its sub-sidiary or affiliate or branch in the foreign country, and the principal product line or service of the parent.

In addition, see the *Directory of Foreign Manufacturers in the U.S.* (Georgia State University Press). This directory lists foreign firms with branches in the United States and includes full citations of names, addresses, products lines, and other company information for both the parent firm and its United States branches.

To check on the often-tangled ownership relations among domes-tic and foreign companies, look in *Dun & Bradstreet's Who Owns Whom*, 1989. You'll find cross-listings of American companies with foreign subsidiaries as well as foreign companies with United States subsidiaries. Who would have thought, for example, that the plethora of Food-4-Less stores in the United States were actually owned by Franz Hariel & Cie, West Germany.

For information on European companies, see *Major Companies of Europe*, 1989. It gives executive names and addresses, telephone, cable, telex, and FAX numbers, along with financial data for hundreds of major European firms.

Also helpful is *Dun & Bradstreet's Principal International Busi-nesses*, 1990, giving basic company information and application data for companies on all continents.

If you've found country and company information but are strug-gling to put down a career you might pursue there, see the *American Almanac of Jobs and Salaries*, 1989 edition. It will define job titles and typical responsibilities for virtually any industry or organization you're considering. Also helpful is *Dun & Bradstreet's The Career Guide*, 1989. It organizes by discipline the kinds of jobs companies offer and goes on to give names and addresses for application to those companies.

Step Three

Get Commerce Department information and Embassy information for every country in your stack of cards.

To accomplish this, you'll need to write two letters for each country, both quite brief: First, a letter to the United States Department of Commerce asking for their latest economic and social information on the country at hand; and second, a letter to the country's own embassy, requesting information on the country.

Letter 1

```
(your return address)

(date)

Director of the Foreign Commercial Service
United States Department of Commerce
Washington, D.C. (ZIP)

Dear Director:
    I am considering professional involvement
in the country of _____, and would ap-
preciate receiving any general information
you have regarding that nation—its people,
business climate, social conditions, living
standards, customs, and so forth.
    May I also ask that you forward my name to
your Commerce Officer in _____? I
plan to be in touch with him or her in the
near future, and would appreciate your word
of introduction. I appreciate your efforts on
my behalf.

Sincerely,

(your typed name)
```

Letter 2

```
The Ambassador to the United States
Embassy of _____
Address
Washington, D.C. (ZIP)
```

Dear Ambassador:

   I am considering professional involvement in and relocation to your country. To learn as much as possible about _____, I would appreciate receiving general information on the country's people, history, business climate, and development plans.

   Thank you for your kindness in this matter. I look forward to our future association as my professional plans take shape.

Sincerely,

(your typed name)

From this mailing—the work of a single hour if you use mail merge on your word processor—you'll receive back a cornucopia of information of the countries of your choice. The Department of Commerce will send a wealth of data on trade forecasts, business predictions, and local economic statistics. In addition, the Department will probably offer a wide menu of further information resources available upon your request.

What you receive from the country's own embassy will vary according to country, but in general it will fill in the gaps in the Department of Commerce depiction of the country. From most embassies you'll receive a sell job, describing the country's wonderful opportunities, locales, and customs. You'll probably also receive the names of one or business or government leaders in the country who can prove extremely helpful to you in later correspondence with companies and organizations.

The whole process, from mailing your letters to receiving the information requested, seldom takes more than ten days. Your investment of a bit of time and a few stamps has given you an up- to-date library of information on the countries that interest you most.

Step Four

Narrow your job search to your five most attractive cards. Save the others for back-up consideration.

After receiving glowing reports from embassies and commerce officers, you may have trouble settling on which cards you want to earmark for action. The decision can be quite personal, involving your own best guess as to which cultural experience you would prefer to have. Your own likes and dislikes in matters of taste, politics, religion, and the consideration of family and friends become important factors when choosing a country.

Once you've wrestled successfully with these matters, begin the final research stage of your application process by deepening your understanding of the countries and companies you've selected.

First, find the latest *Overseas Business Report* on the country at hand. Single copies are available from the Publication Sales Branch of the United States Department of Commerce, Room 1617D, Washington, D.C. 20230. (A year's subscription at $14 can be ordered from the Superintendent of Documents, United States Government Printing Office, Washington, D.C. 20402.) These reports will tell you the following about the country you're interested in:

Foreign Trade Outlook
Promising Export Areas
Industry Trends
Trade Regulations
Distribution and Sales Channels
Transportation and Utilities
Advertising and Market Research
Credit
Investment

Taxation

Selling to the Government

Guidance for Business Travelers (including business
etiquette, language, and dress)

Sources for Economic and Commercial Information

Second, use the expertise of your reference librarian to locate recent books or articles on your chosen country. Global Quest, Inc. of Arlington, VA 22202 publishes a growing series of handbooks on commercial and cultural aspects of different countries.

Magazines such as *Fortune, Business Week, Forbes,* and others regularly present major articles on foreign trade developments and possibilities. For specific company information, as contained in foreign and United States business publications, see Predicasts F & S Index.

After all this research, what do you have besides a drawer full of information? You have, first, a basis on which to decide what jobs you want to pursue with vigor. You have, second, the kinds of company and country information that will make you credible as a candidate for an international position. And finally, you have the kind of insider's knowledge that will help you recognize overclaim and understatement on the part of foreign companies that want your services.

You're now ready to assemble your application package and pack your bags.

Chapter Six

Making Over the Ugly American

Ugly? Certainly not you or me—at least when we look into our own cultural mirror. In fact, we like what we see there: a go-getter, a high-energy type with no time to waste and eyes focused on the bottom line.

But those traditional American strong points may stick out like Pinocchio's nose when viewed from another culture's perspective. This chapter obviously can't point out each landmine in the treacherous terrain of intercultural business life. But we can take a few minutes simply to *listen* to what other cultures are saying about us. (Certainly we don't have to agree with their judgments, but we should hear them out.) Then we'll list and discuss twenty areas of cultural sensitivity, areas you should investigate and reflect upon before stepping into an international interview or other business circumstance.

Listening in on the World

The following quotations were collected by J. P. Fieg and J. G. Blair* to demonstrate that people aren't the same everywhere. As you read each opinion expressed, try to resist the temptation to "fight

---

* Fieg, J.P. and Blair, J.G., *There Is A Difference: Seventeen Intercultural Perspectives*. Meridian House International, Washington, D.C., 1985.

back" as a red-blooded Yankee. Try instead to understand what lies behind the negative impressions—the attitudes, beliefs, customs, and assumptions that lie at the heart of another culture. As an international worker, you'll spend your career learning to make cultural adjustments. There's no time like the present to begin.

From India
   "Americans seem to be in a perpetual hurry. Just watch the way they walk down the street. They never allow themselves the leisure to enjoy life; there are too many things to do."

From Japan
   "Family life in the United States seems harsh and unfeeling compared to the close ties in our country. Americans don't seem to care for their elderly parents."

From Kenya
   "Americans appear to us rather distant. They are not really as close to other people—even fellow Americans—as Americans overseas tend to portray. It's like building a wall. Unless you ask an American a question, he will not even look at you . . . individualism is very high."

From Turkey
   "Once . . . in a rural area in the middle of nowhere, we saw an American come to a stop sign. Though he could see in both directions for miles and no traffic was coming, he still stopped!"

From Colombia
   "The tendency in the United States to think that life is only work hits you in the face. Work seems to be the one motivation."

From Indonesia

"The atmosphere at a sorority party looks very intimate, but if the same people met on the street, they might just ignore one another. Americans look warm, but when a relationship starts to become personal, they try to avoid it."

From Indonesia

"In the United States everything has to be talked about and analyzed. Even the littlest thing has to be 'Why? Why? Why?' I get a headache from such persistent questions. I still can't stand a hard-hitting argument."

From Ethiopia

"The American seems very explicit; he wants a Yes or No—if someone tries to speak figuratively, the American is confused."

From Ethiopia

"Trying to establish an interpersonal relationship in the United States is like trying to negotiate over or break down a wall; it is almost like a series of concentric circles. You have to break down different levels before you become friends."

From Iran

"It is puzzling when Americans apply the word friend to acquaintances from almost every sector of one's past or present life, without necessarily implying close ties or inseparable bonds."

From Iran

"The first time my professor told me: 'I don't know the answer—I will have to look it up,' I was shocked. I asked myself, 'Why is he teaching me?' In my country a professor would give a wrong answer rather than admit ignorance."

From Iran

"To place an aged or senile parent in a nursing home is appalling for our people; taking care of one's parents is the children's duty. Only primitive tribes send their old and infirm off to die alone!"

From Indonesia

"The American wife of my English professor in Indonesia once asked me why I never invited her to my house. I frankly could not give her a direct answer. There was no reason why I should invite her since there were no parties being held by my family . . . if she really wanted to come to the house, she was always welcome at any time. I know now that in America you cannot come freely to any place unless you are invited."

From Hong Kong

"I was surprised [in American families] to see the servant eating with the children and calling the children by their Christian names."

From Australia

"I am impressed by the fact that American teachers never stop going to school themselves."

From Vietnam

"Americans are handy people, even the women. They do almost everything in the house by themselves, from painting walls and doors to putting glass in their windows. Most of them showed me the pretty tables and bookshelves they made by themselves in their spare time."

From Kenya

"In American schools, the children are restless, inattentive, and rebellious, and the teachers have poor class discipline."

From Japan

"Unfortunately, I have been given a bad impression of some Americans who speak of their own country very badly, especially of its foreign policy. I knew all the foreign policy of America isn't good, but I did not want to be told so by a native. I hate people who speak badly of their own land, even if they speak the truth."

From Korea

"In a twelfth-grade American social studies class, the teacher gave choices of assignments for the next class. I didn't like the idea of pupils choosing the assignment. I wonder what these pupils will do later in life when there are no choices in the duty assigned to them. They must learn while they are in school how to do well the jobs assigned to them from above."

From Afghanistan

"I was so much surprised by the many people in America who were under special diet to lose weight. In our society, we are in search of food in order to gain weight."

From Algeria

"I was horrified at the ignorance of Americans about my country—Algeria. They knew nothing at all about it—location, people, language, political condition."

From the Philippines

"They say children are everywhere the same. In my observations I found out a couple of ways where children differ. Children in the United States are very forward in their way of speaking, even to their parents and elders. Children in America show a lack of respect for old age. Also, I have observed that children here do not offer their services to the parents willingly. They either have to be told what is to be done or they have to be given some reward or compensation for what they do."

From Indonesia

"The questions Americans ask me are sometimes very embarrassing, like whether I have ever seen a camera. Most of them consider themselves the most highly civilized people. Why? Because they are accustomed to technical inventions. Consequently, they think that people living in bamboo houses or having customs different from theirs are primitive or backward."

From Egypt

"My American hostess asked me, 'Would you like to settle down in our country for good?' She was surprised when my answer was in the negative, though I took great pains to make it as diplomatic as possible."

From listening to these actual responses to American behavior, you may begin to appreciate the importance of the "Five Intercultural Commandments" much of the rest of the world would like to teach many the Americans headed abroad:

I. *Thou shalt not be Ameri-centric.*

Our nation, God love it, has existed for a mere two centuries. Other cultures, some of them thousands of years old, resent our cultural myopia and lack of interest in their ways and accomplishments.

II. *Thou shalt not assume.*

Americans get into cultural trouble most quickly when they rush to apply American answers to foreign circumstances. Americans should look before they leap.

III. *Thou shalt not be a money-grubber.*

As quaint as it may seem, many cultures value social standing, friendship, family relations, and inner peace more than money. (In fairness, many Americans hold these same values.) But foreign cultures often make negative judgments about Americans and money: our zest in spending it, talking about it, and acting as if it mattered most of all.

IV. *Thou shalt slow down.*

Much of the world runs at a slower pace than do American business people. Our frenetic schedules and antsy antics raise questions for foreign cultures about our stability, trustworthiness, and general sanity. When you're dancing with a foreign company, don't set the tempo yourself.

V. *Thou shalt try to fit in.*

American enclaves exist in every international capital—areas where Americans feel comfortable because they don't have to adjust their living styles to the surrounding culture. They can speak American English to their neighbors, throw steaks on the barbecue, and, in general, maintain the illusion that they're back home in Indiana. Foreign cultures resent such unwillingness to give new experiences, attitudes, and customs a try.

Again, the intent of rehearsing these reminders is not to suggest that you leave your own beliefs and habits behind when you go abroad. Instead, the goal is to remove obstacles from your international employment path. You have to see the fallen branch to avoid tripping over it.

A Checklist of Cultural Pitfalls

Perhaps within a matter of weeks you'll be participating in an intercultural interview, social occasion, or company visit that may make or break an opportunity for an international career. Don't blow it. Take time to think through your possible interactions with a foreign culture in each of the following areas:

1. *Greeting behaviors*

   How do people in the culture say hello and goodbye? Do they touch? How? What do they say?

2. *Visits to homes and offices*

   How should you relate to your host? Is a gift in order? What seating arrangements are expected? What topics are appropriate for conversation, and in what order? What compliments are customary?

3. *Presentations*

   What will you be expected to say? How should your presention begin? How should you show respect for those present? What pattern of organization and persuasion will be most effective? How should you close? How long should you speak? Is it appropriate to ask for or receive questions? Should you use visual aids and handouts? What personal information should you disclose?

4. *Meetings*

   How should you interact with others around the table? Where should you sit? How should you receive recognition to speak? How should your speaking differ from participation in a typical American meeting?

5. *Gestures*

   What meaning does the culture attach to eye contact, arm and hand movements, posture, touching, laughing, yawning, crossing the legs, and so forth? Which movements indicate a lack of respect or unprofessionalism?

6. *Dress and Grooming*

   How should you look for professional purposes? Which aspects of traditional American dress, grooming, and accessories (such as sunglasses, jewelry, and so forth) will strike the culture as out-of-place?

7. *Gender Relations*

How do men relate to men? Men to women? Women to men? Women to women? What topics of conversation are appropriate or inappropriate? What degree of touching is allowed? What limits are established on giving or receiving criticism? What compliments can be given?

8. *Language*

When is it appropriate to speak the foreign language, and when English? If your language skills in the foreign language are limited, when should you attempt to speak or write it?

9. *Religion and Morals*

What are the predominant beliefs and moral attitudes of the culture? What topics, jokes, suggestions, and political assertions are acceptable and unacceptable in the culture? What social behaviors, including smoking, drinking, and gambling, are out of bounds for the culture? How are you expected to act when others around you are observing religious or cultural/political customs?

10. *Work Relations*

How are you expected to relate to superiors and subordinates? What topics are appropriately discussed with each? Do relationships differ during the workday and after work?

I hope that, in contemplating a particular culture, you drew a blank on several of these items. Simply recognizing that, as an American, you may have much to learn about other cultures is a big step in the right direction.

Now how do you go about learning as much as possible about another culture before putting your neck (and possible career future) on the line in an interview or company visit? First, read about the culture (perhaps using one of the books listed in Appendix J). Your librarian can assist you in finding colorful and fascinating books and articles. Second, take the initiative and *talk* to a recent visitor to the culture or, better yet, a native. Perhaps someone in your present company or social circle has visited or even comes from the country. Steer conversation toward the ten points of cultural sensitivity listed above. Ask questions and show interest. Finally, use vacation time to learn about other cultures through *travel*. If you can't afford to visit your target culture, try to spend time in a similar, nearby culture. You can learn much about France, for example, by spending time in Quebec, and much about Spain by visiting Mexico. (Granted, there are also substantial differences.)

In evaluating your potential for employment, an international personnel director or other interviewer will be asking, "How will he or she fit in with our present staff and our clientele?" The answer to that question will be determined not by your impressive educational credentials, long list of work experiences, or desktop-published resume. Your potential to fit in will be appraised by your interpersonal and intercultural awareness and sensitivity. The key to success lies in showing sincere interest in others, no matter how different they may be from residents of Main Street, U.S.A.

Chapter Seven

Preparing for an International Job Interview

You've on the phone with an employer based in London. Jill Trevorson, personnel manager for an investment banking firm, has just called to express her interest in interviewing you for a summer internship, with long-term career possibilities.

What should you expect? No, she probably won't offer to send you a ticket for the Concorde, or any other airliner for that matter. In most cases, foreign employers will arrange an in-the-States interview, at least for the first screening. Jill's company, for example, is associated with Lloyd's Bank in New York. You're invited there for the interview. But wait a minute. You live in Cincinnati. Does she expect you to get to New York at your own expense, simply in hopes of getting the internship?

The painful answer to that question is yes. In many cases, international employers, particularly in Europe, think of major cities as closely linked by rail and air. A London student, for example, would think nothing of popping up to Manchester on the train for an interview. International employers often aren't aware that distances and transportation costs within the United States can pose a significant hurdle for the job-seeker on a budget.

Be sure to clarify, therefore, who's picking up the tab for your interview travel and lodging. For example you may ask, "Does your company usually pay for travel and lodging expenses, or would these be my responsibility?" Jobseekers often discover that the foreign employers think Oklahoma City is just down the road from Minneapolis. Once they understand the distances involved, most companies are willing to assist with transportation and lodging costs. By clarifying where you are in relation to where they plan the interview, you may save yourself needless expense.

I'm not suggesting, by the way, that all international employers will arrange a first interview for you within the United States. Some, particularly in Asia and South America, will assume that you plan a trip to their region in the near future and can be interviewed on-site at that time. Use vacation travel wisely, therefore, in coordination with your international job search.

But back to the future: You're invited to an interview at Lloyd's Bank in New York City. Jill Trevorson tells you that the company's London-based recruiting director will be in New York to interview you and other candidates. Here are ten things you can expect in an international employment interview. Forewarned is forearmed!

1. You will be judged in part by how you look.

Like it or not, your clothing and grooming play a significant (though not decisive) role in your hiring. And "Dress for Success" books notwithstanding, there is no one formula for how to dress. (For instance, personnel managers scoff one popular book's advice on "power suits" for women. "I'm so sick of seeing a gray suit, white blouse, and red accessories," one personnel manager told me. "We're not going to hire someone who thinks professionalism means a certain uniform.")

Better advice, he says, is to "dress to express, not impress." Wear business attire that suits you and the situation. If you have to choose between more conservative or liberal clothing, lean toward the conservative side.

2. You may overlook some of the key decision-makers.

Many job candidates have sat silently, even sullenly, waiting in a reception room for their interview. They make no effort to get to know the secretary, and may even be curt with him or her. What a mistake! The impressions of the office staff are often invited by the interviewing manager or volunteered by staff members. The intuitions of a seasoned secretary mean much to his or her superior.

Take time, therefore, to make appropriate small talk with people you meet before the interview. Often they can give you valuable information ("Mr. Sajaki loves to talk about golf") and tips ("The company seems especially interested in your proposal-writing skills"). For that matter, look around the reception room. If annual reports, company literature, or company-related business articles are set out on the tables, they're probably there for a reason. Be the one candidate who can say in the interview, "Yes, I noticed in your annual report that . . ."

3. First impressions matter.

The first five minutes of an interview are crucial. Interview research suggests that many interviewers make up their minds about a candidate in those first few minutes, and then spend the remainder of the interview confirming their impressions. But what sort of questions make up the first five minutes, and how can a job candidate prepare?

In most international employment interviews, the "tough" questions for which you have rehearsed answers don't occur at the outset of the interview. Instead, this time is devoted to ice-breakers—small talk about the weather, parking, traffic, your hometown, your hotel, and so forth. Too many candidates make the mistake of giving minimal "yes/no" responses to these efforts of the interviewer to become acquainted. Don't make this mistake. It is as much your responsibility to put the interviewer at ease as it is his or her responsibility to make you feel comfortable. You have everything to gain by presenting yourself at the beginning of the interview as a sociable, friendly conversationalist.

You may, for example, want to notice what's on your interviewer's walls or desk. Are those soccer (i.e., "football") trophies on top of the cabinet? Is that a picture of a large family or new baby on the desk? Many of the most productive topics for opening "small talk" are staring at you from the interviewer's office.

4. Your interview answers shouldn't sound like lectures.

Watch the hands and eyes of your interviewer to know when enough is enough. Nonverbal signals such as averted eyes, hand movements, shifting posture, and other signs tell you that the interviewer has heard enough in response to one question and is ready to move on.

5. Give headlines before launching into a long story.

It is not uncommon in international employment interviews to face unwieldy, complex questions such as "Tell me about your preparation" or "What challenges do you foresee in this position?" If you know in advance that you'll be talking for two minutes or more in response to such questions, establish the structure of your answer at the outset. For example, your answer to the question regarding your preparation might begin with this kind of headline: "I'll try to answer that question by telling you about my education, my primary work experiences, and my work habits." There—you've established an agenda, a shopping list, for both you and the interviewer. Your answer seems organized and satisfying precisely because you have set out the ground rules for what you will and won't discuss. The much less attractive alternative to such headlining is the kind of rambling answer we've all heard in interviews: "Well, let's see. I graduated from high school in 1982 and then . . ."

6. Give eye contact to all participants in the interview.

When being interviewed by more than one person in a room, it's common to give eye contact almost exclusively to the person asking the questions. Let's take the case of an interview I observed recently in San Juan, Puerto Rico. The candidate faced an interview panel of three executives—a bank vice president, the personnel manager, and the marketing manager. You can guess who did virtually all of the questioning: the two subordinates in the room. The vice president sat back as a silent observer, only nodding occasionally. In this hour-long interview, the candidate made the mistake of looking only at the personnel manager and marketing manager. He never once met and held the eyes of the vice president.

When the interview ended, the interviewers' impressions of the candidate fell strictly in line with the amount of eye contact they received during the interview (a phenomenon borne out by interview research). The personnel manager and marketing manager liked the candidate, and used words such as "direct," "honest," and "personable" to describe her characteristics. But the most important decision-maker in the room—the vice president who had received virtually no eye contact—had different impressions: "a bit stand-offish," "not a good fit," and "nervous or somewhat hostile."

Obviously, the candidate should have looked directly at her questioner at the beginning of her answer, and then distributed her direct eye contact to each person in the room for the remainder of the answer. Remember, the most important people in the room usually ask the fewest questions.

7. Expect interruptions and deal with them graciously.

In many, if not most, international employment interviews, the phone will ring, the secretary will pop in for an urgent question, or the intercom will blare. Don't show even the hint of annoyance at such interruptions, even if your interviewer shows his or her irritation. If you've lost your train of thought due to such intrusions, politely ask the interviewer's help in getting back on track: "May I ask you to repeat your question?" "We were discussing my educational background. Did you want to hear more about my graduate degrees?"

8. Your responses should sound natural, not memorized.

You score no points with an interviewer by rattling off a rehearsed answer. When the international interviewer's English skills are less than yours, you may actually sabotage the interview by a slick answer delivered at machine-gun pace. Instead, try to give the interviewer the impression that the question interests you and deserves your careful thought (even if you've read the question in this book or heard it a dozen times before in other interviews). Do you recall those awful, stilted answers given by Miss America candidates in the interview stage of that competition? That's exactly the way you don't want to sound in your answers. Respond naturally, sincerely, and conversationally.

If you are temporarily stumped by a question or "go blank," tell the interviewer politely that you need a moment to answer the question: "Please give me just a moment to think about my best answer to that question" or "That's a good question—let me think for a moment to give you a complete answer." No interviewer reacts negatively to such requests. If anything, interviewers feel that you are dignifying the question (and, by extension, the question-asker) by taking time to really think about your response.

9. Adapt all terms and references to your interview audience.

In an international interview, you can't assume that common United States terms will be understood by your audience. High school means very different things in various parts of the world, and your references to your junior year, whether in high school or college, can often be confusing to international interviewers. In such cases, you may want to refer to your education by year—"grade twelve in America's twelve-year system"—or in relation to understood terms— "the first year of my Master's program." Initials such as B.A. may confuse an audience more familiar with A.B. or other terms.

Similarly, in referring to past employers, you may often want to explain their type of business or relative prominence to your questioners. The Big Eight accounting firms, for example, aren't so big everywhere in the world, and you may need to explain exactly what Ernst, Whinney or Price Waterhouse does.

10. Ask questions that show your sincere interest in the international company.

Candidates obsessed with "scoring" in interviews often forget that they are judged as much by the quality of their questions as by their answers. In most interviews, you will be asked, "Do you have any questions about the company?" The only wrong answer to this question is, "No, I think we've covered everything." Consider: You're asking for the company's interest in you as an employee but, in return, aren't able to come up with a single expression of interest in the company? It doesn't compute.

Some good stand-by questions are the following:

(asked of the interviewer) "What has been your experience with the company? Have you been happy here?"

"Where do you see the company going in the next three (five, etc.) years?"

"How would you describe employee relations at the company?"

It's tempting, but usually unwise, to ask self-serving questions regarding raises, vacations, and so forth. (There will be an appropriate time for such questions after you've established the company's interest in hiring you.) You may want or need to ask rather blunt questions about salary. This line of questioning can be pursued without putting interviewers off: "What is the usual salary range for this position?" Notice that you haven't asked "What will I be paid?" Interviewers may not be willing or able to name an exact number in the interview. And by asking for the usual pay range you have put yourself in position to ask for more, because you are by no means a usual employee, right?

What Will They Ask?

Bearing in mind that your answers should never sound memorized, you may nevertheless want to think through and practice answering aloud the most common interview questions:

Questions about Your Education
* What do you consider your successes in school?

* What kinds of subjects did you dislike or avoid in school?

* What kind of jobs did you hold while in school?

* How did you decide which college (school) to attend?

* How would you evaluate the school you attended in relation to other programs?

Questions about Your Skills and Work Experience

* What can you offer this company at the beginning of your job here?

* What specific strengths made you effective in previous positions?

* How would you go about managing a budget for your work-unit?

* What do you consider some of the most important ideas you contributed in previous positions?

* Describe a typical day in a previous position.

* Evaluate a previous boss. What did you like or dislike about his or her managerial style?

* Tell me about some of the people you worked with in previous positions. How did you relate to them?

* What do you think it takes to be successful in the position you seek?

Questions about Your Attitudes and Intelligence

* What would you like to be doing two years from now?

* What risks did you take in a previous position, and what were the results of those risks?

* Tell me about a failure of some sort in your professional life, and how you handled that failure.

* Describe the best boss you ever had.

* What kinds of things do you think this company might do to make you more successful in your position?

*   What do you know about this company?

Such challenging interview questions, of course, are open-ended, requiring more than a "yes/no" response. You may want to talk out answers to these questions into a tape recorder. Simply listening to the quantity, quality, stops, and starts of your answers can be the best way to improve your interviewing manner. As you listen (sometimes a painful experience), jot down notes on specific ways in which you can improve. For example, you might want to note "avoid umms, get right to the point, keep examples and anecdotes brief," and so forth. With these goals in mind, practice your answers again on tape. With even a few practice sessions, you'll hear definite improvement and feel your confidence rising.

Here are sixty-five more questions that I've collected over the years from observing and participating in employment interviews:

1. Please tell me about your previous job.

2. What do you believe were your major responsibilities in that job?

3. What kind of job experiences have you had that relate to this position?

4. What aspects of your previous job did you like?

5. What aspects of your previous job did you dislike?

6. What are some of the things you spent the most time on in your previous job?

7. What are some of the assignments in your previous job that you did particularly well? Why?

8. What are some of the assignments in your previous position that you found difficult to do? Why?

9. Tell me about a problem you solved on your previous job.

10. What did you do when you couldn't solve a problem in your job?

11. Describe your boss's method of management.

12. For what things did your boss compliment you?

13. In your previous job, how much work was done on your own? As part of a team?

14. What was the most innovative idea you introduced in your previous job?

15. Describe your techniques for getting the job done.

16. What school have you have that can be helpful in performing the job for which you are applying?

17. What are your own objectives with regard to this position?

18. What are your long-term career objectives?

19. In your own career, where do you want to be one (three, five) year(s) from now?

20. What do you plan to do to reach your career objectives?

21. How do you feel about the progress you've made so far in your present or previous job?

22. Do you believe your talents and abilities are well matched to this job? How and why?

23. What are your greatest assets?

24. How did you choose the school you attended?

25. Did you change your course of study? Why?

26. Did you change schools? Why?

27. Why did you major in your particular field?

28. In what extracurricular activities were you involved in school?

29. What made you choose those particular activities?

30. What accomplishments did you feel proud of at school?

31. What experiences at school do you wish you had a chance to do over? Why?

32. How did you pay for your education?

33. Did you hold any leadership positions in school?

34. What things interest you outside of work?

35. What do you like to do best?

36. What things give you the greatest satisfaction?

37. Have your interests changed in recent years?

38. How well did you do in school?

39. What grades did you receive?

40. In what courses did you do best? Why?

41. With what courses did you have the most trouble?

42. From what courses did you get the most benefit? Why?

43. From what courses did you get the least benefit? Why?

44. Do you feel that your grades fairly reflect your ability? Why or why not?

45. If you had it to do over again, would you take the same course of study?

46. How do you view the job for which you are applying?

47. If you were to get this job, in what areas could you contribute immediately? Where would you need training?

48. What barriers do you see that might prevent you from performing your job as effectively as would like?

49. Do you have the tools and support that you need to do your job?

50. What do you understand to be the purpose or mission of the company?

51. How do you feel about the day-to-day work tasks involved with this position?

52. How well do you work under pressure? Give me some examples.

53. How well do you get along with your peers?

54. What kind of people rub you the wrong way?

55. How do you go about motivating people?

56. What kinds of problems do you enjoy solving?

57. What can you tell me about your level of ambition?

58. How do you spend your free time?

59. What newspapers and magazines do you read regularly?

60. What is your definition of success?

61. What did you learn from a previous position?

62. What can you tell me about your level of creativity?

63. Do you work better alone or as part of a team? Explain.

64. What motivates you?

65. Why should this company hire you?

After the Interview

Few job offers are made on the spot. Within a matter of days (sometimes weeks), you may receive a verbal or written job offer, or you may be invited for further interviews. Given the distances involved, some of these later interviews may be by phone.

But the period immediately following your initial interview shouldn't be considered merely a waiting game. You should write a thank-you letter to your company host and/or interviewer. This message need not be long, but should express your appreciation for their interest in you and your impression of the company. Here's a sample:

```
Dear Sr. Ortiz:
    I enjoyed our discussion yesterday and want
to thank you for your hospitality during my
visit to Zapata Industries. I was particular-
ly impressed by my tour of the new Juarez
production facility and by the cooperative
spirit among your employees.
```

```
    Please don't hesitate to contact me if you
need further information helpful to your
decision-making. I look forward to hearing
from you.
```

If you spent time with several employees during your visit, name them in your thank-you letter: "I enjoyed meeting Frank Rodriguez, Rosa Sanchez, and you during my visit, and thank you all for . . . " In the rush and possible anxiety of an interview visit, you may tend to forget the names of people you meet. Get business cards or jot down names in preparation for writing a thank-you letter.

The days immediately following a job interview are an excellent time to check out the claims made by the company during your visit. You may soon be asked to commit a significant portion of your life to the company—you certainly want to make sure that you haven't been hyped during your interview. Relocating to Calcutta for a company that will go into receivership within six months isn't what you had in mind by an international work experience.

If you receive no word for ten days after an interview, it's appropriate to write a brief, polite letter of inquiry or make a phone call to your contact at the company. Here's a sample "what's-going-on" letter:

```
Dear M. Villan:
    I'm writing to re-emphasize my interest in
the position we discussed during my visit to
your corporate headquarters on May 9. If I
can be helpful in supplying further informa-
tion or materials, please don't hesitate to
call or write.
I look forward to our next conversation.
With best regards,
```

Accepting, Postponing or Refusing an International Job Offer

Just as you had hoped, you receive the job offer by phone. If you like what you hear, you may want to give your tentative acceptance on the phone—subject to your review of the written job offer (which you have every right to request). In that written offer you should ask that the following matters be specified:

* The job for which you are being hired, including any provisions or terms you have negotiated with the company.

* The amount you will be paid, and any currency or tax understanding you've reached with the company. Is the stated salary in American dollars? In highly inflationary economies, have you protected yourself drastic losses in the real value of your salary? Do you know how that salary will be taxed?

* The kind of benefits package, severance agreement, and other matters that have been agreed upon.

* Who will pay for relocation expenses.

* The date you are expected to report for work.

It's crucial to get these matters in writing prior to formal acceptance of an international job offer. Too often, some presumed understandings get "lost in translation," leaving both employer and new employee unsure of who said what. If a company representative is unwilling to put the job commitment in writing, you've located a definite red flag to your future association.

Your formal acceptance should similarly be in writing, as in this sample letter:

Dear Mr. Peters:

  I am pleased to accept the position as described in your letter of May 18. I understand that the company wishes to approve my relocation expenses in advance of my move. After receiving bids this week from trans-Atlantic shippers, I'll forward them to you by express mail.

  Thank you for your kind offer to meet me at Heathrow airport at 9 a.m., June 1, gate 37. I'll look forward to seeing you then.

With best regards,

If you're fortunate enough to have more than one international employment offer on your desk at the same time, you will want to send a postponement letter. Sending this communication is much better than simply letting time pass without any message to prospective employers.

```
Dear Mr. Peters:
    I deeply appreciate the position offered in
your letter of May 18. May I request a period
of ten days to consider it? You'll have my
answer by express mail no later than May 28.
    Thank you for considering this request and,
again, for the position offered.
Sincerely,
```

Or you may have changed your mind about the position altogether. In this case, take the time to thank the company that has probably invested a thousand dollars or more in the hiring process for you. It's not only the right thing to do, but makes good business sense. You may be knocking on this employer's door at some point in the future.

```
Dear Mr. Peters:
    Thank you for offering the position
described in your letter of May 18. Unfor-
tunately, I have made other professional com-
mitments that will not make it possible for
me to accept your offer.
    Please accept my very best wishes for the
future.
Sincerely,
```

If you're new to the international interview process entirely, or need to brush up your skills, three helpful videotapes may be available through your local university or public library:

Face to Face Payoff: Dynamics of Interviewing Available through Video Software and Production, Yonkers, New York.

The Colonel Comes to Japan Available through LCA Video Films, New York.

Going International: Bridging the Culture Gap Available through Copeland Griggs Productions, San Francisco, CA

Chapter Eight

Facing the Facts
about Work Permits

The story of your right to work in other countries is short to tell: You
have no rights. Countries ranging from Australia to EEC nations to
Japan welcome your tourist dollars but have severely restricted your
ability to find legal employment during your stay.

For example, in France an employer must demonstrate that virtually no French citizen available for work possesses the same skills
as a non-French citizen applying for work. In New Zealand, there is
a two-month waiting list even for a required in-person interview for
a one-month work permit (the usual tourist visa limit for Americans).
In Holland, official literature tells non-EEC nationals that it is illegal
even to seek employment in the country. A Dutch work permit
(*tewerkstellingsvergunning*) is occasionally granted to a non-EEC national, but almost always in connection with a government-negotiated
deal with a major Dutch company. In Switzerland, each canton
receives a very limited quota of 9-month work permits (*Aufen-
thaltsbewillingung*) that turn out to be about as desirable (and rare) as
Super Bowl tickets. Once these have been passed out, only the 3-
month *Saisonbewilligung* are available, and these too prove difficult
to obtain without the aid of a Swiss employer. (Australians and New
Zealanders, it is interesting to note, cannot obtain work permits of any

kind in Switzerland.) In Scandinavia, non-native work permits are granted only when there is no unemployment in the field in question. And when granted, these permits are good only for three months.

What to do? A United States citizen's alternatives come down to four:

1. *Find employment with a United States company doing business abroad.* These companies have usually worked out country-by-country agreements whereby they can place employees for extended periods in international positions. These agreements often involve some kind of reciprocity, in which the company brings foreign nationals to United States-based positions. (See the extensive list of such companies in the appendix.)

2. *Work through an influential foreign employer who is able to pull strings to obtain the permits you require.* Important foreign corporations sometimes have unpublicized exemptions or special ins with regard to work laws. This is especially true in high- need areas of employment such as TEFL (teaching English as a foreign language), computer science, health care, engineering, and some agricultural fields.

3. *Work through international exchange and trainee programs that have already negotiated work permits for participants.* You can contact these four organizations for more information on such programs:

Council on International Educational Exchange (CIEE)
205 E. 42nd St.
New York, NY 10017
Tel. (212) 661-1450

International Agriculture Exchange Association (IAEA)
National Agricultural Centre
Kenilworth, Warwickshire CV8 2LG, England
Tel. (0203) 22890.

International Association for the Exchange of Students for
   Technical Experience (IAESTE)
Seymour Mews, London W1, England
Tel. 01-486-5101.

International Secretaries
174 New Bond St.
London W1Y 9PB, England
tel. 01-491-7100

4. *Work on the black market.* The great majority of these jobs are casual labor in restaurants, hotels, construction sites, and on farms. Depending on the country in which you are working, deportation is a day-to-day possibility, and your employer faces the threat of heavy fines. You have little protection against employers who decide not to pay you.

It's unrealistic, therefore, to think that you will find lasting international employment in the black labor market. It's equally unrealistic to list international employers who regularly hire black market workers—such a list, though it could be created, would be a virtual shopping list for enforcement authorities within the country.

Students and others who have returned safely from an effort to work around the world often give this advice to friends contemplating a similar trip: Work an extra few months in the United States to save up travel money. Then go abroad as what you are—a tourist, not a laborer. As the information on work permits suggests, most foreign economies are highly protected against unauthorized intrusion by nonnational workers.

For Non-U.S. Nationals: How to Work Legally in the United States

As is true in most countries, United States laws related to immigration and work permits change frequently. The following information is based on legislation in effect at the time of publication.

Since the passage of the 1986 Immigration Reform and Control Act, United States employers face legal and financial penalties if they do not verify the citizenship and work status of their employees. As a non-U.S. national, therefore, you should not expect to talk your way into long-term or career-oriented work experiences in the United States. Employers have too much at stake to accept you. Even traditionally loose areas of black market labor such as agriculture, kitchen help, and hotel services are now heavily scrutinized by the Immigration and Naturalization Service (INS).

The easiest legal route to a United States job, therefore, is enter the country under a student visa. These are relatively simple to obtain once you have been accepted for study by an American college or university. You will be classified as an F-1 or J-1 student, depending upon your country of origin, proposed college program, and other factors. In either case, you are granted substantial access to American jobs.

For example, during the period of your student visa you can work on campus up to twenty hours per week during the school session and up to forty hours per week during vacations without authorization from the INS. It is more difficult, but not impossible, to work off-campus as a foreign student. You must demonstrate to the INS that you have experienced an unforeseen financial need; this need must be documented thoroughly on form I-538. Typical circumstances justifying such INS authorization are the death of a supporting parent, a parent's bankruptcy, or a natural disaster affecting your level of support from your home country. If granted, the permit for off-campus employment allows you work up to twenty hours per week off-campus.

The INS also has a program for practical training authorization for qualifying foreign students. Practical training is work experience related to the student's course of study and not available in the home country. A computer science student, for example, could apply for practical training with IBM on the grounds that state-of-the-art computing facilities were unavailable in his or her home country.

Students holding F-1 visas are allowed a total of twelve months practical training eligibility before graduation and twelve months after graduation. The pre-graduation period of practical training is often used in co-op work/study programs. The post- graduation portion of the practical training allowance is granted by the INS in two 6-month segments. The first segment can be authorized by the foreign student advisor on campus. The second segment is granted by the INS only if you can demonstrate that you have a job. (Certain forms and binding deadlines pertain to this application; get the latest information from your student advisor.)

Students holding J-1 visas cannot obtain practical training before graduation, but are eligible for eighteen months of such work experience following graduation. Like F-1 students, they must prove that the work experience is related to their course of study and is not available in their home country. If you do not have a job at the time of application, you may be granted only six months of practical training authorization which then may be extended if you find a job within that period.

To work in the United States beyond the time limits granted under practical training, students must undergo the lengthy and often difficult process of switching their visa status. You will want to investigate H-1 and J-2 visas (usually applied for through your employer) or permanent residency status.

To achieve permanent residency status, you will have to obtain one of the very limited numbers of green card visas given by the INS through a complex system of quotas and categories. Having a spouse or relative in the United States is usually helpful, but by no means decisive, in this long application process. Nonnationals can also obtain a coveted green card through Labor Certification—that is, by demonstrating with the help of their employer that no United States citizen with comparable skills is available for employment. Non-United States nationals frequently find it advantageous to pursue specialized fields in which they do not compete directly with large numbers of native United States job applicants.

But be forewarned: The road to longterm legal employment in the United States is by no means easy. The patient cooperation of your employer and often the services of an immigration attorney may be required.

Major U.S. Employers with Foreign Offices

The following company names and descriptions are offered for investigation by those seeking international positions. The list is selective to feature a wide range of companies and potential occupations. No recommendation or endorsement is implied by this selection. The inclusion of a company name here does not imply current solicitation of job applications by the company or the company's willingness to supply job-related information to applicants. In some cases, the company branch listed here will refer you to a parent company or subsidiary for the latest information on international hiring by the company.

Companies are listed by state. You may want to begin your job search with companies in your region. If you are invited to interview for an international position, your first interview will probably be at the company's in-state offices.

(Company descriptions originally appeared in *The National Job Bank*, Bob Adams, Inc., 1990, and are reprinted by permission.)

ALABAMA

ALLIED CORPORATION/BIRMINGHAM

P.O. Box 593, Fairfield AL 35064. 205/787-8605. Contact Manager. An area producer of coal tar pitch, creosote and coal tar solutions, and refined tars. Parent company, Allied Signal Corporation, serves a broad spectrum of industries through its more than 40 strategic businesses, which are grouped into five sectors: Aerospace; Automotive; Chemical; Industrial and Technology; and Oil and Gas. Allied Signal is one of the nation's largest industrial organizations, and has 115,000 employees in over 30 countries. Corporate headquarters location: Morristown, NJ.International: Australia, Belgium, Canada, England, Hong Kong, Mexico, New Zealand, Switzerland, Venezuela.

AMPEX COORPORATION

P.O. Box 190, Opelika AL 36803-0190. 205/749-7678. Contact John B. Cotton, Divisional Manager of Professional Recruiting. A world leader in professional audio-video systems and recording tape. Also engaged in the manufacture of computer peripheral and instrumentation technology. Introduced the first audio tape recorder in the U.S. and developed the first successful video cassette recorder. Company has designed products for the broadcast industry: video tape and disc recorders, computer graphics, special effect systems, editing and switching systems for television and mastering and mix-down audio recorders for the music business. Common positions include: Accountant; Buyer; Chemist; Computer Programmer; Draftsperson; Chemical Engineer; Electrical Engineer; Industrial Engineer; Mechanical Engineer; Operations/Production Manager. Principal educational backgrounds sought: Accounting; Chemistry; Computer Science; Engineering; Finance. Company benefits include: medical insurance; dental insurance; pension plan; life insurance; tuition assistance; disability coverage; employee discounts; savings plan. Corporate headquarters located in Redwood City, CA. Operations at this facility include: manufacturing. International: Argentina, Australia, Bahamas, Belgium, Brazil, Colombia, Canada, England, France, Germany, Greece, Hong Kong, Israel, Italy, Japan, Mexico, Netherlands, Spain, Sweden.

SCI SYSTEMS, INC.

2109 West Clinton, Huntsville AL 35805. 205/882-4800. Contact Personnel Director. Designs and develops electronic products for government and commercial clients. Corporate headquarters location. International: Scotland, Singapore.

SINCLAIR & VALENTINE

2200 Industrial Street, P.O. Box 7284, East Mobile AL 36607. 205/456-4559. Contact Branch Operations Manager. An area producer of specialty printing inks and coatings, press chemicals, and printing supplies. Parent company, Allied Signal Corporation, serves a broad spectrum of industries through its more than 40 strategic businesses, which are grouped into five sectors: Aerospace; Automotive; Chemical; Industrial and Technology; and Oil and Gas. Allied Signal is one of the nation's largest industrial organizations, and has 115,000 employees in over 30 countries. Corporate headquarters location: Morristown, NJ. International: Canada, Colombia, Germany, Mexico, Netherlands.

ALASKA

ATLANTIC RICHFIELD COMPANY/ ALASKA REGION

P.O. Box 100360, Anchorage AK 99510. 907/276-1215 Contact Len Dasho, Employee Relations Manager. A major energy and natural resources firm with operations in petroleum, natural gas, and exploration. Corporate headquarters location: Los Angeles, CA. Numerous area facilities. International: Argentina, Australia, Belgium, China, Colombia, England, France, Germany, Greece, Italy, Ivory Coast, Japan, Mexico, Singapore, Switzerland, Zimbabwe.

XEROX CORPORATION

4341 B Street, Anchorage AK 99503. 907/561-8200 Contact Personnel Coordinator. Offers a wide range of office products, as well as sales and service operations. Products include copiers and telecommunications equipment, as well as office and printing systems. Other Alaska facilities include: Fairbanks, Juneau, Kenai, Prudhoe Bay and Valdez. Corporate headquarters location: Stamford, CT. International: Australia, Austria, Belgium, Colombia, Denmark, England, France, Germany, Hong Kong,

Ireland, Italy, Japan, Kenya, Malaysia, Netherlands, New Zealand, Nigeria, Norway, Portugal, Singapore, Spain, Sweden, Switzerland, Venezuela.

ARIZONA

AMERON PIPE DIVISION/SOUTHWEST

P.O. Box 20505, Phoenix AZ 85036. 602/252-7111. Contact Alan L. Rhea, Personnel Manager. Produces a wide range of pipe products, including concrete reinforced steel pipe, concrete pipe, and reinforced concrete pipe for drainage and irrigation. Nationally, company is engaged principally in four product areas: pipe products, construction products, steel products, and corrosion control products. Pipe products include concrete and steel pressure and non-pressure pipe for water transmission and storm, industrial waste water, and sewage control. Construction products include ready-mix cement, steel reinforced concrete pipe, welded wire mesh and various other constructio materials. Steel products include carbon and alloy steel rod and wire products, such as wire and cold-heading products. Corrosion control produces coatings to prevent or control corrosion during repair, construction and maintenance of facilities in the marine, sanitation, chemical, petrochemical and nuclear industries. International operations. Corporate headquarters location: Monterey Park, CA. New York Stock Exchange. International: Brazil, Colombia, France, Germany, Hong Kong, Mexico, Netherlands, Saudi Arabia, Spain.

BURR-BROWN CORPORATION

6730 South Tucson Boulevard, Tucson AZ 85706. 602/746-1111. Contact Shari Hickox, Employment Manager. A leading supplier of precision microelectronic devices and microcomputer-based systems for use in data acquisition, signal conditioning, and industrial control. Operates in five market segments: Instrumentation (including electronic test, analytical, and medical); Industrial (including process control, factory data collection, and environmental/geophysical measurement); Military/Aerospace (including navigation/guidance/control, radar/sonar/ECM, and test and measurement; Computers (including industrial measurement and control systems, peripheral equipment, and graphics and image processing equipment); and Communications (including data communications, telecommunications, and audio/visual signal processing). Operating divisions are: Industrial Systems Products Division, Military Products Division, Micro Technology Division, and International. International: Austria, England, France, Germany, Holland, Japan, Scotland

GARRETT AIRLINE SERVICES DIVISION
P.O. Box 52170, Phoenix AZ 85072. 602/731-5145. Contact Chuck Johnson, Director of Human Resources. Provides spare parts and aftermarket services to the aviation industry. Parent company, Allied Signal Corporation, serves a broad spectrum of industries through its more than 40 strategic businesses, which are grouped into five sectors: Aerospace; Automotive; Chemical; Industrial and Technology; and Oil and Gas. Allied Signal is one of the nation's largest industrial organizations, and has 115,000 employees in over 30 countries. Common positions include: Accountant; Administrator; Commercial Artist; Computer Programmer; Customer Service Representative; Aerospace Engineer; Electrical Engineer; Mechanical Engineer; Technical Writer/Editor. International: Australia, Brazil, Canada, England, Frnace, Germany, Ireland, Japan, Singapore, Spain, Sweden, Switzerland.

GENERAL DYNAMICS CORPORATION NAVAJO FACILITY
P.O. Box 679, Fort Defiance AZ 86504. 602/729-5711. Contact Sylvia Duboise, Personnel Assistant. Manufactures printed circuit board assemblies, harness assemblies, and related electronic components. Nationally, company is a major diversified corporation with manufacturing interests in aircraft, space systems, missiles, ships, electronics, mining, tanks, and other military equipment. Cororate headquarters location: St. Louis, MO. New York Stock Exchange. International: Australia, Belgium, Denmark, Egypt, Germany, Greece, Israel, Japan, Korea, Netherland, Norway, Spain.

REVLON INC.
4301 West Buckeye Road, Phoenix AZ 85043. 602/272-7661. Contact Bob Simmons, Director of Personnel. Produces a wide variety of cos-

metics, toiletries, and perfumes. Nationally, company is engaged in the manufacture of a diverse range of products, including beauty products, health care products, ethical pharmaceuticals, and optical products. Corporate headquarters location: New York, NY. New York Stock Exchange. International: Argentina, Australia, Belgium, Bermuda, Canada, England, France, Germany, Hong Kong, Ireland, Israel, Italy, Japan, Mexico, New Zealand, Singapore, Spain, Venezuela.

ARKANSAS

AMERICAN GREETINGS CORPORATION
Route 2, Box 131, Harrisburg AR 72432. 501/578-2486. Contact Bob Parker, Personnel Manager. Produces a wide variety of greeting cards. Corporate headquarters location: Cleveland, OH. Other facilities include McCrory and Osceola. International: Canada, England, Mexico, Monaco, Switzerland.

INTERNATIONAL PAPER PINE BLUFF MILL
P.O. Box 7069, Pine Bluff AR 71611. 501/541-5700. Contact Manager/ Management Development. A major paper mill producing coated publication papers and bleached board. Common positions include: Accountant; Chemical Engineer; Civil Engineer; Electrical Engineer; Mechanical Engineer. Principal educational backgrounds sought: Accounting; Engineering. Company benefits include: medical, dental, and life insurance; pensionplan; tuition assistance; savings plan. Corporate headquarters location: Purchase, NY. Operations at this facility include: manufacturing. New York Stock Exchange. International: Greece, Israel, Japan, Spain, Switzerland.

WHIRLPOOL CORPORATION
6400 South Jenny Lind, Fort Smith AR 72903. 501/648-2000. Contact Director/Human Resources. A major manufacturer of refrigerators and freezers. Divisional headquarters location. Corporate headquarters location: Benton Harbor, MI. New York Stock Exchange. Common positions include: Accountant; Chemist; Electrical Engineer; Industrial Engineer; Mechanical Engineer. Principal educational background sought: Engineering. Company benefits include: medical insurance;

dental insurance; pension plan; life insurance; tuition assistance; disability coverage; profit sharing; employee discounts; savings plan. International: Brazil, Canada.

CALIFORNIA

BELL & HOWELL COMPANY

819 Cowan Road, Burlingame CA 94010. 415/692-4550. Contact Mrs. A. Gilly, Office Manager. Parent company is a diversified corporation doing business in three major areas: Specialized Business Equipment, which produces items such as microfilm recorders, readers, jackets, and services, as well as micropublishing, and office collation and mailing machines; Learning and Materials, which operates technical training shools in electronics and computer science, publishers textbooks, and produces a variety of instructional materailas at all levels; and Instrumentation, which produces measuring and recording equipment, magnetic tape instrumentation, and a variety of semi-conductor compounds, optics equipment,a nd photoplates for integrated circuits. This facility is part of the Speicalized Business Equipment Group, and produces microfilm goods while providing related services. Corporate headquarters location: Chicago, IL. New York Stock Exchange. International: Australia, Belgium, Canada, England, France, Germany, Ireland, Japan.

BRUNSWICK CORPORATION/DEFENSE DIVISION

3333 Harbor Boulevard, Costa Mesa CA 92628. 714/546-8030. Contact Joan McGary, Personnel Director. A division of Brunswick Corporation. Primarily engaged in scientific, engineering, and manufacturing projects serving the United States military and its supporting defense operations. Products include tactical weapons and aerospace systems. Other plants located in Nebraska, Virginia, and Ohio. Operations include: manufacturing; research/development. Corporate headquarters location: Skokie, IL. New York Stock Exchange. Common positions include: Accountant; Attorney; Buyer; Commercial Artist; Draftsperson; Engineer; Aerospace Engineer; Electrical Engineer; Industrial Engineer; Mechanical Engineer; Personnel & Labor Relations Specialist; Physicist; Systems Analyst; Technical Writer/Editor; Materials Engineer. Principal educational backgrounds sought: Business Administration; Computer Science; Engineering; Physics. Company benefits include: medical, dental and life insurance; pension plan; tuition assistance; disability coverage; employee discounts. International: Argentina, Belgium, Brazil, Canada, Guatemala, Japan, Korea, Mexico, Switzerland.

CARNATION COMPANY

5045 Wilshire Boulevard, Los Angeles CA 90036. 213/932-6000. Contact Frank Slohn, Manager/Personnel & Recruiting. A major firm which manufactures and sells awide range of food products, pet foods, containers, and dietary products. Among many major products are Coffee-Mate, Instant Breakfast, hot cocoa mix, Contadina tomato products, Trio and Chef-Mate food service products, dairy items, metal containers and Friskies, Fancy Feast and Mighty Dog pet foods. Common positions include: Accountant; Computer Programmer; Agricultural Engineer; Chemical Engineer; Electrical Engineer; Industrial Engineer; Mechanical Engineer; Financial Analyst; Management Trainee; Operation/Production Manager; Marketing Specialist; Purchasing Agent; Quality Control Supervisor; Sales Representative; Statistician; Systems Analyst; Transportation and Traffic Specialist. Principal educational backgrounds sought: Accounting; Business Administration; Communications; Computer Science; Economics; Engineering; Finance; Marketing. Company benefits include: medical, dental and life insurance; pension plan; tuition assistance; disability coverage; profit sharing. Parent company: Nestle. International: Australia, Belgium, Dominican Republic, France, Germany, Greece, Jamaica, Japan, Mexico, Netherlands, Peru, Philippines, Singapore, Spain, Thailand.

COMPUTER SCIENCES CORPORATION

2100 East Grand, El Segundo CA 90245. 213/615-0311. Contact Scott Sharpe, Vice President of Corporate Personnel. A major provider of computer services and consultation to industry and government. Works primarily in two operations areas: Contract Services, offering such capabilities as the development of custom-designed computer systems; and Data Systems, handling the firm's INFONET service, which provides remote datta processing and value-added services via an international data communications network. Corporate headquarters location. New York Stock Exchange. International: Belgium, Canada, England, Germany, Netherlands.

FIRESTONE TIRE AND RUBBER COMPANY
25375 Cabot #210, Hayward CA 94545. 415/786/0420. Contact Personnel Department. Primarily engaged in the sale of a broad line of tires for the original equipment and replacement markets of the world. Manages its business through three primary operating groups: the World Tire Group is responsible for the design, development, testing, and manufacturing of tires throughout the world; the Sales and Marketing Group is a nationwide sales network which includes dealer outlets and automotive service centers; and the Corporate Development Group has the reponsibility for corporate strategic planning activities. Employs approximately 60,000 people worldwide. Considers people for whole region, which includes California, Washington, Oregon, Montana, Idaho, Wyoming, Arizona, Utah, and Hawaii. Corporate headquarters location: Akron, OH. New York Stock Exchange. International: Argentina, Belgium, Brazil, Chile, Costa Rica, France, Ghana, Haiti, Italy, Ivory Coast, Japan, Kenya, Liberia, Monaco, Netherlands, New Zealand, Philippines, Portugal, Switerland, Thailand, Tunisia, Uruguay, Venezuela.

FLUOR CORPORATION
3353 Michelson Drive, Irvine CA 92730. 714/975-2000. Contact Employee Office. Primarily engaged in engineering and construction, as well as the production of various natural resources. Provides worldwide engineering and related services to energy, natural resource, industrial, commercial, utility, and government clients. International: France, Ivory Coast, Netherlands, Singapore.

GARRETT AIRESEARCH
2525 West 190th Street, Torrence CA 90509. 213/776-1010. Contact Jon Hansen, Manager, Employment. Engaged primarily in the design and manufacture of systems, products, and components for the aerospace industry, as well as such related fields as surface transportation. An Allied

Signal Company. Common positions include: Accountant; Computer Programmer; Draftsperson; Aerospace Engineer; Ceramics Engineer; Chemical Engineer; Electrical Engineer; Industrial Engineer; Mechanical Engineer; Metallurgical Engineer; Financial Analyst; Industrial Designer; Operations/Production Manager; Physicist; Purchasing Agent; Quality Control Supervisor; Systems Analyst; Technical Writer/Editor. Principal educational backgrounds sought: Accounting; Business Administration; Computer Science; Economics; Engineering; Liberal Arts; Physics. Company benefits include: medical insurance; dental insurance; pension plan; life insurance; tuition assistance; disability coverage; profit sharing; vacations and holidays. Corporate and divisional headquarters location. Parent company: Garrett Corporation. Operations at this facility include: manufacturing; research/development; administration. Allied Signal is listed on the New York Stock Exchange. International: Australia, Brazil, Canada, England, France, Germany, Ireland, Japan, Singapore, Spain, Sweden, Switzerland.

GREYHOUND CORPORATION
90 New Montgomery, San Francisco CA 94105. 415/495-1533. Contact Samantha Stoker, Personnel Coordinator. Nationally, company is a diversified holding company operating through several subsidiary and affiliated corporations. Subsidiaries operate in four cohesive groups: Greyhond Lines is a common carrier bus firm, with operations throughout the United States with more than 5,000 busses and more than 3,000 stop facilities; Greyhound Manufacturing Group operates in the United States and Canada, and builds bus shells, assembles intercity busses for sale to company and unaffiliated customers, and fabricates and sells bus parts; financial operations consist of companies engaged primarily in equipment financing, computer leasing, and money order and insurance services in the United States and abroad (includes Greyhound Computer Corporation); Armour & Company divisions and subsidiaries are engaged in the slaughter of livestock and poultry, purchases and sells meats and animal products and by-products, and manufactures, processes and sells other food products including cheese, butter and food oil products; services subsidiaries provide services directed to business markets, including aircraft ground handling ser-

vices, temporary help services, convention and exhibition services, and other products and services directed to consumer markets, including hobby craft kits. Corporate headquarters location: Phoenix, AZ. International. New York Stock Exchange. International: Australia, Canada, England, France, Netherlands, Saudi Arabia.

HEWLETT-PACKARD COMPANY

3000 Hanover Street, Department 20AC, Palo Alto CA 94304. Mailed inquiries only. Contact Jo Ann Taylor, Manager, Employment Administration. A worldwide firm engaged in the design, manufacture, marketing, and servicing of a broad array of precision electronics instruments and systems for measurement, analysis, and computation. Company's line of over 10,000 products are used in business, industry, science, education, and medicine. The company employs approximately 84,000 people in 24 U.S. cities, Europe, Japan, Canada, Australia, the Far East and Latin America. Common positions include: Accountant; Administrator; Attorney; Blue-Collar Worker Supervisor; Buyer; Chemist; Computer Programmer; Customer Service Representative; Chemical Engineer; Electrical Engineer; Industrial Engineer; Mechanical Engineer; Financial Analyst; Industrial Designer; Operations/Production Manager; Marketing Specialist; Personnel and Labor Relations Specialist; Physicist; Public Relations Worker; Purchsing Agent; Quality Control Supervisor; Sales Representative; Systems Analyst; Technical Writer/Editor. Principal educational backgrounds sought: Accounting; Business Administration; Communications; Computer Science; Engineering; Finance; Marketing; Mathematics; Physics. Company benefits include: medical, dental and life insurance; pension plan; tuition assistance; disability coverage; profit sharing; employee discounts; savings plan; flexible work hours; credit union; income protection plan; recreational activities. Corporate headquarters location. Operations include: administration. New York Stock Exchange. International: Argentina, Australia, Austria, Belgium, Brazil, France, Hong Kong, Ireland, Italy, Japan, Korea, Lebanon, Luxemborg, Malaysia, Mexico, Netherland, New Zealand, Norway, Scotland, Singapore, Spain, Sweden, Switzerland, Taiwan, Venezuela.

LOCKHEED CORPORATION

P.O. Box 551, Burbank CA 91520-9044. 818/847-4734. Contact Professional Staffing. Other area facilities include: Ontario. A major aerospace corporation. Conducts aerospace research and development and produces advanced aircraft and aerospace systems; also constructs and repairs ships, and provides aircraft maintenance and modification and other related technical support. Most business is conducted in sour industry segments: Missiles, Space and Electronics, including activities in space exploration, weaponry, and communications; Aircraft and Related Services, maintaining operations in such diverse areas as strategic airlifters, tactical reconnaissance aircraft, and software servies; Aerospace Support, encompassing the fields of aircraft modification and aviation services; and Shipbuilding, including operations in new ship construction and ship overhaul. United States Government is a major client. New York Stock Exchange. Corporate headquarters location. International: Australia, Bahrain, Canada, China, England, France, Hong Kong, Ivory Coast, Japan, Kenya, Lebanon, Singapore, Spain, Switzerland.

SRI INTERNATIONAL

333 Ravenswood Avenue, Menlo Park CA 94025. 415/326-6200. Contact Michael Patrick (Engineering) or Beth Solomon (Sciences). A multi-disciplinary research, development, and consulting organization engaged in government and private industry research. Corporate headquarters location. Common positions include: Biochemist; Biologist; Chemist; Economist; Biomedical Engineer; Chemical Engineer; Electrical Engineer; Mechanical Engineer; Financial Analyst; Personnel & Labor Relations Specialist; Physicist; Systems Analyst; Technical Writer/Editor. Principal educational backgrounds sought: Biology; Business Administration; Chemistry; Communications; Computer Science; Economics; Engineering; Finance; Mathematics; Physics. Company benefits include: medical, dental and life insurance; pension plan; tuition assistance; disability coverage; employee discounts. International: Australia, Canada, England, France, Germany, Italy, Japan, Netherlands, Philippines, Saudi Arabia, Singapore, Sweden, Switzerland, Taiwan.

COLORADO

DANA CORPORATION/ENGINE PRODUCTS DIVISION

P.O. Box 666 Pueblo CO 81002. 303/948-3311. Contact Personnel Department. A manufacturer of aluminum pistons and bell housings. Common positions in this facility include: Accountant; Blue-Collar Worker Supervisor; Computer Programmer; Industrial Engineer; Mechanical Engineer; Operations/Production Manager; Personnel & Labor Relations Specialist; Quality Control Supervisor. Principal educational backgrounds sought: Accounting; Engineering. Company benefits include: medical insurance; dental insurance; pension plan; life insurance; tuition assistance; disability coverage; savings plan. Corporate headquarters location: Toledo, OH. Operations at this facility include: Manufacturing. New York Stock Exchange. International: Brazil, India.

PAINE WEBBER

1600 Broadway, Denver CO 80202. 303/861-2400. Contact Branch Manager. Denver office of the well-known financial stock-brokerage firm. International: England, France, Hong Kong, Japan, Switzerland.

RALSTON PURINA COMPANY

4555 York Street, Denver CO 80216. 303/295-0818. Contact Office Manager. Produces a nationally-advertised line of dog foods, cat foods, and feed for other domestic animals. Overall, company is the world's largest producer of dog and cat foods, commercial livestock feeds, cereals, canned goods (tuna and mushrooms), soybean meal, and soybean oil. Also involved in various diversified businesses. Employs more than 63,000 people worldwide at 250 facilities. Corporate headquarters location: St. Louis, MO. New York Stock Exchange. International: Australia, Belgium, Brazil, Canada, Colombia, France, Germany, Guatemala, Italy, Japan, Korea, Mexico, Netherlands, Panama, Peru, Spain.

TEXAS INSTRUMENTS INC.

5825 Mark Dabling Boulevard, Colorado Springs CO 80919. 719/593-5142. Contact Staffing Administrator. Produces precision machined products and electronic components for government electronics systems. Nationally, company is engaged in the design, development and manufacture of semiconductor memories, microprocessors, large scale integrated circuits and other semiconductor devices and materials, clad metal systems, industrial and commercial electronic controls, optoelectronics, airborne and ground-based radar systems, electro-optics equipment and services for global oil and mineral exploration. Operations include: manufacturing and administration. Corporate headquarters location: Dallas, TX. International facilities. New York Stock Exchange. Common positions include: Blue-Collar worker Supervisor; Buyer; Draftsperson; Electrical Engineer; Industrial Engineer; Mechanical Engineer; Financial Analyst; Department Manager; Operations/Production Manager; Personnel and Labor Relations Specialist; Purchasing Agent; Quality Control Supervisor; Technical Writer/Editor. Principal educational backgrounds sought: Business Administration; Computer Science; Engineering. Company benefits include: medical, dental and life insurance; pension plan; tuition assistance; disability coverage; profit sharing; employee discounts; savings plan. International: Argentina, Australia, Brazil, Canada, England, France, Germany, Italy, Japan, Malaysia, Mexico, Netherlands, Philippines, Portugal, Singapore, Taiwan.

TRW ELECTRONIC PRODUCTS INC.
3650 North Nevada Avenue, Colorado Springs CO 80907. 303/475-0660. Contact Employment Manager. Produces a variety of electronics signal processing equipment and systems, including encoders and decoders, as a part of TRW Electronic Systems group (Redondo Beach, CA). Nationally, TRW operates in three industry segments: Car and Truck Components; Electronics and Space Systems (including this facility); and Industrial and Energy (products include fasteners, tools, and bearings for industrial users, pumps and valves used by petroleum companies, and aircraft components for commercial and military aircraft). Common positions include: Accountant; Administrator; Blue-Collar Worker Supervisor; Computer Programmer; Draftsperson; Electrical Engineer; Industrial Engineer; Mechanical Engineer; Financial Analyst; Department Manager; Operation/Production Manager; Personnel and Labor Relations Specialist; Purchasing Agent; Quality

Control Supervisor; Systems Analyst; Technical Writer/Editor. Educational backgrounds sought: Accounting; Business Adminstration; Engineering; Mathematics; Physics. Company benefits include: medical insurance; dental insurance; pension plan; life insurance; tuition assistance; disability coverage; savings plan. Corporate headquarters location: Cleveland, OH. Parent company: TRW Inc. Operations at this facility include: manufacturing. New York Stock Exchange. International: Australia, Austria, Belgium, Canada, England, France, Germany, Italy, Japan, Mexico, Ireland, Singapore, Spain, Switzerland, Taiwan, United Arab Emirates.

CONNECTICUT

AMAX INC.
Amax Center, Greenwich CT 06836-1700. 203/629-6369. Contact Joe Pereira, Supervisor Employee Relations. A diversified minerals and energy development company with worldwide operations. The company explores for, mines, refines, and sells a wide variety of minerals and metals, and has interests in coal, petroleum, and natural gas. Principal products are molybdenum, coal, zinc, petroleum and natural gas, potash, tungsten, silver, gold, and magnesium. Through Alumax, Inc., company is also involved in the production of aluminum and the fabrication and marketing of aluminum products. Common positions include: Accountant; Computer Programmer; Financial Analyst. Principal educational backgrounds sought: Accounting; Finance. Company benefits include: medical, dental, and life insurance; pension plan; tuition assistance; disability coverage; profit sharing; savings plan. Corporate headquarters location. Operations at this facility include: administration; sales. New York Stock Exchange. International: Canada, England, Netherlands.

AMPHENOL/HAMDEN
720 Sherman Avenue, Hamden CT 06514. 203/281-3200. Contact Personnel Director. An area producer of flat ribbon cable. Parent company, Allied Signal Corporation, serves a broad spectrum of industries through its more than 40 strategic businesses, which are grouped into five sectors: Aerospace; Automotive; Chemical; Industrial and Technology; and Oil and Gas. Allied Signal is one of the nation's largest industrial or-

ganizations, and has 115,000 employees in over 30 countries. Corporate headquarters location: Morristown, NJ. International: Austria, Canada, England, France, Germany, Hong Kong, India, Italy, Japan, Netherlands, Sweden.

GERBER SCIENTIFIC

83 Gerber Road West, South Windsor CT 06074. 203/644-1551. Contact Anthony Pagliuco, Personnel Manager. A company engaged in the manufacture of high tech drafting equipment such as photo plotters. International: Belgium, England, Finland, Germany, Sweden.

THE STANLEY WORKS

P.O. Box 7000, New Britain CT 06050. 203/225-5111. Contact Eileen Smith, Personnel Manager. Several area locations, including Farmington, New Britain and Plantsville, CT. A worldwide marketer and manufacturer of quality tools for do-it-yourselfers and professionals, including carpenters, mechanics, electricians, plumbers, and industrial maintenance engineers. Manufactures hardware and complementary products for the home, the factory, and the building industry. Its industry segments are: Consumer Products, including hand tools, fasteners, home hardware, garage door openers, and residential entry doors for the do-it-yourself market; Builders Products, which provides products to the professional construction industry, including architectural and residential hardware, pedestrian power-operated doors, insulated steel entry doors, garage doors and openers, and automatic parking gates and commercial doors. and Industrial products, which includes products sold to industrial and automotive customers, including professional hand tools, 'MAC' mechanics tools, air tools, hydraulic tools, industrial storage systems, and industrial hardware and stampings. Plants are located throughout the United States (significant Connecticut operations), and in more than 30 foreign countries. Corporate headquarters location. New York Stock Exchange. International: Australia, Belgium, Brazil, Canada, Colombia, Denmark, England, Finland, France, Germany, Greece, Hong Kong, Italy, Mexico, Netherland, New Zealand, Norway, Philippines, Portugal, Singapore, Taiwan.

DELAWARE

CHRYSLER CORPORATION

500 South College Avenue, Newark DE 19713-1302. 302/453-5619. Contact Mrs. Delores Perna, Personnel Administrator. An auto assembly warehouse plant for the major manufacturer of automobile parts for Chrysler dealers. Corporate headquarters location: Detroit, MI. International: Canada, England, Israel, Japan, Mexico, Switzerland.

DU PONT COMPANY

1007 Market Street, Wilmington DE 19898. 302/774-3366. Contact Harold Flood, Personnel Director. A major corporation whose diverse activities include the manufacture of biomedical products; the manufacture of industrial and consumer products, such as photographic, data-recording and video devices; the production of man-made fibre products, with applications in a variety of consumer and commercial industries; the production of polyier products, such as plastic resins, elastomers and films; the production of agricultural and industrial chemicals, such as herbicides and insecticides, and pigments, fluorochemicals, petroleum additives and mineral acids; the exploration for and production of crude oil and natural gas, internationally; the refining, marketing and downstram transportation of petroleum; and the mining and distribution of steam and metallurgical coals, exported mainly to overseas steel producers. Corporate headquarters location. International: Argentina, Australia, Belgium, Brazil, Canada, Colombia, England, Finland, Germany, Guatemala, Hong Kong, Ireland, Japan, Mexico, Netherlands, New Zealand, Norway, Peru, Singapore, Spain, Sweden, Switzerland, Taiwan, Thailand, Venezuela.

J.C. PENNEY CO.

U.S. Route 113, Blue Hen Mall, Dover DE 19901. 302/674-4200. Contact Patricia Collins, Personnel Assistant. A national company which operates a chain of department stores and thrift drug stores, and which also provides banking services. Area locations in Wilmington (302/998-1131) and Newark (302/366-7680). International: Belgium, Italy.

DISTRICT OF COLUMBIA

SHERATON/CARLTON HOTEL
923 16th Street NW, Washington DC 20006. 202/638-2626. Contact Vivian Grant, Personnel Director. A major downtown hotel facility, with 250 rooms and complete dining facilities. Second area hotel nearby. Part of the international hotel chain, offering hotel, dining, convention, and meeting facilites at major metropolitan locations throughout the country. Corporate headquarters location: Boston, MA. Common positions include: Accountant; Administrator; Computer Programmer; Credit Manager; Customer Service Representative; Electrical Engineer; Mechanical Engineer; Hotel Manager/Assistant Manager; Department Manager; General Manager; Management Trainee; Personnel & Labor Relations Specialist; Public Relations Worker; Purchasing Agent; Sales Representative; Systems Analyst. Principal educational backgrounds sought: Accounting; Business Administration; Communications; Computer Science; Economics; Engineering; Finance; Liberal Arts; Marketing; Mathematics. International: Argentina, Australia, Austria, Bahamas, Bahrain, Belgium, Bermuda, Bolivia, Brazil, Camaroon, Canada, Chile, China, Colombia, Costa Rica, Cyprus, Denmark, Dominican Republic, Ecuador, Egypt, El Salvador, England, Finland, France, Germany, Greece, Guatemala, India, Italy, Mexico, Spain, Sweden, Thailand, Venezuela, and others.

FLORIDA

WALT DISNEY WORLD
P.O. Box 10000, Lake Buena Vista FL 32830-1000. 407/824-2222. Contact Professional Staffing Department. Corporate office for the internationally renowned theme park. International: Belgium, Canada, Denmark, England, France, Germany, Italy, Japan, Portugal, Spain.

MOTOROLA, INC./COMMUNICATIONS SECTOR
8000 West Sunrise Boulevard, Plantation FL 33322. 305/475-5700 Contact Allen H. Waters, Staffing Manager. Manufacturers of two-way radios, special applications products and pagers for commercial and government markets. Common positions include: Accountant; Com-

puter Programmer; Chemical Engineer; Electrical Engineer; Industrial Engineer; Mechanical Engineer; Metallurgical Engineer; Financial Analyst; Industrial Designer; Marketing Specialist; Personnel & Labor Relations Specialist; Purchasing Agent; Systems Analyst; Technical Writer/Editor. Principal educational backgrounds sought: Accounting; Chemistry; Computer Science; Engineering; Finance; Marketing. Company benefits include: medical, dental, and life insurance; pension plan; tuition assistance; disability coverage; profit sharing; employee discounts; savings plan. Corporate headquarters location: Schaumburg, IL. Operations at this facility include: divisional headquarters; manufacturing; research/development; administration. New York Stock Exchange. International: Australia, Austria, Belgium, Canada, Costa Rica, Denmark, England, France, Germany, Hong Kong, Ireland, Japan, Korea, Malaysia, Mexico, Netherlands, Norway, Philippines, Singapore, Spain, Sweden, Switzerland, Taiwan.

PARKER HANNIFIN CORPORATION/AUTOMOTIVE AFTERMARKET GROUP

3200 Parker Drive, St. Augistine FL 32084. 904/829-1000. Contact Personnel Supervisor. Operations include the production of a broad line of safety products, cooling systems products, specialty tools, and equipment sold primarily in the automotive aftermarket, and air conditioning components sold primarily to original equipment manufacturers. Parent company (Cleveland, OH), operates in two other major business segments: Industrial, which includes a broad line of fluid system components used in virtually every major agricultural, manufacturing, and processing operation; and Aviation/Space/Marine, whose operations design and produce fluid system equipment for hydraulic, pneumatic, fuel and cryogenic applications in military aircraft, spacecraft, commercial airliners, general aviation aircraft, and marine operations. International operations in England and West Germany. Corporate headquarters location. International: Argentina, Australia, Austria, Belgium, Brazil, Canada, Denmark, England, Finland, Germany, Italy, Japan, Korea, Mexico, Netherlands, Norway, Singapore, Spain, Sweden.

SCHERING LABORATORIES

50 NW 176th Street Miami FL 33169-5086 305/654-2200 Contact William E. Vandervalk, Manager of Employee Relations. Manufacturers of physician recommended and prescribed products. A major pharmacy hospital and physicians' office supplier. Common positions include: Accountant; Administrator; Blue-Collar Worker Supervisor; Biomedical Engineer; Chemist; Chemical Engineer; Industrial Engineer; Mechanical Engineer; Operations/Production Manager; Purchasing Agent; Quality Control Supervisor; Research Scientist. Principal educational backgrounds sought: Accounting; Business Administration; Chemistry; Engineering; Liberal Arts; Pharmacy. Company benefits: medical insurance; dental insurance; pension plan; life insurance; tuition assistance; disability coverage; profit sharing; employee discounts; savings plan; credit union. Corporate headquarters: Madison, NJ. Parent company: Schering-Plough. Operations at this facility include: manufacturing; research/development. New York Stock Exchange. International: Argentina, Australia, Brazil, Germany, France, India, Ireland, Japan, Kenya, Peru.

SENSORMATIC ELECTRONICS CORPORATION

500 North West 12th Avenue Deerfield Beach FL 33442 Mailed inquiries only Contact Ellen Burne, Manager of Employment. Manufacturing and engineering of electronic article surveillance equipment and sensor vision. Common positions include: Accountant; Blue-Collar Worker Supervisor; Buyer; Computer Programmer; Customer Service Representative; Draftsperson; Electrical Engineer; Industrial Engineer; Mechanical Engineer; Financial Analyst; Industrial Designer; Department Manager; Management Trainee; Operations/Production Manager; Personnel and Labor Relations Specialist; Purchasing Agent; Quality Control Supervisor; Sales Representative; Systems Analyst. Principal educational backgrounds sought: Accounting; Business Administration; Communications; Computer Science; Engineering; Finance; Marketing. Company benefits include: medical insurance; dental insurance; pension plan; life insurance; tuition assistance; disability coverage; profit sharing. Corporate headquarters location. Operations at this facility include:

manufacturing; research/development; administration; service; sales. International: Austria, Belgium, France, Germany, Spain, Switzerland.

GEORGIA

THE COCA-COLA COMPANY

P.O. Drawer 1734, Atlanta GA 30301. 404/676-2121. Contact Personnel Office. One of the world's leading producers of soft drinks; among the world's largest citrus processors; and the third largest wine company in the United States. Company operates nationwide in twwo primary areas: Soft Drink Sector (Coca-Cola, Tab, Sprite, Fresca, and many others); and Food and Wine Sector (Minute Maid orange juice, Hi-C drinks, Presto plastic wraps and films, Taylor wines, Sterling wines, Great Western sparkling wines, and other products). Corporate headquarters location. International: Argentina, Australia, Bahamas, Belgium, Bermuda, Brazil, Camaroon, China, Colombia, Costa Rica, Denmark, Ecuador, Finland, Greece, Guatemala, Hong Kong, India, Italy, Japan, Kenya, Korea, Mexico, Morocco, Netherlands, New Zealand, Norway, Pakistan, Panama, Peru, Philippines, Spain, Sweden, Switzerland, Thailand, Tunisia, Turkey, Uruguay, Venezuela, Zimbabwe.

CONTAINER CORPORATION OF AMERICA

5853 East Ponce de Leon Avenue, Stone Mountain GA 30083. 404/469-4111. Contact John Mundt, Employee Relations Manager. Produces corrugated and fiber boxes. Nationally, company is one of the world's largest producers of paperboard packaging, with major manufacturing facilities located throughout the United States and throughout the world. Some major products include shipping containers, folding cartons, composite cans, plastic drums, and many others. A major operating subsidiary of MObil Corporation (New York, NY). International: Colombia, Italy, Mexico, Netherlands, Spain, Venezuela.

GLIDDEN COATINGS AND RESINS

1065 Glidden Street, Atlanta GA 30318. 404/355-4760. Contact Thomas D. Cifaldi, Personnel Representative. Produces a wide variety of paints for use in the home, as well as industrial coatings and pigments, and other specialty paint products. Company is a well-known manufacturer of paints, coatings, resins, and lacquers, with divisions located throughout the United States. A subsidiary of ICI Corporation, a diversified corporation with interests in paper, consumer goods, chemical, metals, foods, and other areas. Common positions include: Accountant; Administrator; Blue-Collar Worker Supervisor; Buyer; Credit Manager; Customer Service Representative; Department Manager; Management Trainee; Personnel & Labor Relations Specialist; Purchasing Agent; Quality Control Supervisor; Sales Representative. Principal educational backgrounds sought: Accounting; Business Administration; Chemistry; Engineering; Finance; Liberal Arts. Company benefits include: medical, dental and life insurance; pension plan; tuition assistance; disability coverage; profit sharing; employee discounts; savings plan. Corporate headquarters location: Cleveland, OH. Operations at this facility include: regional headquarters; manufacturing; administration; service; sales. International: Canada, Costa Rica, Guatemala, Mexico.

THE SHERWIN-WILLIAMS COMPANY
6795 South Main Street, Morrow GA 30260. 404/961-7780. Contact Jo Ann Hanson, Director of Personnel. Engaged in coatings manufacturing and distribution, and related research and product development. Nationally, company operates in six business segments: Retail Stores, Coatings, Chemicals, Packaging Products, Specialty Products, and International. Products include Sherwin-Williams, Dutch Boy, Martin Senour, Baltimore, an Kem paints as well as related packaging. Common position include: Accountant; Blue-Collar Worker Supervisor; Buyer; Chemist; Customer Service Representative; Mechanical Engineer; Operations/Production Manager; Purchasing Agent; Quality Control Supervisor. Principal educational backgrounds sought: Business Administration; Chemistry. Company benefits include: medical insurance; dental insurance; pension plan; life insurance; tuition assistance; disability coverage; employee discounts; savings plan. Operations at this facility include: manufacturing; research/development. Corporate headquarters location; Cleveland, OH. New York Stock Exchange. International: Argentina, Belgium, Bolivia, Brazil, Canada, China, Colombia, Costa Rica, Dominican Republic, Ecuador, Finland, France, Germany, Haiti, Honduras, India, Ireland, Italy, Jamaica, Japan, Korea, Mexico,

Netherland, New Zealand, Panama, Peru, Philippines, Saudi Arabia, Spain, Switzerland.

HAWAII

CHEVRON USA (HAWAII DIVISION)
1001 Bishop Street, Pauahi Tower, Suite, Honolulu HI 96813. 808/527-2700. Contact Gloria Castro, Personnel Director. Parent company, Chevron Corporation, refines and sells petroleum. Chevron Chemical (Ortho gardening and home products) is a subsidiary. International: Saudi Arabia, Uruguay.

DILLINGHAM CONSTRUCTION PACIFIC
P.O. Box 4088, Honolulu HI 96812. 808/735-3218. Contact Thomas Jackson, Manager-Employment. A general construction contractor. Parent company, Dillingham Construction, is in Pleasanton, CA. Other subsidiaries include: Dillingham Construction Guam, Dillingham Construction (H.K.), Hawaiian Dredging & Construction, HD&C Glass, Hawaiian Bitumuls & Paving, Hawaiian Rock Products. Common positions include: Civil Engineer; Mechanical Engineer; Construction Engineer. Principal educational background sought: Engineering. Company benefits include: medical, dental and life insurance; pension plan; tuition assistance; disability coverage; profit sharing; savings plan. Corporate headquarters location: Pleasanton, CA. Operations at this facility include: divisional headquarters. International: Australia, Canada, Guam, Hong Kong, Pakistan.

IDAHO

BOISE CASCADE CORPORATION
P.O. Box 50, Boise ID 83728. Mailed inquiries only. Contact Corporate College Recruitment. An integrated forest products company, engaged principally in the manufacture, distribution and sale of paper, office products, and building products and in the management of timberland resources to support these operations. Common positions include: Accountant; Computer Programmer; Chemical Engineer; Electrical Engineer; Mechanical Engineer; Financial Analyst; Forester; Management

Trainee; Operations/Production Manager; Marketing Specialist; Sales Representative. Principal educational backrounds sought: Accounting; Business Administration; Computer Science; Engineering; Finance; Marketing. Company benefits include: medical, dental, and life insurance; pension plan; tuition assistance; disability coverage; profit sharing; savings plan. Operations at this facility: divisional headquarters; administration. New York Stock Exchange. International: Austria, Canada, France, Germany.

SEARS, ROEBUCK & COMPANY

300 North Milwaukee, Boise ID 83788. 208/345-6100. Contact Mitzi Holt, Personnel Director. Operates a chain of department stores. Corporate headquarters location: Chicago, IL. International: Brazil, Canada, Guatemala, Honduras, Mexico, Panama, Peru, Spain, Venezuela.

WESTINGHOUSE ELECTRIC CORPORATION

P.O. Box 2068, Idaho Falls ID 83401. 208/526-5483. Contact Personnel Director. Research and development lab. Corporate headquarters location. International: Argentina, Australia, Canada, England, Germany, Ireland, Korea, Mexico, Netherlands, Singapore.

ILLINOIS

BRUNSWICK CORPORATION

One Brunswick Plaza, Skokie IL 60077. 312/470-4700. Contact Mr. Chris Buitron, Personnel Director. Several area locations including: Niles, Morton Grove, Libertyville, St. Charles. A multi-industry firm engaged primarily in four industry segments: Technical Group, including manufacturing facilities in Niles, Morton Grove, and St. Charles (Vapor Division), Skokie (Defense Division and Technetics Division), and Libertyville (Ozite Division); Medical Group (manufactures disposable equipment, industrial gloves, diagnostic equipment, and other products—no Illinois facilities); Marine Power Group (inboard and outboard motors, marine accessories—no Illinois facilities); and the Recreation Group, with headquarters for more than 250 recreation centers (bowling alleys) located in Skokie, as well as the group's Brunswick and Consumer Divisions, which produce a variety of bowling products, billiard tables, and other recreational products. The Technical Group's Vapor Division produces process control products; Defense Division manufactures products such as motor cases and pressure vessels, fire detection systems, launch and weapons systems, honeycomb and metal-bonded structures, camouflage, and others; Technetics produces industrial filters, valves, jet engine seals, metal fiber products, golf club shafts, and other products; Ozite Division produces residential and commercial carpets, and specialty automotive and industrial coverings. Corporate headquarters location. New York Stock Exchange. International: Argentina, Belgium, Brazil, Canada, Guatemala, Japan, Korea, Mexico, Switzerland.

CATERPILLAR TRACTOR COMPANY

P.O. Box 504, Joliet IL 60434. 815/729-6250. Contact Employee Relations Manager. A multi-national company which designs, manufactures and markets earthmoving equipment, materials handling equipment, and diesel engines. Common positions include: Blue-Collar Worker Supervisor; Electrical Engineer; Metallurgical Engineer (company has current hiring freeze). Principal educational backgrounds sought: Accounting; Computer Science; Engineering. Company benefits include: medical insurance; dental insurance; pension plan; life insurance; tuition assistance; disability coverage; profit sharing; savings plan. Operations at this facility include: manufacturing. Corporate headquarters location: Peoria, IL. New York Stock Exchange. International: Australia, Belgium, Brazil, Canada, England, France, Hong Kong, India, Japan, Mexico, Scotland, Singapore, Switzerland.

INTERNATIONAL MINERALS & CHEMICAL CORP.

421 East Hawley Street, Mundelein IL 60060. 312/949-3458. Contact Debra Gold, Supervisor, Corporate Human Resources. Corporate, regional and divisional headquarters location for a Fortune 500 company consisting of two wholly owned subsidiaries. Since the company is a decentralized organization, resumes should be forwarded directly to desired business group: Pitman-Moore, Inc. or Mallinckrodt, Inc. Common positions include: Accountant; Administrator; Attorney; Computer Programmer; Draftsperson; Financial Analyst; Personnel & Labor Rela-

tions Specialist; Public Relations Worker; Systems Analyst. Principal educational backgrounds sought: Accounting; Business Administration; Communications; Computer Science; Finance; Liberal Arts. Company benefits include: medical insurance; dental insurance; tuition assistance; disability coverage; profit sharing; employee discounts; savings plan. Operations at this facility include: administration. New York Stock Exchange. International: Colombia, England, Japan, Mexico, Netherlands, Switzerland, Zimbabwe.

MEAD CONTAINER
7601 South 78th Avenue, Bridgeview IL 60455. 312/458-8100. Contact Beverly Grybas, Administrative Manager. Several area locations including: Chicago (2) and Hillside. A multi-industry firm with segments operating primarily in the forest products industry (paper, pulp, lumber, etc.), but also in such areas as balance-engineered castings, molded rubber parts, distribution of piping and electrical supplies, and the manufacture of advanced digital information systems. Forest products segment includes three major subsidiaries: Georgia Kraft Company, Brunswick Pulp and Paper, and Northwood Forest Industries. Bridgeview facility produces corrugated shipping containers; facility at 9540 South Dorchester Avenue, Chicago (60628) produces folding cartons; subsidiary facility (Bermingham and Prosser) at 125 Fencl Lane, Hillside (60162) is responsible for distributing paper products; and subsidiary Ft. Dearborn Paper Company, 2901 West 36th Place, Chicago (60632) produces and converts paper. Parent company is divided into five operating segments: Paper, Paperboard, Consumer and Distribution, Industrial Products, and Advanced Systems. Corporate headquarters location: Dayton, OH. International: Canada, England, France, Germany, Italy, Japan, Netherlands, Switzerland.

OWENS-ILLINOIS INC./MACHINE DIVISION
315 Tolle Lane, Godfrey IL 62035. 618/466-8811. Contact Personnel Department. One of several area divisions of the well-known diversified manufacturer of packaging products. Company's principal products are glass containers, although the company also produces and sells containerboard, corrugated containers, printing plates and ink, plywood and

demension lumber, blown plastic containers, plastic beverage bottles, plastic drums, metal and plastic closures, tamper-resistant closures, plastic and glass presciption containers, pharmaceutical items, labels, and mulipack plastic carriers for containers. Specialized glass products made and sold by the company include Libbey Tumblers, stemware, and decorative glassware, television bulbs for picture tubes, and Kimble scientific and laboratory ware. Some overseas affiliates also manufacture flat glass and related products. International: Australia, Brazil, Canada, Colombia, Germany, Italy, Japan, Singapore, Switzerland, Venezuela.

OZITE CORPORATION
1755 Butterfield Road, Libertyville IL 60048. 312/362-8210. Contact Kathy Fox, Director of Industrial Relations. Manufactures commercial, automotive, and industrial carpeting and wall covering. Corporate headquarters location. Common positions include: Accountant; Administrator; Bank Officer/Manager; Blue-Collar Worker Supervisor; Buyer; Chemist; Claim Representative; Computer Programmer; Credit Manager; Customer Service Representative; Industrial Engineer; Personnel & Labor Relations Specialist; Purchasing Agent; Quality Control Supervisor; Sales Representative. Principal educational backgrounds sought: Accounting; Business Administration; Engineering; Liberal Arts; Marketing. Company benefits include: medical insurance; dental insurance; pension plan; life insurance; tuition assistance; disability coverage; profit sharing; employee discounts; savings plan. International: Canada, Saudi Arabia.

SARA LEE
31st National Plaza, 70 West Madison, Chicago Il 60602. 312/726-2600. Contact Philip Temple, Vice President of Human Resources. The corporate office of the cake, cake-mix, and dessert snacks producer. International: Australia, France, Netherlands.

SKIL CORPORATION
4300 West Peterson Avenue, Chicago IL 60646. 312/286-7330. Contact Michael McMinn, Personnel. Several area locations including: Skokie,

and Elk Grove Village. Manufacturers of hand and power tools. A subsidiary of Emerson Electric Company. Corporate headquarters location. International: Australia, Austria, Mexico, Netherlands, Sweden, Switzerland.

INDIANA

BRISTOL-MYERS U.S. PHARMACEUTICAL AND NUTRITION

400 West Lloyd Expressway, Evansville IN 47721. 812/429-5000. Contact Employment Office. Engaged in the research, manufacture, and marketing of pharmaceutical and nutritional products for the consumer and pharmaceutical markets. Operations include administration, marketing, and research at the Bristol Myers USPNG Research Center. Common positons include: Accountant; Biochemist; Chemist; Computer Programmer; Biomedical Engineer; Chemical Engineer; Electrical Engineer; Industrial Engineer; Mechanical Engineer; Financial Analyst; Personnel & Labor Relations Specialist; Quality Control Supervisor; Sales Representative; Statistician; Systems Analyst; Technical Writer/Editor. Principal educational backgrounds sought: Accounting; Chemistry; Computer Science; Engineering; Marketing (MBA). Company benefits include: medical insurance; dental insurance; life insurance; tuition assistance; disability coverage; employee discounts; savings plan; pension plan. Corporate headquarterslocated in New York, NY. New York Stock Exchange. International: Egypt, Hong Kong, Italy, Japan, Panama, Spain, Venezuela.

ELI LILLY AND COMPANY

Lilly Corporate Center, Indianapolis IN 46285. 317/276-2165. Contact Corporate Recruitment. A major researcher and producer of pharmaceuticals, cosmetics, medical instrument systems and animal health products. International: Argentina, Australia, Austria, Belgium, Brazil, Canada, Chile, Colombia, Denmark, England, France, Germany, Greece, Guatemala, Italy, Japan, Korea, Malaysia, Mexico, Netherlands, New Zealand, Peru, Philippines, Singapore, Switzerland, Taiwan, Thailand, Venezuela.

STEWART-WARNER CORP./SOUTH WIND DIVISION

1514 Drover Street, Indianapolis IN 46221. 317/267-1677. Contact Manager/Personnel. Develops, manufactures and markets heat transfer and combustion heating equipment. Primary customers include commercial and military aircraft manufacturers, truck, off-the-road, and bus manufacturers. Divisional headquarters. Operations include: manufacturing; research/development; administration; sales. Corporate headquarters location. Common positions include: Accountant; Computer Programmer; Industrial Engineer; Mechanical Engineer; Financial Analyst; Department Manager; Operations/Production Manager; Marketing Specialist; Sales Representative; Systems Analyst. Principal educational backgrounds sought: Accounting; Business Administration; Computer Science; Engineering; Finance; Marketing. Company benefits include: medical insurance; pension plan; life insurance; tuition assistance; credit union. International: Australia, England, Germany, India, Italy, Mexico.

IOWA

DUNHAM-BUSH INC.

811 East Main, P.O. Box 498, Marshalltown IA 50158. 515/752-4291. Contact James B. Hart, Industrial Relations Manager. Manufacturer of commercial steam and hot water systems and components. Corporate headquarters location: West Hartford, CT. Operations include: manufacturing; service; sales. Common positions include: Accountant; Administrator; Advertising Worker; Blue-Collar Worker Supervisor; Buyer; Draftsperson; Engineer; Industrial Engineer; Mechanical Engineer; Manager; Branch Manager; Department Manager; General Manager; Management Trainee; Operations/Production Manager; Marketing Specialist; Personnel & Labor Relations Specialist; Purchasing Agent. Principal educational backgrounds sought: Accounting; Business Administration; Engineering; Marketing. Company benefits include: medical insurance; pension plan; life insurance; tuition assistance; disability coverage; employee discounts; savings plan. International: Canada, England, Germany.

NORPLEX DIVISION/ALLIED SIGNAL

P.O. Box 370, N.E. County Road, Postville IA 52162. 319/864-7321. Contact Personnel Director. Engaged in the manufacture of copper clad and unclad plastic laminates. Parent company, Allied Signal Corporation, serves a broad spectrum of industries through its more than 40 strategic businesses, which are grouped into five sectors: Aerospace; Automotive; Chemical; Industrial and Technology; and Oil and Gas. Allied Signal is one of the nation's largest industrial organizations, and has 115,000 employees in over 30 countries. Corporate headquarters location: Morristown, NJ. International: Brazil, China, France, Japan.

ROCKWELL INTERNATIONAL/AVIONICS GROUP

400 Collins Road NE, Cedar Rapids IA 52498. 800/835-9355. Contact John P. Gorman, Professional Staffing Specialist. Operates three divisions—Collins Air Transport Division, Collins General Aviation Division, and Collins Government Avionics Division— which provide aviation electronics products, systems and services to the air transport, business and general aviation, and military and government aircraft markets worldwide. Common positions include: Electrical Engineer; Mechanical Engineer; Marketing Specialist. Principal educational backgrounds sought: Computer Science; Engineering. Company benefits include: medical insurance; dental insurance; pension plan; life insurance; tuition assistance; disability coverage; employee discounts; savings plan; company pharmacy; child care center; recreation center. Corporate headquarters location: El Segundo, CA. Parent company: Rockwell International. Operations at this facility include: group headquarters; manufacturing; research/development; administration; service; sales. New York Stock Exchange. International: Australia, Belgium, Brazil, Canada, Egypt, England, France, Germany, Hong Kong, Israel, Italy, Japan, Korea, Mexico, Philippines, Saudi Arabia, Singapore, Spain, Taiwan.

SHELLER-GLOBE CORPORATION

P.O. Box 727, 3200 Main Street, Keokuk IA 52632. 319/524-4560. Contact Darlene Busey, Employment/Training Supervisor. A diversified manufacturer serving the auto, industrial, and consumer markets.

Produces automotive equipment and aftermarket parts. Corporate headquarters location: Toledo, OH. Operations include: manufacturing. New York Stock Exchange. Common positions include: Accountant; Blue-Collar Worker Supervisor; Chemist; Computer Programmer; Draftsperson; Engineer; Electrical Engineer; Industrial Engineer; Mechanical Engineer; Financial Analyst; Management Trainee; Operations/Production Manager; Personnel & Labor Relations Specialist; Quality Control Supervisor; Statistician; Transportation & Traffic Specialist. Principal educational backgrounds sought: Accounting; Business Administration; Chemistry; Computer Science; Engineering; Finance; Liberal Arts. Company benefits include: medical insurance; dental insurance; life insurance; pension plan; tuition assistance; disability coverage; profit sharing; employee discounts; savings plan. International: Canada, England, France, Mexico.

KANSAS

CESSNA AIRCRAFT COMPANY
P.O. Box 7704, Wichita KS 67277. 316/946-7249. Contact Mr. Dale Greenlee, Professional Placement Representative. Engaged in the engineering; fabrication, assembly, and marketing of light commercial and business aircraft. Primary customers are corporations with limited sales to individuals. Common positions include: Accountant; Buyer; Computer Programmer; Draftsperson; Aerospace Engineer; Electrical Engineer; Industrial Engineer; Mechanical Engineer; Personnel & Labor Relations Specialist; Systems Analyst; Technical Writer/Editor. Principal educational backgrounds sought: Accounting; Computer Science; Engineering; Marketing. Company benefits include: medical, dental, and life insurance; pension plan; tuition assistance; disability coverage; savings plan. Corporate headquarters location. Parent company: General Dynamics. Operations at this facility include: divisional headquarters; manufacturing; research/development; administration; service; sales. International: France, Scotland.

MANVILLE BUILDING MATERIALS
Box 1287, County Road 319, McPherson KS 67460. 316/241-6260. Contact Georgeanne Peterson, Personnel Director. A manufacturer and

distributor of fiberglass insulation products. International: Argentina, Australia, Belgium, Bermuda, Canada, England, France, Germany, Italy, Japan, Mexico, Saudi Arabia, Singapore, Spain, United Arab Emirates, Venezuela, Zaire.

OLIN WATER SERVICES

9393 West 110th Street, Suite 600, Overland Park KS 66210. 913/451-3100, ext. 223. Contact Ronald W. Major, Director/Personnel and Safety. A water treatment company. A subsidiary of Olin Corporation (Stamford, CT). Divisional headquarters. New York Stock Exchange. Common positions include: Accountant; Computer Programmer; Department Manager; General Manager; Marketing Specialist; Purchasing Agent; Sales Representative. Principal educational backgrounds sought: Chemistry; Marketing. Company benefits include: medical, dental and life insurance; pension plan; tuition assistance; disability coverage; employee discounts; savings plan. International: Australia, Belgium, Colombia, England, France, Germany, Ireland, Japan, Mexico, New Zealand, Singapore, Spain, Taiwan, Venezuela.

KENTUCKY

ASHLAND PETROLEUM CO

P.O. Box 391, Ashland KY 41114. 606/329-3862. Contact Marc E. Washington, Manager, Professional Employment. Ashland Oil, the 60th largest industrial company in the United States, is a large diversified corporation with a strong base in its traditional refining, marketing, and transportation businesses and an equally strong group of non-refining operations. These operatons include: retail marketing, motor oil marketing, chemicals, engineering and construction, and oil and gas exploration and production. Common positions include: Accountant; Attorney; Chemist; Computer Programmer; Chemical Engineer; Civil Engineer; Electrical Engineer; Industrial Engineer; Sales Representative; Systems Analyst. Principal educational backgrounds sought: Accounting; Business Administration; Chemistry; Computer Science; Engineering; Marketing. Company benefits include: medical insurance; dental insurance; pension plan; life insurance; tuition assistance; disability coverage; savings plan; employee stock ownership plan; credit union.

Corporate headquarters location. Operations at this facility include: divisional headquarters; manufacturing; research/development. Company is listed on the New York Stock Exchange. International: England, India.

BROWN & WILLIAMSON TOBACCO CORPORATION

P.O. Box 35090, Louisville KY 40232. 502/568-7703. Contact Gary Rosentreter, Corporate Recruiter. Researches, develops, manufactures, and markets tobacco products, principally cigarettes. Emphasis is on research, development, and engineering; finance; management information systems; and marketing. Division of BATUS, subsidiary of British American Industries, London, England. Corporate headquarters location. Common positions include: Accountant; Attorney; Buyer; Chemist; Computer Programmer; Engineer; Chemical Engineer; Civil Engineer; Electrical Engineer; Industrial Engineer; Mechanical Engineer; Food Technologist; Marketing Specialist; Physicist; Statistician; Systems Analyst. Principal educational backgrounds sought: Business Administration; Chemistry; Computer Science; Engineering; Finance; Marketing; Mathematics. Company benefits include: medical, dental, and life insurance; pension plan; tuition assistance; disability coverage; profit sharing; savings plan. International: Costa Rica, Turkey.

SARGENT & GREENLEAF INC.

One Security Drive, Nicholasville KY 40356. 606/885-9411. Contact Ms. Shirlean Herron, Industrial Relations Manager. Produces high security locks, access controls and devices. Corporate headquarters location. Operations include: manufacturing; research/development; administration; service; sales. Common positions include: Accountant; Blue-Collar Worker Supervisor; Buyer; Computer Programmer; Credit Manager; Customer Service Representative; Draftsperson; Engineer; Industrial Engineer; Mechanical Engineer; Financial Analyst; Industrial Designer; Department Manager; General Manager; Operations/Production Manager; Marketing Specialist; Personnel & Labor Relations Specialist; Purchasing Agent; Quality Control Supervisor; Sales Representative; Systems Analyst. Principal educational backgrounds sought: Accounting; Business Administration; Engineering; Finance; Marketing. Company benefits include: medical insurance; pension plan; life insurance; tuition assistance; disability coverage. International: England, Switzerland.

LOUISIANA

ALLIED CHEMICAL/MENICKENS

P.O. Box 2830, Baton Rouge LA 70821. 504/383-5222. Contact Personnel Director. An area producer of chemicals, including genetron, muriatic acid, zinc, hydrofluoric acid, sulfuric acid, oleum, and calcium chloride. Parent company, Allied Signal Corporation, serves a broad spectrum of industries through its more than 40 strategic businesses, which are grouped into five sectors: Aerospace; Automotive; Chemical; Industrial and Technology; and Oil and Gas. Allied Signal is one of the nation's largest industrial organizations, and has 115,000 employees in over 30 countries. Corporate headquarters location: Morristown, NJ. International: Australia, Belgium, Canada, England, Hong Kong, Mexico, New Zealand, Switzerland, Venezuela.

GRACE OFFSHORE

701 Poydras, Suite 4700, New Orleans LA 70139. 504/584-9600. Contact Personnel Department. Engaged in offshore oil well work-over and completion services. Parent company, W.R. Grace & Co., is a diversified worldwide enterprise consisting of specialty and agricultural chemicals, energy production and services, retailing, restaurants, and other businesses; the firm operates over 2,500 facilities in 47 states and 42 foreign countries and employs 80,000 people. Corporate headquarters location: New York, NY. International: Argentina, Australia, Brazil, Canada, Denmark, England, Finland, France, Germany, Greece, Guatemala, Hong Kong, Ivory Coast, Japan, Malaysia, Mexico, New Zealand, Norway, Philippines, Portugal, Singapore, Spain, Sweden, Switzerland, Venezuela.

MAINE

BURNHAM & MORRILL DIVISION/IC INDUSTRIES

One Beanpot Circle, Portland ME 04104. 207/772-8341. Contact Bruce Tupper, Benefits Manager. A manufacturer of a variety of food products, including brown bread, puddings, and baked beans. Corporate head-quarters location: Chicago, IL. International: Australia, China, Colombia, India, Italy, Malaysia, Mexico, New Zealand, Philippines, Switzerland, Venezuela.

MARYLAND

BLACK & DECKER

701 East Joppa Road, Towson MD 21204. 301/583-3900. Contact Human Resources Department. Engaged in manufacturing, selling, and servicing electric, pneumatic, and gasoline-powered tools, including accessories geneally used in homes and home worrkshops, for lawn care and maintenance, in timbering, in the service and maintenance trades, and on farms. International: Argentina, Australia, Austria, Belgium, Brazil, Canada, China, Colombia, Costa Rica, Denmark, Ecuador, El Salvador, England, Finland, Germany, Greece, Hong Kong, India, Ireland, Israel, Italy, Kenya, Korea, Mexico, Netherlands, New Zealand, Nigeria, Norway, Panama, Portugal, Singapore, Spain, Sweden, Switzerland, Taiwan, Venezuela, Yugoslavia, Zambia.

DRESSER INDUSTRIES INC./WAYNE DIVISION

P.O. Box 1859, 124 West College Avenue, Salisbury MD 21801. 301/546-6623. Contact Linas Orentas, Human Resources Administrator. Develops, manufactures, markets and services Globe automobile hoists and Wayne gasoline dispensing systems for the domestic and export markets. Common positions include: Accountant; Administrator; Advertising Worker; Blue-Collar Worker Supervisor; Buyer; Computer Programmer; Credit Manager; Customer Service Representative; Draftsperson; Economist; Industrial Engineer; Mechanical Engineer; Operations/Production Manager; Marketing Specialist; Personnel & Labor Relations Specialist; Public Relations Worker; Purchasing Agent; Quality Control Supervisor; Sales Representative; Systems Analyst; Technical Writer/Editor; Tool Engineer; Design Engineer; Inventory Control; Export Personnel. Principal educational backgrounds sought: Accounting; Business Administration; Communications; Computer Science; Economics; Engineering; Finance; Liberal Arts; Marketing; Mathematics; Physics. Company benefits include: medical insurance;

dental insurance; pension plan; life insurance; tuition assistance; disability coverage; savings plan. Corporate headquarters location: Dallas, TX. Operations at this facility include: divisional headquarters; manufacturing; research/development; administration; service; sales. New York Stock Exchange.International: Argentina, Australia, Belgium, Brazil, Canada, Chile, Colombia, China, England, Germany, Greece, Hong Kong, Indonesia, Italy, Japan, Kuwait, Luxemborg, Mexico, Netherlands, Nigeria, Norway, Peru, Saudi Arabia, Scotland, Singapore, Spain, Sweden, Switzerland, Thailand, Taiwan, USSR, Venezuela.

NATIONAL CAN CORPORATION
2010 Reservoir Road, Sparrows Point MD 21219. 301/477-3131. Contact Personnel. Produces metal cans, including sanitary containers, and beverage and other containers. Nationally, company is one of the world's leading manufacturers of packaging products, manufacturing and marketing aluminum and steel cans, glass and plastic blow-molded containers, steel crowns, aluminum closures, and metal and plastic caps for a variety of end-uses. Operates more than 70 manufacturing and support facilities in 10 countries and Puerto Rico. Principal markets include the beer, soft drink, and food processing industries around the world. Corporate headquarters location: Chicago, IL. New York Stock Exchange. International: England, Greece.

WESTVACO CORPORATION
3400 East Biddle Street, Baltimore MD 21213. 301/327-7376. Contact Margaret Sponaugle, Personnel Administrator. Manufactures corrugated fiber cartons. Nationally, company is an international firm specializing in the manufacture of high-quality papers for communications, packaging, and high-technology applications. Products include packaging for both industrial and consumer markets, and envelopes (where company is among the world's largest producers). Other area facilities in Luke, Baltimore, Pasadena, and Laurel, MD. Corporate headquarters location: New York, NY. International: Australia, Belgium, Brazil.

MASSACHUSETTS

BAIRD CORPORATION

125 Middlesex Turnpike, Bedford MA 01730. 617/276-6000. Contact Ronald Babineau, Personnel Manager. Principally engaged in the design, development, manufacture, and sale of a variety of analytic and optical instruments and systems for the industrial, defense, and medical diagnostic markets. Operates in three business segments: Analytical Instruments, used to provide information on the chemical, physical, and structural properties of materials: Optical Systems, including night driver's viewers and daytime periscopes for armored vehicles, other night vision equipment, and photographic equipment; and Medical Diagnostic Systems, whose chief product is a gamma camera used in cardiovascular nuclear medicine diagnostics. Corporate headquarters location. International: Brazil, England, Netherlands.

BORG-WARNER CORPORATION/NEW BEDFORD GEAR

Theodore Rice Boulevard, Industrial Park, New Bedford MA 02745. 508/995-2616. Contact Paul Humason, Personnel Manager. The New Bedford Gear Division specializes in metal cutting, primarily for transmission gears and timing sprockets for automobiles. Nationally, the company is a $2.7-billion diversified manufacturing and services firm, with some 50 divisions operating in 20 countries on six continents. Most products are made for manufacturers serving the transportation, construction, consumer products, machinery, agribusiness, and energy markets. The company also has extensive operations that provide financial and protective services for business. The company's major divisions are: Air Conditioning, primarily through subsidiary York Air Conditioning; Chemicals and Plastics, including a family of engineering thermoplastics designed for abuse-resistance in hundreds of consumer products, as well as other resin and chemical products; Financial Services, primarily operating through Borg-Warner Acceptance Corporation, one of the leading independent finance companies in the United States; Protective Services, which operates through subsidiary Baker Industries, parent company of Wells Fargo armored, alarm, and guard services, and Pony Express courier service; Energy and Industrial Equipment, whose major products include centrifugal pumps for power generating plants, pipelines, water plants, and irrigation, precision seals for pumps and compressors, valves, automotive and industrial chain, bearings, and a wide range of power transmission products, as well as other products; and Transportation Equipment, supplied to original equipment manufacturers and the automotive aftermarket, including automatic and manual transmissions and transmission components, carburetion and ignition equipment, clutches, four-wheel drive units, axles, emission controls, and radiators. These components are supplied for passenger cars, trucks, and off-highway vehicles and equipment. Corporate headquarters location: Chicago, IL. New York Stock Exchange. International: Argentina, Australia, Austria, Belgium, Brazil, Canada, England, France, Germany, Italy, Japan, Mexico, Netherlands, New Zealand, Panama, Scotland, Singapore, Spain, Venezuela.

ARTHUR D. LITTLE INC.
25 Acorn Park, Cambridge MA 02140. 617/864-5770. Contact Lewis Rambo, Personnel Director. A worldwide contract research, engineering, and management consulting organization whose business is to help industry, institutions, and governments manage the problems and opportunities created by change. Professional staff includes some 1,400 members, representing experts in hundreds of different disciplines and industries; also has approximately 450 specialized consultants, drawn largely from universities and colleges. Affiliated business units include: Arthur D. Little Systems (Burlington), which specializes in the development of computer software, computer systems design, and implementation; Delphi Associates (Lowell—a subsidiary of ADL Systems); Pilgrim Health Applications (Lowell), which processes medical claims for third-party payment; and a wide range of other companies providing diverse consulting services. Corporate headquarters location. International: Belgium, Brazil, Canada, England, France, Germany, Greece, Portugal, Saudi Arabia, Spain.

RAYTHEON COMPANY
141 Spring Street, Lexington MA 02173. 617/862-6600. Contact Employment Manager. A major high-technology electronics firm, actively engaged in the conception, development, manufacture, and sale of

electronic systems and subsystems, equipment, and components for government and commercial use. Corporate headquarters location. New York Stock Exchange. International: Argentina, Australia, Belgium, Brazil, Canada, Chile, Denmark, Egypt, England, France, Germany, Hong Kong, Israel, Italy, Japan, Kenya, Mexico, Netherlands, New Zealand, Saudi Arabia, Singapore, Spain, Switzerland, Taiwan, Turkey, Venezuela.

STONE & WEBSTER ENGINEERING

P.O. Box 2325, Boston MA 02107. 617/589-5111. Contact Nancy Chamberlain, Professional Employment Representative. Provides a wide range of engineering consulting services, including design and construction, on large-scale projects, primarily for the power generation industry. Also provides consulting services for other industries, including petrochemicals, industrial manufacturing, and others. Offices located throughout the United States and in some international locations. Employs 12,000 people worldwide. Corporate headquarters location. International: Canada, England, France, Indonesia, Korea, Malaysia, Mexico, Saudi Arabia, United Arab Emirates.

MICHIGAN

EMHART CORPORATION/WARREN DIVISION

P.O. Box 868, Mount Clemens MI 48403. 313/949-0440. Contact Mr. Morris, Director of Human Resources. A leading area manufacturer of plastic products. Employs 500. International: Argentina, Australia, Autria, Belgium, Brazil, Canada, Chile, Denmark, Egypt, Finland, France, Germany, Hong Kong, Ireland, Italy, Japan, Mexico, Netherlands, new Zealand, Norway, Portugal, Singapore, Spain, Sweden, Switzerland, Taiwan.

JOHNSON CONTROL INC. AUTOMOTIVE SYSTEMS GROUP

P.O. Box 1003, Ann Arbor MI 48106. 313/665-1500. Contact Employee Relations, Staffing and Development. Engaged in the manufacture of automotive seating and body systems for the automotive industry. Employs over 5,000. Common positions include: Accountant; Administrator; Chemist; Computer Programmer; Customer Service Representative; Draftsperson; Industrial Engineer; Mechanical Engineer; Financial Analyst; Industrial Designer; Department Manager; General Manager; Personnel and Labor Relations Specialist; Purchasing Agent; Sales Representative; Systems Analyst. Principal educational backgrounds sought: Accounting; Business Administration; Chemistry; Computer Science; Engineering; Marketing; Mathematics. Company benefits include: medical, dental, and life insurance; pension plan; tuition assistance; disability coverage; employee discounts; savings plan. Corporate headquarters location: Milwaukee, WI. Operations at this facility include: divisional headquarters; research/development; administration; sales. New York Stock Exchange.

PARKE DAVIS-ROCHESTER

870 Parkdale Road, Rochester MI 48063. 313/651-9081. Contact Angelo Rizzo, Manager of Employee Relations. A major Southeastern Michigan manufacturer of pharmaceutical products. Employs 600. International: Argentina, Australia, Brazil, Ecuador, Egypt, England, Germany, Hong Kong, India, Italy, New Zealand, Nigeria, Pakistan, Panama, Peru, Portugal, Saudi Arabia, Spain, Sweden, Taiwan, Thailand, Venezuela.

STEELCASE INC.

P.O. Box 1967, Grand Rapids MI 49501. 616/247-2710. Contact Jeanne West, Employment Representative. A large manufacturer of furniture. International: Canada, England, France, Germany, Japan.

MINNESOTA

GAF CORPORATION

50 Lowry Avenue North, Minneapolis MN 55411. 612/529-9121. Contact Mary Hall, Personnel Director. Regional prodution facility of the well-known chemicals, building materials, photographic and reprographic products manufacturer. A grocery store chain. International: Australia, Austria, Belgium, Brazil, Canada, England, France, Germany, Italy, Japan, Mexico, Netherlands, New Zealand, Singapore, Spain, Sweden, Switzerland.

MAICO HEARING INSTRUMENTS INC.

7375 Bush Lake Road, Minneapolis MN 55435. 612/835-4400. Contact Human Resources Manager. A producer of audiometers and hearing aids. Common positions include: Accountant; Aministrator; Advertising Worker; Buyer; Credit Manager; Customer Service Representative; Draftsperson; Electrical Engineer; Mechanical Engineer; General Manager; Operations/Production Manager; Marketing Specialist; Personnel and Labor Relations Specialist; Purchasing Agent; Quality Control Supervisor; Sales Representative; Technical Writer/Editor; Assembler; Principal educational backgrounds sought: Accounting; Business Administration; Communications; Engineering; Marketing. Company benefits include: medical insurance; dental insurance; pension plan; life insurance; tuition assistance; disability coverage. Corporate headquarters location. Parent company: Gfeller, US. Operations at this facility include: manufacturing; research/development; administration; service; sales. International: Uruguay.

NORTHERN TELECOM, INC.

Mail Station H-103, P.O. Box 1222, Minneapolis MN 55440. 612/932-8000. Contact Personnel Department. A major manufacturer of computers and telephones. International: Australia, Belgium, Canada, France, Germany, Ireland, Italy, Netherlands, Spain, Switzerland.

PILLSBURY COMPANY

Pillsbury Center, Mail Station 0110, Minneapolis MN 55402. 612/330-8196. Contact David Magy, Manager, Staffing and College Relations. Manufactures and markets food products for consumer, industrial, and international markets. Corporate headquarters location. International: Canada, England, France, Germany, Guatemala, Mexico, Venezuela.

MISSISSIPPI

COLT INDUSTRIES/HOLLEY CARBURETOR DIVISION

P.O. Drawer 727, Water Valley MS 38965. 601/473-3100. Contact Personnel Director. Manufacture carburetors, pistons. Employs 1,000. International: Canada, England, France.

GENESCO INC.

1208 Bethdale Drive, Iuka MS 38852. 601/423-3254. Contact Terry Harrell, Personnel Manager/Safety Coordinator. Manufactures men's and women's leather shoes. Corporate headquarters location: Nashville, TN. Operations include: manufacturing. New York Stock Exchange. Common positions include: Blue-Collar Worker Supervisor; Buyer; Industrial Engineer; Department Manager; Operations/Production Manager; Personnel & Labor Relations Specialist; Maintenance Manager; Plant Superintendent. Principal educational backgrounds sought: Engineering; Management; Personnel Management. Company benefits include: medical insurance; pension plan; life insurance; tuition assistance; disability coverage; employee discounts; savings plan; credit union. International: Canada.

TECUMSEH PRODUCTS/TUPELO DIVISION

P.O. Box 527, Tupelo MS 38802. 601/566-2231. Contact Human Resources Director. Manufactures compressors for use in industrial and residential air conditioning and heating systems. Employs 700. International: Brazil, Canada, Germany, Italy.

MISSOURI

ANHEUSER-BUSCH COMPANIES INC.

One Busch Place, St. Louis MO 63118. 314/577-2000. Contact Charles DiMercurio, Manager/Recruiting Services and College. A diversified corporation whose products include beer, agricultural operations and products, and family entertainment complexes. Corporate headquarters location. International: England, Japan.

EMERSON ELECTRIC CO./ELECTRONICS AND SPACE DIVISION

8100 West Florissant, St. Louis MO 63136. Contact Bill Kellenberger, Director of Personnel Resources. The Government and Defense Group (Electronics and Space Division) is engaged in the design and manufacture of electro-mechanical armaments for aircraft, ships and ground vehicles; automatic test equipment and electronic warfare wquipment. A subsidiay of Emerson Electric Company, the major worldwide electronics and manufacturing firm (same location). Divisional headquarters location. Operations include: manufacturing. Common positions include: Accountant; Computer Programmer; Engineer; Electrical Engineer; Programmer; Systems Analyst; Technical Writer/Editor. Principal educational background sought: Engineering. Company benefits include: medical, dental, and life insurance; pension plan; tuition assistance; disability coverage; employee discounts; savings plan. International: Belgium, Japan, Saudi Arabia.

THE HERTZ CORPORATION
Lambert Field, P.O. Box 10014, St. Louis MO 63145. 314/426-7555. Contact Amber Johnston, Personnel Director. Area offices for one of the nation's leading transporation services organization. Company operates nationally through several divisions: Rent-A-Car Division (car rental services); Car Leasing Division; and Equipment Rental and Leasing Division. Also engaged in joint venture truck leasing operations with Penske Corporation (Hertz Penske Truck Leasing) at 600 locations. A major subsidiary of RCA Corporation (New York, NY). Corporate headquarters location: New York, NY. International: Australia, Austria, Japan, Denmark, England, Germany, Ireland, Israel, Italy, Japan, Netherlands, Panama, Portugal, Spain, Switzerland.

PINKERTON'S INC.
7730 Carondelet, St. Louis MO 63105. 314/725-8100. Contact Ed Delanty, Personnel Director. St. Louis office of the oldest and largest non-governmental security service organization in the world today, operating for over 130 years. Principal business is providing high-quality security, investigative, and consulting services to a multitude of commercial, industrial, institutional, governmental, and residential clients. Operates from 129 offices in the United States, Canada, and Great Britain. Major services include: industrial plant security, retail security, nuclear plant security, institutional security, commercial and residential building security, construction security, patrol and inspection service, courier service, inventory service, community security, sports and special events service, K9 patrol service, investigation service,

security consultation, and equipment evaluation. Employs more than 35,000 people worldwide. International: Canada, England.

MONTANA

CHAMPION INTERNATIONAL/BONNER

Bonner MT 59823. 406/258-5511. Contact Ed Roberts, Personnel Director. A producer of a variety of packaging goods, including pulp and linerboard. Nationally, company is a major integrated forest products firm. Corporate headquarters location: Stamford, CT. International: Brazil.

CONOCO INC.

Box 2548, Billings MT 59103. 406/255-2500. Contact Personnel Director. A refinery which processes asphalt, diesel fuel, gasoline, Jet 50, and propane. Corporate headquarters location: Houston, TX. International: Argentina, Australia, Austria, Bahrain, Belgium, Brazil, Chad, Egypt, England, France, Germany, Indonesia, India, Italy, Japan, Netherlands, Nigeria, Norway, Scotland, Singapore, Spain, Sweden, Switzerland, Tunisia, United Arab Emirates.

NEBRASKA

CAMPBELL SOUP COMPANY

P.O. Box 778, Omaha NE 68101. 402/342-8118. Contact Mike Field, Manager of Human Resources. The Omaha division of the well-known food producer manufactures frozen convenience meals. Common positions include: Accountant; Blue-Collar Worker Supervisor; Buyer; Chemist; Computer Programmer; Draftsperson; Electrical Engineer; Industrial Engineer; Mechanical Engineer; Food Technologist; Personnel and Labor Relations Specialist; Purchasing Agent; Quality Control Supervisor; Statistician; Systems Analyst. Principal educational backgrounds sought: Accounting; Biology; Business Administration; Chemistry; Computer Science; Engineering. Company benefits include: medical insurance; dental insurance; pension plan; life insurance; tuiton assistance; disability coverage; employee discounts; savings plan. Corporate headquarters location: Camden, NJ. Operations at this facility include: manufacturing. New York Stock Exchange. International: Argentina, Australia, Belgium, Canada, England, France, Germany, Hong Kong, Italy, Japan, Mexico, Netherlands.

CONAGRA

1 Central Park Plaza, Conagra Center, Omaha NE 68102. 402/978-4000. Contact Personnel Office. A diversified family of companies operating across the food chain. Products range from supplies farmers need to grow crops to prepared food items. ConAgra operates in three segments of the food chain: Agriculture, Trading and Processing, and Prepared Foods. The company has major businesses in agricultural chemicals, animal feed, fertilizer, specialty trading, grain processing, beef, pork, lamb, poultry, processed meats, dairy products, seafood and frozen prepared foods. International: Spain.

MUTUAL/UNITED OF OMAHA INSURANCE CO.

Mutual of Omaha Plaza, Omaha NE 68175. 402/342-7600. Contact Employment Manager. Mutual of Omaha offers a full portfolio of (insurance) coverages and services with $25.4 billion paid in benefits to policy holders. United of Omaha Life Insurance Company ranks among the top 2% of all life insurance companies in the United States with more than $53 billion of life insurance in force. Common positions include: Accountant; Actuary; Attorney; Claim Representative; Computer Programmer; Customer Service Representative; Financial Analyst; Marketing Specialist; Personnel & Labor Relations Specialist; Systems Analyst; Underwriter. Principal educational backgrounds sought: Accounting; Business Administration; Computer Science; Finance; Liberal Arts; Marketing; Mathematics. Company benefits include: medical, dental, and life insurance; pension plan; tuition assistance; disability coverage; employee discounts; savings plan. Corporate headquarters location. Operations at this facility include: regional headquarters; divisional headquarters; administration; service. International: Canada, Panama.

UNION PACIFIC CORPORATION

1416 Dodge Street, Suite 400, Norchem Building Omaha NE 68179. 402/271-3643. Contact J.A. Hale, Jr., Director/Audit Personnel & Planning. Principal industry areas are energy, transportation, and natural resources. Divisional headquarters location. Corporate headquarter location: New York, NY. New York and American Stock Exchanges. Common positions include: Accountant; Auditor. Principal educational backgrounds sought: Accounting; Business Administration; Computer Science. Company benefits include: medical insurance; dental insurance; pension plan; life insurance; tuition assistance; disability coverage; profit sharing. International: Canada.

NEVADA

WACKENHUT SERVICES INC
3052 South Highland, Las Vegas NV 89109. 702/295-3575. Contact Personnel Department. A leading Nevada detective agency. Employs 400. International: Argentina, Bermuda, Canada, Chile, Colombia, Costa Rica, Dominican Republic, Ecuador, England, Germany, Hong Kong, Japan, Korea, Mexico, Panama, Philippines, Saudi Arabia, Scotland, Venezuela.

NEW HAMPSHIRE

GTE PRODUCTS CORPORATION
Portsmouth Avenue, Exeter NH 03833. 603/772-4331. Contact Human Resources Manager. Operations in the following divisions: Coated Coil operation, which involves production of tungsten filaments coated with high performance insulator aluminum oxide used in television electron guns; Special Refractory Products, which manufactures products made from refractory metals that are used as furnace hardware; Ceramics Department, which produces various types of steatite ceramic electrical insulators used in bases of light bulbs; and the Quartz Department, which produces and finishes quartz crucibles for use by the semiconductor industry. Divisional headquarters location. Corporate headquarters location: Stamford, CT. Operations include: manufacturing. New York Stock Exchange. Common positions include: Accountant; Computer Programmer; Customer Service Representative; Ceramics Engineer; Metallurgical Engineer. Principal educational backgrounds sought: Engineering; Marketing. Company benefits include: medical insurance;

dental insurance; pension plan; life insurance; tuition assistance; disability coverage; employee discounts; savings plan; 401 K plan. International: Argentina, Australia, Belgium, Brazil, Canada, England, France, Germany, India, Italy, Japan, Kenya, Mexico, Switzerland, Thailand.

MARKEM CORPORATION

150 Congress Street, Keene NH 03431. 603/352-1130, ext. 230. Contact Manager, Human Resources Division. An international firm providing complete in-plant printing systems to industry throughout the world. Specializes in the design, manufacturing, sales and service of printing elements, various in-line and independent printing mechanisms and the accompanying chemical supplies. Corporate and regional headquarters. Operations include: manufacturing; research/development. Common positions include: Accountant; Advertising Worker; Buyer; Commercial Artist; Computer Programmer; Customer Service Representative; Draftsperson; Engineer; Chemical Engineer; Electrical Engineer; Mechanical Engineer; Management Trainee; Marketing Specialist; Personnel & Labor Relations Specialist; Sales Representative; Technical Writer/Editor. Principal educational backgrounds sought: Business Administration; Computer Science; Engineering; Liberal Arts; Marketing. Company benefits include: medical insurance; pension plan; life insurance; tuition assistance; disability coverage; profit sharing; employee discounts; savings plan; in-plant library, bank, cafeteria, greenhouse; training. International: Canada, England, France, Germany, Italy, Japan, Mexico, Netherlands, Sweden.

MPB CORPORATION

P.O. Box 547, Keene NH 03431. 603/352-0310. Contact Robert Rooney, Personnel Director. A stand-alone company owned by a group of investors headed by Harold S. Geneen. Common positions include: Accountant; Administrator; Blue-Collar Worker Supervisor; Buyer; Computer Programmer; Customer Service Representative; Draftsperson; Aerospace Engineer; Industrial Engineer; Mechanical Engineer; Metallurgical Engineer; Department Manager; General Manager; Operations/Production Manager; Personnel and Labor Relations Specialist;

Purchasing Agent; Quality Control Supervisor; Systems Analyst. Educational backgrounds sought include: Business Administration; Engineering. Company benefits include: medical insurance; dental insurance; pension plan; life insurance; tuition assistance; disability coverage; profit sharing; employee discounts; savings plan. Corporate headquarters location: Keene,NH. Operations at this facility include: manufacturing. International: Germany.

NEW JERSEY

AMERICAN CYANAMID COMPANY
One Cyanamid Plaza, Wayne NJ 07470. 201/831-3081. Contact Leo J. Medicus, Manager/College Relations & Prof. Plcmnt. Several area locations, including Princeton, NJ; Pearl River, NY; and Stamford, CT. A diversified, multinational organization, engaged in the research, development, manufacture, and marketing of agricultural, chemical, consumer, and medical products. Operates 17 research laboratories and nearly 100 plants nationwide; offers 2,500 products in more than 135 countries. Medical business consists of both prescription and non-prescription pharmaceutical products and hospital products, made and marketed by Lederle Laboratories Division (in United States). Agricultural business consists of animal feed and health products; insecticides, fungicides, herbicides and plant regulators; and fertilizers. Chemical business consists of more than 5,000 organic and inorganic chemicals and related products in six operating divisions: Chemical Products; Polymer Products; Glendale Optical Company; Fibers; and Industrial Products. Consumer products operates in three divisions: Shulton Inc./USA makes and markets personal care and grooming products (brand names such as 'Old Spice,' 'Breck,' and others); and household maintenance and cleaning aids (including 'Pine Sol' cleaner); Jacqueline Cochran Inc., which makes and markets men's and women's prestige fragrances; and Shulton International, which manufactures and markets the above products internationally. Corporate headquarters location. New York Stock Exchange. Common positions include: Biochemist; Chemist; Engineer; Agricultural Engineer; Chemical Engineer; Industrial Engineer; Mechanical Engineer; Metallurgical Engineer; Mining Engineer; Petroleum Engineer; Marketing Specialist; Statistician;

Systems Analyst. Principal educational backgrounds sought: Business Administration; Chemistry; Computer Science; Engineering; Marketing. International: Australia, Austria, Belgium, Brazil, Canada, Colombia, Denmark, Egypt, England, France, Germany, Greece, Guatemala, Hong Kong, India, italy, Japan, Kenya, Korea, Mexico, Netherlands, new Zealand, Nigeria, Pakistan, Peru, Philippines, Portugal, Spain Sweene, Switzerland, Taiwan, Turkey, Venezuela.

CURTISS-WRIGHT CORPORATION
1200 Wall Street West, Lyndhurst NJ 07071. 201/896-8400. Contact Mr. Cap W. Orr, Corporate Director of Labor Relations. A diversified multinational manufacturing concern. The corporation manufactures and markets products and provides services to industrial customers and under Government contracts in four broad areas: Aerospace; Flow Control and Marine; Industrial; and Electrical Generating. Aerospace segment produces jet engine and reciprocating engine parts, control and actuation components and systems, shot-peening and peen-forming services, and custom extruded shapes and shafts, for U.S. Government agencies, foreign governments, commercial/military/general aviation airframe manufacturers, commercial/military helicopter manufacturers, jet aircraft engine manufacturers, and commercial airlines. Flow Control and Marine segment produces globe, gate, solenoid and safety relief valves, and custom extruded shapes and seamless alloy pipe for U.S. Navy propulsion systems, commercial power systems, and U.S. Navy shipbuilders. Industrial segment produces precision spring clutches, manual impact wrenches, and aircraft windshield wiper systems for the office machine, industrial/military hand tool and general aviation markets, custom extruded shapes and seamless alloy pipe for the shipbuilding, oil/petrochemical/chemical construction industries, shot-peening and heat treating for the general metal working, and oil and gas drilling and exploration industries. The industrial compressor industry, and U.S. Government agencies, and Canadian operations, which manufactures air compressors and distributes small reciprocating engines for commercial/industrial, and lawn and garden uses. Area subsidiaries include Curtiss-Wright Flight Systems, Inc., a manufacturer of aerospace control and actuation components and systems (300 Fairfield Road, Fairfield NJ

07006); Metal Improvement Company, which performs shot-peening, peen-forming, and heat-treating services (10 Forest Avenue, Paramus NJ 07652); and Target Rock Corporation, a manufacturer of flow control valves. (East Farmingdale NY 11735). Common positions include: Accountant; Administrator; Attorney; Computer Programmer; Draftsperson; Aerospace Engineer; Electrical Engineer; Industrial Engineer; Mechanical Engineer; Metallurgical Engineer; Financial Analyst; Operations/Production Manager; Personnel & Labor Relations Specialist; Quality Control Supervisor; Systems Analyst. Principal educational backgrounds sought: Accounting; Business Administration; Engineering; Finance. Company benefits include: medical, dental, and life insurance; pension plan; tuition assistance; disability coverage; savings plan. Corporate headquarters location. New York Stock Exchange. International: Australia, Canada, England, France, Germany, India, Israel, Kuwait, Netherlands.

McGRAW-EDISON COMPANY

7 Fairfield Crescent, West Caldwell NJ 07006. 201/575-0760. Contact Michael Gerardi, Plant Manager. A major manufacturer and supplier of electrical and mechanical products and related services designed for a wide range of industrial, utility, commercial, and automotive applications. Operates nationally in six business segments: Power Systems, Process Equipment, Service, Industrial, Automotive, and Commercial. Corporate headquarters location: Rolling Meadows, IL. New York Stock Exchange. International: Brazil, Canada, England, France, Singapore, United Arab Emirates.

OWENS-ILLINOIS INC.

Park 80, Plaza West One, Saddle Brook NJ 07662. 201/845-5030. Contact Mrs. S.L. Donovan, Sales Service Manager. Multiple area locations, including Bridgeton, East Brunswick, Edison, Wayne, Glassboro, and Vineland, NJ; Brockport and Volney, NY; Milford, CT. One of the world's leading and most diversified manufacturers of packaging products. The company produces and sells glass containers, multiwall paper and plastic shipping sacks, plastic shrink and stretch film, printing plates and ink, plywood and dimension lumber, blown plastic containers, plastic beverage bottles, plastic drums, metal and plastic closures, tamper-resistant closures, plastic and glass prescription containers, pharmaceutical items, labels, and multipack plastic carriers for containers. Specialized glass products made and sold by the company include 'Libbey' tumblers, stemware, and decorative glassware, television bulbs for picture tubes, 'Kimble' scientific and laboratory ware, and 'SUNPAK' evacuated glass tubes for use in solar energy collectors. Some overseas affiliates also manufacture flat glass and related products. Operates through five segments: Glass Container Group (facilities in Bridgeton, NJ; Brockport and Volney, NY, and many other domestic and international locations); Forest Products Group (no area facilities); Plastics & Closure Group (facilities in East Brunswick and Edison, NJ; Milford, CT; and in other domestic and international locations); Consumer Products Group (no area facilities); and Health Care Group (plant located in Vineland, NJ). This is a major sales facility for the company's complete line of products. Corporate headquarters location: Toledo, OH. New York Stock Exchange. International: Austria, Brazil, Canada, Colombia, Germany, Italy, Japan, Singapore, Switzerland, Venezuela.

PUROLATOR COURIER
131 Morristown Road, Basking Ridge NJ 07920-1652. 201/953-6400. Contact Personnel Director. Other area location: Rahway, NJ. A diversified corporation operating through the following divisions: Purolator Courier Corporation (Basking Ridge, NJ), which provides overnight delivery of time-sensitive materials by ground and air transportation throughout the United States; Purolator Products Inc. (970 New Brunswick Avenue, Rahway NJ 07065), which manufactures and markets automotive, truck, and off-road vehicle filters and related products in the United States and Canada; Purolator Courier Ltd., which provides identical services to Purolator Courier Corporation in Canada; and Stant, Inc. (Connersville, IN), which manufactures and markets fuel caps, oil caps, radiator caps, and other related automotive products. Corporate headquarters location. New York Stock Exchange. International: Austria, Canada, Denmark, Egypt, England, France, Germany, Ireland, Italy, Spain, Sweden, Switzerland.

SCHERING-PLOUGH CORPORATION

2000 Galloping Hill Road, Kenilworth NJ 07033. 201/298-4373. Contact Richard Happel, Director of Personnel. Several area locations, including Kenilworth. A worldwide company primarily engaged in the discovery, development, manufacturing, and marketing of pharmaceutical and consumer products. Pharmaceutical products include prescription drugs, over-the-counter medicines, eye-care products, and animal-health products promoted to the medical and allied professions. The consumer products group consists of proprietary medicines, toiletries, cosmetics, and foot-care products marketed directly to the public. Well-known products include 'Coricidin' cough/cold medicines; 'Maybelline' eye, face, lip, skin-care, and nail-color products; 'Wesley-Jessen' vision-care products; 'Coppertone' sun care products; 'Dr. Scholl' foot-care products; and 'St. Joseph' line of children's over-the-counter analgesics. Corporate headquarters location: Madison, NJ. New York Stock Exchange. International. Operations include: manufacturing; research/development; administration; service; sales. New York Stock Exchange. Common positions include: Accountant; Administrator; Advertising Worker; Attorney; Biochemist; Biologist; Blue-Collar Worker Supervisor; Buyer; Chemist; Computer Programmer; Credit Manager; Customer Service Representative; Draftsperson; Economist; Biomedical Engineer; Chemical Engineer; Electrical Engineer; Industrial Engineer; Mechanical Engineer; Financial Analyst; Branch Manager; Department Manager; General Manager; Management Trainee; Operations/Production Manager; Marketing Specialist; Personnel & Labor Relations Specialist; Physicist; Programmer; Public Relations Worker; Purchasing Agent; Quality Control Supervisor; Reporter/Editor; Sales Representative; Statistician; Systems Analyst; Technical Writer/Editor. Principal educational backgrounds sought: Accounting; Biology; Business Administration; Chemistry; Communications; Computer Science; Economics; Engineering; Finance; Marketing; Mathematics; Pharmacy; Physics; Nursing. Company benefits include: medical insurance; dental insurance; pension plan; life insurance; tuition assistance; disability coverage; profit sharing; employee discounts; savings plan; employee stock ownership. International: Argentina, Australia, Brazil, Canada, France, India, Ireland, Japan, Kenya, Peru.

NEW MEXICO

AMAX CHEMICAL

P.O. Box 279, Carlsbad NM 88220. 505/885-3157. Contact Personnel Director. This facility produces muriate of potash. Nationally, this company is engaged in the exploration for and mining of ores and minerals and the smelting, refining, and other treatment of minerals and metals, as well as the production of coal, oil, and natural gas. Its principal products are coal, iron ore, copper, lead, zinc, potash, nickel, silver, and magnesium. Corporate headquarters location: Greenwich, CT. New York Stock Exchange. International: Canada, England, Netherlands.

DIGITAL EQUIPMENT CORPORATION

P.O. Box 499, Albuquerque NM 87103. 505/345-3311. Contact Ralph Paez, Personnel Manager. Designs, manufactures, sells, and services computers and associated peripheral equipment and related software and supplies. Applications and programs include: scientific research, computation, communications, education, data analysis, industrial control, time sharing, commercial data processing, graphic arts, word processing, health care, instrumentation, engineering, and simulation. Employs 63,000 people in the United States and 37 foreign countries. Albuquerque facility produces computers. Corporate headquarters location: Maynard, MA. New York Stock Exchange. International: Australia, Austria, Denmark, England, France, Germany, Japan, Ireland, Switzerland, Taiwan.

MOTOROLA INC.

4800 Alameda Boulevard NE, Albuquerque NM 87113. 505/822-8801. Contact Personnel Manager. One of the world's leading manufacturers of electronic equipment and components, engaged in the design, manufacture, and sale of a diversified line of products, including two-way radios and other electronic communications systems; semiconductors, including integrated circuits; electronic engine controls; digital appliance controls; automobile radios; citizens' band radios, and other automotive and industrial electronic equipment; and data communications products for a wide range of users, including low, medium, and high-speed modems, multiplexors, and network processors. Albuquerque facility produces ceramic products for electronics applications, including optics and audio uses. Corporate headquarters location: Chicago, IL. New York Stock Exchange. International: Australia, Austria, Belgium, Canada, Costa Rica, Denmark, England, France, Germany, Hong Kong, Ireland, Italy, Japan, Korea, Malaysia, Mexico, Netherland, Norway, Philippines, Singapore, Spain, Sweden, Switzerland, Taiwan.

NEW YORK

AMERICAN HOME PRODUCTS CORPORATION

685 Third Avenue, New York NY 10017. 212/986-1000. Contact Employment Specialist. A leading manufacturer and marketer of prescription drugs and medical supplies, packaged medicines, food products, and household products and housewares. Prescription Drugs and Medical Supplies segment operates through the following subsidiaries: Wyeth Laboratories (produces ethical pharmaceuticals, biologicals, and nutritional products); Ayerst Laboratories (produces ethical pharmaceuticals, over-the-counter antacids, vitamins, and sunburn remedies); Ives Laboratories (ethical pharmaceuticals); Fort Dodge Laboratories (veterinary pharmaceuticals and biologicals); Sherwood Medical (medical devices, diagnostic instruments, test kits, bacteria identification systems); and Corometrics Medical Systems (medical electronic instrumentation for obstetrics and neonatology). Packaged Medicines segment operates through subsidiary Whitehall Laboratories (produces analgesics, cold remedies, and other packaged medicines). Food Products segment operates through subsidiaries American Home Foods (canned pasta, canned vegetables, specialty foods, mustard, popcorn); and E.J. Brach & Sons (assorted chocolates, novelties, and other general line candies). Household Products and Housewares segment operates through subsidiaries Boyle-Midway (cleaners, insecticides, air fresheners, waxes, polishes, and other items for home, appliance, and apparel care); Dupli-Color Products (touch-up, refinishing, and other car-care and shop-use products); Ekco Products (food containers, commercial baking pans, industrial coatings, food handling systems, foilware, plasticware); Ekco Housewares (cookware, cutlery, kitchen tools, tableware and accessories, padlocks); and Prestige Group (cookware,

cutlery, kitchen tools, carpet sweepers, pressure cookers). Corporate headquarters location. International: Argentina, Australia, Belgium, Brazil, Canada, Chile, Colombia, England, France, Germany, Greece, Guatemala, Italy, Japan, Kenya, Mexico, New Zealand, Nigeria, Pakistan, Peru, Portugal, Spain, Sweden, Switzerland, Turkey, Uruguay, Venezuela.

GRUMMAN CORPORATION
1111 Stewart Avenue, Bethpage NY 11714. 516/575-0574. Contact Personnel Recruiter. One of the nation's largest diversified high-technology manufacturers, operating more than 110 manufacturing plants, field offices, and test sites, as well as 75 sales offices and other small facilities in the United States and around the world. Employs more than 28,000 people worldwide. Company is one of the United States' ten largest defense contractors, and a major developer of military aircraft and spacecraft (including craft used in moon landings). Operates through several divisions, including Grumman Aerospace Corporation, Grumman Allied Industries, Grumman Data Systems Corporation, Grumman Credit Corporation, and Grumman International. Grumman Aerospace manufactures various military aircraft, including the F-14 Tomcat, the A-6E Intruder, the EA-6B Prowler, the E-2C Hawkeye, the EF-111A Tactical Jamming System, and many other related systems and components. Grumman Allied Industries manufactures buses, energy systems, aluminum trucks, fire-trucks, yachts, canoes, boats, and temperature-controlled trucks. Grumman Data Systems provides computer services to government, business, and industry, as well as to other Grumman subsidiaries. Grumman International performs marketing and sales activities for Grumman products and services overseas, and initiates collaborative programs with foreign industries. Corporate headquarters location. New York Stock Exchange. International: France, Kuwait.

MACMILLAN INC.
866 Third Avenue, 15th Floor, New York NY 10022. 212/702-5541. Contact Abby Miller, Employment Manager. Company's core businesses are educational publishing, instruction, and information services.

Operates in five segments: Publishing, including the School Division, which publishes textbooks and instructional materials for elementary and high schools; College Division, which publishes textbooks for both undergraduate and graduate levels of higher education, and which owns the Dellen Publishing Corporation and certain textbook lists of the Penn-Well Publishing Company; Professional Books Division, which publishes text and reference books for business, medicine, government, and academia; Glencoe Publishing, which publishes textbooks and materials for Catholic education; G. Schirmer, publishers of scores of educational, traditional, and contemporary music; Harper & Row School Text Division, which includes an elementary phonics-based reading program, high school mathematics texts and other textbooks to complement Macmillan's school text programs; Scribner, which publishes college texts, reference works and trade books; Macmillan Educational Company, which supplements other divisions and provides editorial and production services to outside publishers; Macmillan Software Company, which markets ASYST to the scientific community; and General Books Division, which publishes fiction and nonfiction books for adult and juvenile readers, and which incorporates Four Winds Press, a premier juvenile imprint. Instruction segment operates through Berlitz operations (see separate listing), which provide intensive language instruction programs, home self-teaching programs, language reference works, travel guides, dictionaries, and translation services; Katharine Gibbs Schools, which provide office skills training and business education; United Electronics Institute, which offers a two-year vocational program in electronics technology training; and the Stone School, offering business training programs. Information Services segment operates through Standard Rate & Data Service, the nation's leading publisher of advertising reference works; National Register Publishing, a business and institutional directory publisher; Macmillan Professional Journals, which publishes and sells to healthcare advertisers; Business Mailers, managing over 60 commercial mailing lists; and Macmillan Book Clubs, the largest special-interest book club in the country. Home Learning and Reference Materials segment operates through P.F. Collier encyclopedia publishers. Retail and Mail Order Distribution segment operates through Gump's, which offers fine quality merchandise at retail locations in San Francisco, Houston, Dallas, Beverly Hills and Los Angeles, and through mail order operations. Corporate headquarters location. International. New York Stock Exchange. Common positions include: Accountant; Advertising Worker; Attorney; Customer Service Representative; Financial Analyst; Marketing Specialist; Personnel & Labor Relations Specialist. Principal educational backgrounds sought: Accounting; Art/Design; Business Administration; Communications; Computer Science; Economics; Finance; Liberal Arts; Marketing. Company benefits include: medical insurance; dental insurance; pension plan; life insurance; tuition assistance; disability coverage; employee discounts; savings plan. International: Australia, Brazil, Canada, Egypt, England, Germany, Ireland, Japan, Mexico, Netherlands, New Zealand, Switzerland, Venezuela.

PHILIP MORRIS INC.

120 Park Avenue, New York NY 10017. 212/679-1800; 880-5000. Contact Director/Employee Relations. Several area locations. A leading company operating in three industries: cigarettes, beer, and soft drinks. Diversified operations now include the manufacture of specialty papers, tissues, and packaging materials, as well as community development. Operates through six subsidiaries: Philip Morris U.S.A., Philip Morris International, Philip Morris Industrial (all in New York City), The Seven-Up Company (St. Louis, MO; international division in New York City), Miller Brewing Company (Milwaukee, WI), and Mission Viejo Company (Mission Viejo, CA), a community development firm. Other area subsidiaries include Philip Morris Credit Corporation (New York, NY). Corporate headquarters location. New York Stock Exchange. International: Australia, Canada, Hong Kong, Switzerland.

SALOMON BROTHERS

Two New York Plaza, 33rd Floor, New York NY 10004. 212/747-7000. Contact Personnel Manager. An international investment banking, market making, and research firm, serving corporations, state and local governments, sovereign and provincial governments and their agencies, supranational organizations, central banks, and other financial institutions. A major operating subsidiary of Phibro-Salomon Inc. Corporate headquarters location. International: England, Hong Kong, Japan.

STERLING DRUG INC.

90 Park Avenue, New York NY 10016. 212/907-2342. Contact Shelden Dixon, Personnel Administrator. Multiple area locations, including Montvale, NJ. A diversified transnational company engaged in the manufacture and sale of prescription and over-the-counter health-care medicines, household and personal products, specialty chemicals and pigments. Operates 77 manufacturing facilities in 47 countries, employing 22,500 people. Subsidiary operations include: Sterling Pharmaceutical Group (New York, NY); Lehn & Fink Products Group (Montvale, NJ); Sterling Chemical Group (New York, NY). Sterling International Group (New York, NY); Sterling Research Group (Rensselaer, NY); and several international subsidiaries, based in Switzerland, Canada, and Australia. Well-known company products include 'Bayer' aspirin and others. Common positions include: Accountant; Computer Programmer; Customer Service Representative; Engineer; Financial Analyst; Marketing Specialist; Sales Representative; Systems Analyst. Principal educational backgrounds sought: Accounting; Finance. Company benefits include: medical insurance; dental insurance; pension plan; life insurance; tuition assistance; disability coverage; employee discounts; savings plan. Corporate headquarters location. New York Stock Exchange. International: Argentina, Australia, Belgium, Canada, Ecuador, England, France, Germany, Greece, Guatemala, Indonesia, Italy, New Zealand, Nigeria, Philippines, Portugal, Singapore, Switzerland, Venezuela, Zaire.

JOHN WILEY & SONS INC.

605 Third Avenue, New York NY 10158. 212/850-6000. Contact Susan Fisher, Personnel Recruiter. Several area locations, including Somerset, NJ. An independent publisher of educational, business, and professional books, reference works, journals, and related materials. A new subsidiary, Wilson Learning Corporation (Eden Prairie, MN), produces adult learning programs for industry. Company's publications and programs are edited, produced, and marketed worldwide through a

diversified group of domestic and international subsidiaries, foreign affiliates, and overseas sales offices. Company's Educational, Professional, Medical, and International Groups are all located in New York. Corporate headquarters location. International: Australia, England, India, Singapore.

NORTH CAROLINA

W.R. GRACE & COMPANY/AIRMOLD DIVISION

P.O. Box 610, Roanoke Rapids NC 27870. 919/536-2171. Contact Homer F. Tomes, Industrial Relations Manager. A manufacturer of rigid plastic doublewall cases through a blow-molding process. Divisional headquarters location. Common positions include: Electrical Engineer; Mechanical Engineer. Principal educational backgrounds sought: Engineering. Company benefits include: medical, dental, and health insurance; pension plan; tuition assistance; disability coverage; savings plan. International: Argentina, Australia, Belgium, Canada, Denmark, England, Finland, France, Germany, Greece, Guatemala, Hong Kong, Japan, Malaysia, Mexico, New Zealand, Norway, Philippines, Portugal, Singapore, Spain, Sweden, Switzerland .

RESISTOFLEX COMPANY/DIVISION OF CRANE COMPANY

P.O. Box 1449, Marion NC 28752. 704/724-9524. Contact Human Resources. Manufactures thermoplastic products, including thermoplastic line pipe and flexible hoses. A subsidiary of Crane Company. Corporate headquarters location: New York, NY. Operations include: manufacturing; research/development; administration; sales. New York Stock Exchange. Common positions include: Accountant; Administrator; Blue-Collar Worker Supervisor; Buyer; Customer Service Representative; Draftsperson; Industrial Engineer; Mechanical Engineer; Financial Analyst; Operations/ Production Manager; Marketing Specialist; Personnel & Labor Relations Specialist; Programmer; Purchasing Agent; Quality Control Supervisor; Systems Analyst. Principal educational backgrounds sought: Accounting; Business Administration; Computer Science; Engineering; Finance; Marketing; Mathematics. Company benefits include: medical insurance; dental insurance; pension plan; life insurance; tuition assistance; disability coverage; savings plan. International: Belgium, Canada, England, Spain.

NORTH DAKOTA

AMOCO OIL COMPANY

P.O. Box 5000, Mandan ND 58554. 701/667-2400. Contact Jim Collui, Personnel Director. An operating facility of the major petroleum firm. Corporate headquarters location: Chicago, IL. International: England, Hong Kong, Switzerland.

OHIO

ALLEN-BRADLEY/SYSTEMS DIVISION

747 Alpha Drive, Highland Heights OH 44143. 216/449-6700. Contact Professional Employment Representative. Engaged in the design and production of distributed process and numerical control equipment for industrial automation. Also involved in the design of automation systems. Operations at this facility include: research/development; administration. Corporate headquarters location: Milwaukee, WI. Common positions include: Accountant; Draftsperson; Biomedical Engineer; Electrical Engineer; Mechanical Engineer; Industrial Designer; Marketing Specialist; Physicist; Programmer; Purchasing Agent; Quality Control Supervisor; Statistician; Systems Analyst; Technical Writer/Editor; Test Engineer; Quality/Reliability Engineer. Principal educational backgrounds sought: Accounting; Computer Science; Engineering; Finance; Marketing; Mathematics; Physics. Company benefits include: medical, dental, and life insurance; pension plan; tuition assistance; disability coverage; employee discounts; savings plan. International: Australia, Belgium, Brazil, Canada, England, France, Germany, India, Italy, Japan, Mexico, Saudi Arabia, Spain.

BEATRICE/HUNT-WESSON, INC.

P.O. Box 450, 29180 Glenwood Road, Perrysburg OH 43551. 419/666-2134. Contact Jim Martin, Personnel Manager. A manufacturer of tomato products. Corporate headquarters location: Fullerton, CA. Common positions include: Accountant; Buyer; Electrical Engineer; Industrial Engineer; Mechanical Engineer; Department Manager; Operations/ Production Manager; Personnel and Labor Relations Specialist; Purchasing Agent; Quality Control Supervisor. Principal educational backgrounds sought: Accounting; Business Administration; Engineering; Finance. Company benefits include: medical insurance; dental insurance; pension plan; life insurance; tuition assistance; disability coverage; 401K. International: Australia, Belgium, Canada, Colombia, England, France, Germany, Ireland, Jamaica, Japan, Malaysia, Mexico, Netherlands, Norway, Peru, Singapore, Spain, Switzerland, Thailand, Venezuela.

THE B.F. GOODRICH COMPANY

3925 Embassy Parkway, Department 0007, Akron OH 44313. Contact Mr. James B. Boles, Director of Corporate Group Human Resources. A diversified manufacturer of plastics, specialty chemicals, and products for the aerospace and defense industries. Common positions include: Accountant; Attorney; Buyer; Claim Representative; Computer Programmer; Editor; Financial Analyst; Personnel Specialist; Purchasing Agent; Systems Analyst; Principal educational backgrounds sought: Accounting; Business Administration; Communications; Computer Science; Finance; Human Resources; Law; Liberal Arts. Company benefits include: medical insurance; pension plan; life insurance; tuition assistance; disability coverage; employee discounts; savings plan; stock purchase plan; prescription drug plan; 401K plan. Corporate headquarters location. Operations at thsi facility include: administration. New York Stock Exchange. International: Australia, Brazil, Hong Kong, India, Italy, Mexico, Netherlands, Philippines, Thailand.

WHITE CONSOLIDATED INDUSTRIES, INC.

11770 Berea Road, Cleveland OH 44111. 216/252-3700. Contact Arthur Depompei, Director of Compensation. A diversified manufacturer of products for both consumer and industrial markets worldwide. Products include: washers and dryers. Corporate headquarters location. New York Stock Exchange. International: Canada, England, Japan, Mexico.

OKLAHOMA

ALLEN BRADLEY COMPANY INC./MAGNETICS DIVISION

5900 North Harrison, Shawnee OK 74801. 405/275-2100. Contact Human Resources Department. Produces ceramic magnets for PM motor applications and ferrite components for electronic, communications and computer applications. Common positions include: Accountant; Chemist; Customer Service Representative; Ceramics Engineer; Electrical Engineer; Mechanical Engineer; Operations/Production Manager; Personnel & Labor Relations Specialist; Purchasing Agent; Quality Control Supervisor; Systems Analyst; Sales Engineers (Electrical Engineer). Principal educational backgrounds sought: Accounting; Chemistry; Engineering; and Marketing. Company benefits include: medical insurance; dental insurance; pension plan; life insurance; tuition assistance; disability coverage; and savings plan. Divisional headquarters. Corporate headquarters location: Milwaukee, WI. Parent company is Ruckwell International, Pittsburgh, PA. Operations at this facility include manufacturing, research & development, administration and sales.International: Australia, Belgium, Brazil, Canada, England, France, Germany, India, Italy, Japan, Mexico, Saudi Arabia, Spain.

TELEX COMPUTER PRODUCTS, INC.

4242 South Sheridan, Tulsa OK 74135. 918/627-1111. Contact Recruiting & Placement Department. A major manufacturer of computers and related information management products, including magnetic tape products and printers. Employs over 2,000 people. Established 1965. International: England.

THE WILLIAMS COMPANIES

P.O. Box 2400, Tulsa OK 74102. 918/588-2234. Contact Mary Waldrond, Manager, Employee Relations. Engaged in three essential industries: energy, fertilizer, and metals. Operates through six companies: Northwest Energy Company (interstate natural gas pipelinesystems), Williams Pipe Line Company (gas pipelines), Williams Natural Gas Company (gas pipelines), Williams Gas Marketing and Williams Telecommunications Group. Corporate headquarters location. Common positions include: Accountant; Attorney; Claim Representative; Commercial Artist; Computer Programmer; Customer Service Representative; Draftsperson; Electrical Engineer; Mechanical Engineer; Mining Engineer; Financial Analyst; Marketing Specialist; Personnel & Labor Relations Specialist; Reporter/Editor; Sales Representative; Systems Analyst. Principal educational backgrounds sought: Accounting; Business Administration; Computer Science; Engineering; Finance; Marketing. Company benefits include: medical insurance; dental insurance; pension plan; life insurance; tuition assistance; disability coverage; profit sharing; savings plan. Corporate headquarters location. Operations at this facility include: administration. International: Australia, England.

OREGON

ESCO CORPORATION

2141 Northwest 25th Avenue, Portland OR 97210. 503/228-2141. Contact Manager of Personnel. A manufacturer of a variety of equipment for a wide range of industries, including mining, food processing, nuclear energy developing, and logging. Products include: dredge cutters; tractor and dozer equipment; chain conveying systems; and custom castings. Corporate headquarters location. Operations at this facility include: manufacturing; service; sales. Common positions include: Accountant; Administrator; Advertising Worker; Attorney; Blue-Collar Worker Supervisor; Buyer; Chemist; Computer Programmer; Credit Manager; Customer Service Representative; Draftsperson; Ceramics Engineer; Industrial Engineer; Mechanical Engineer; Metallurgical Engineer; Financial Analyst; Branch Manager; Department Manager; General Manager; Management Trainee; Operations/Production Manager; Marketing Specialist; Personnel & Labor Relations Specialist; Programmer; Public Relations Worker; Purchasing Agent; Quality Control Supervisor; Sales Representative; Systems Analyst. Principal educational backgrounds sought: Accounting; Business Administration; Computer Science; Engineering. Company benefits include: medical insurance; dental insurance; pension plan; life insurance; tuition assistance; disability coverage; employee discounts; savings plan. International: France.

GENERAL FOODS CORPORATION

P.O Box 2705, Portland OR 97208. 503/639-0641. Contact Betty Jackson, Personnel Director. Nationally, the firm is one of the world's largest processors and marketers of food and beverage products; operates in such areas as packaged convenience foods, processed meats, coffee, and foodservice products. Facilities are located throughout the United States and abroad. Positions available at this location: Department Manager; Sales Representative (4 year degree required). Company benefits include: medical, dental, and life insurance; pension plan; tuition assistance; profit sharing; savings plan. Regional and divisional headquarters. Operations at this facility include: administration; service; sales. Corporate headquarters location: White Plains, NY. New York Stock Exchange. International: Belgium, Brazil, Canada, Colombia, Denmark, England, France, Germany, Hong Kong, Ireland, Italy, Japan, Korea, Mexico, Panama, Philippines, Singapore, Spain, Switzerland.

OMARK INDUSTRIES

4909 International Way, P.O. Box 2127, Milwaukie OR 97222. 503/653-8881. Contact Personnel Department. A leading manufacturer of equipment for harvesting timber and pulpwood, and of expendable products for gun-sportsmen and do-it-yourselfer hobbyists. The company is also a major supplier of chainsaw blades to original equipment manufacturers. Corporate headquarters location. International: Australia, Belgium, Brazil, Canada, England, France, Germany, Japan, Sweden.

WANG LABORATORIES INC.

5 Centerpointe Drive, Suite 300, Lake Oswego OR 97035. 503/624-0268. Contact Personnel. A major producer of office automation systems; products include a wide variety of computers and CRT word processing equipment, systems, and subsystems. Corporate headquarters location: Lowell MA. International: Australia, Austria, Belgium, Canada, Egypt, Germany, Hong Kong, Israel, Japan, Netherlands, New Zealand, Singapore, Switzerland.

PENNSYLVANIA

ALUMINUM COMPANY OF AMERICA

1501 Alcoa Building, Pittsburgh PA 15219. 412/553-4545. Contact Lindy Butler, Manager/Human Resources Staff. The world's leading producer of aluminum products. Employs more than 45,000 people in 150 operating locations and sales offices worldwide. The company's principal operations are in the mining of bauxite, refining it into alumina, smelting the alumina into aluminum, proccessing aluminum and aluminum alloys into milled and finished products, as well as recycling used aluminum products. Operations include manufacturing products from other metals, producing chemicals, and selling engineering and construction services. The firm is engaged in large research and development projects. Other Pennsylvania plants are located in Lebanon and AlcoaCenter. Common positions include: Accountant; Ceramics Engineer; Electrical Engineer; Industrial Engineer; Mechanical Engineer; Metallurgical Engineer; Sales Representative; Business Analyst; Systems Analyst; Marketing Specialist; Personnel and Labor Relations Specialist; Financial/EDP Auditor. Principal educational backgrounds sought include: Accounting; Business Administration; Computer Science; Engineering; Marketing. Company benefits include: medical, dental and life insurance; pension plan; tuition assistance; disability coverage; savings plan; profit sharing. Corporate regional, and divisional headquarters. New York Stock Exchange. International: Australia, Belgium, Jamaica, Japan, Mexico, Norway, Spain, Surinam.

FRUEHAUF CORPORATION

P.O. Box 110, Middletown PA 17057. 717/944-7491. Contact Steve Horney, Personnel Manager. Engaged in the manufacture, sale, leasing, financing, distribution, and servicing of transportation equipment. Operates in three segments: Trailer Operations, Auto Operations, and Maritime and Aerospace Operations. Corporate headquarters location: Detroit, MI. Second major Pennsylvania facility, producing liquid bulk trailers, is located in Uniontown. New York Stock Exchange. International: Australia, Belgium, Canada, England, France, Mexico, Netherlands.

OCCIDENTAL CHEMICAL PVC DIVISIONS

P.O. Box 699, Pottstown, PA 19464. 215/327-6400. Contact Larry Ogden, Human Resources Manager. Manufacturers a wide range of PVC resins, compounds, and fabricated products as a division of Occidental Chemical Corporation, which is a part of Occidental Petroleum Company, a natural resources company engaged in the exploration for and development of oil and natural gas in the United States. Corporate headquarters location: Los Angeles, CA. International: Belgium, Bermuda, Bolivia, Brazil, Canada, Colombia, England, Germany, India, New Zealand, Pakistan, Peru, Saudi Arabia, Scotland, Spain, Switzerland, Tunisia, USSR, United Arab Emirates, Venezuela.

PLAYSCHOOL INC.

110 Pitney Road, Lancaster, PA 19046. 215/572-3400. Contact Rose Bleacher, Personnel Manager. Well-known manufacturer of child guidance, infant and preschool toys. A subsidiary of Hasbro. International: Switzerland.

SPS TECHNOLOGIES

Highland Avenue, Jenkintown, PA 19046. 215/572-3400. Contact Employment Department. Engaged in the design, manufacturing, and marketing of high-technology fastener products, including precision components and high-technology fastener products, including precision components and assembly tools, and material-handling products such as storage systems, steel shelving, shop equipment, and automated material-handling products such as storage systems, steel shelving, shop equipment, and automated material-handling systems. Maintains more than 15 manufacturing plants and sales offices located throughout the world, including Great Britain, Mexico, and Australia. Divisional headquarters location. Operations at this facility include: manufacturing; research/development; administration; service; sales. International: Australia, Belgium, Canada, England, France, Germany, India, Ireland, Italy, Japan, Mexico.

THE WEST COMPANY

West Bridge Street, Phoenixville, PA 19460. 215/935-4500. Contact Employment Department. Engaged in the design, manufacturing, and marketing of high-technology fastener products, including precision components and assembly fastener products, including precision components and assembly tools, and material-handling products such as storage systems, steel shelving, shop equipment, and automated material-handling systems. Maintains more than 15 manufacturing plants and sales offices throughout the world, including Great Britain, Mexico, and Australia. Divisional headquarters location. Operations at this facility include: manufacturing, research/development; administration, service; sales. International: Australia, Austria, Brazil, Colombia, England, Germany, Italy, Japan, Mexico, Singapore, Spain.

RHODE ISLAND

A.T. CROSS COMPANY

1 Albion Road, Lincoln RI 02865. 401/333-1200. Contact Dave Zito, Personnel. A.T. Cross Company is a major international manufacturer of fine writing instruments. These products are sold to the consumer gift market through selected jewelry, department, stationary, gift and book stores, and sold to the business gift market via a network of companies specializing in recognition programs. International: Ireland.

SOUTH CAROLINA

COOPER AIR TOOLS/DIVISION OF COOPER INDUSTRIES

670 Industrial Drive, P.O. Box 1410, Lexington SC 29072. 803/359-1200. Contact Wendell Patton, Manager/Employment and Training. A manufacturer of pneumatic hand tools, air motors, airfeed drills, and hoists. Divisional headquarters location. Operations include: manufacturing; research/devlopment; administration; service; sales. Corporate headquarters location: Houston, TX. New York Stock Exchange. Common positions include: Accountant; Advertising Worker; Blue-Collar Worker Supervisor; Buyer; Commercial Artist; Computer Programmer; Customer Service Representative; Draftsperson; Industrial Engineer; Mechanical Engineer; Metallurgical Engineer; Financial Analyst; In-

dustrial Designer; Department Manager; Marketing Specialist; Personnel & Labor Relations Specialist; Purchasing Agent; Quality Control Supervisor; Sales Representative; Systems Analyst. Principal educational backgrounds sought: Accounting; Business Administration; Computer Science; Engineering; Finance; Liberal Arts; Marketing; Mathematics. Company benefits include: medical, dental, and life insurance; pension plan; tuition assistance; disability coverage; employee discounts; savings plan. International: Canada, Mexico, Netherlands.

RIEGEL TEXTILE CORPORATION

P.O. Box 3478, Greenville SC 29602. 803/233-4151. Contact Dan Scott, Manager of Public Relations. A diversified, integrated company serving many different markets: apparel, industrial, interior furnishings, kitchen textiles, traditional infants' products, disposable diapers, personal care products, and data processing services. Company is decentralized into operating divisions and subsidiaries which are autonomous profit centers, each responsible for its own operation. Corporate headquarters location. New York Stock Exchange. Common positions include: Accountant; Blue-Collar Worker Supervisor; Buyer; Chemist; Computer Programmer; Credit Manager; Customer Service Representative; Electrical Engineer; Industrial Engineer; Mechanical Engineer; Financial Analyst; Marketing Specialist; Personnel & Labor Relations Specialist; Quality Control Supervisor; Sales Representative; Systems Analyst. Principal educational backgrounds sought: Accounting; Business Administration; Chemistry; Computer Science; Engineering; Finance; Marketing. Company benefits include: medical insurance; dental insurance; pension plan; life insurance; tuition assistance; disability coverage; employee discounts; savings plan. International: Canada, France, Ivory Coast, Morocco.

SOUTH DAKOTA

AMOCO FOAM PRODUCTS COMPANY

3803 North 4th Avenue, Sioux Falls SD 57104. 605/335-5521. Contact Bruce Lake, Personnel Director. Manufactures plastic food containers. Corporate headquarters location: Worthington, MN. International: England, Hong Kong, Switzerland.

TENNESSEE

HOLIDAY CORPORATION

3796 Lamar, Memphis TN 38195. 901/362-4881. Contact Pat Ferguson, Director of General Employment. The world's largest hospitality company, operating in two businesses; hotels and hotel/casinos. With some 1,600 properties worldwide, its Holiday Inn hotel system is nearly three times the size of its nearest chain competitor. Three other hotel brands and a casino gaming company round out Holiday's diversified product portfolio. Its other hotel brands are: Embassy Suites, an all-suite full-service hotel chain; Hampton Inn, a limited service, moderately priced chain; and Home Wood Suites, a new extended-stay hotel product introduced in early 1988. Together, the company's four hotel brands comprise more than 1,800 hotels and 353,000 rooms worldwide. Common positions include: Accountant; Architect; Attorney; Computer Programmer; Customer Service Representative; Draftsperson; Mechanical Engineer; Hotel Manager/Assistant Manager; General Manager; Personnel & Labor rlations Specialist; Systems Analyst. Principal educational backgrounds sought: Accounting; Business Administration; Communications; Computer Science; Engineering; Finance; Marketing. Company benefits include: medical, dental, and life insurance; pension plan; tuition assistance; disability coverage; profit sharing; employee discounts; savings plan. Corporate headquarters location. Operations at this facility include: regional headquarters; divisional headquarters; research/development; administration; service; sales. New York Stock Exchange. International: Australia, Belgium, Bolivia, Brazil, Canada, Dominican Republic, France, Germany, Greece, Hong Kong, Italy, Japan, Netherlands, Philippines, Spain, Switzerland, Taiwan, Thailand, United Arab Emirates, Venezuela, Yugoslavia.

THOMAS INDUSTRIES INC./PAINT APPLICATOR DIVISION

P.O. Box 360, Johnson City TN 37605. 615/926-8131. Contact Wayne Steenberg, Personnel Director. Manufacturer of paint brushes, paint rollers and painting accessories, tools, and hardware for the homeowner and professional painter. This facility is a divisional headquarters location. Corporate headquarters location: Louisville, KY. Operations include: manufacturing; administration; sales. New York Stock Exchange.

Common positions include: Accountant; Blue-Collar Worker Supervisor; Buyer; Commercial Artist; Credit Manager; Customer Service Representative; Industrial Engineer; Department Manager; General Manager; Operations/Production Manager; Marketing Specialist; Purchasing Agent; Quality Control Supervisor; Sales Representative; Transportation & Traffic Specialist. Principal educational backgrounds sought: Accounting; Art/Design; Business Administration; Finance; Marketing. Company benefits include: medical insurance; pension plan; life insurance; tuition assistance; disability coverage; profit sharing; employee discounts; savings plan. International: Belgium, Canada, England, Mexico.

TEXAS

BELL HELICOPTER/TEXTRON
P.O. Box 482, Department 19, Plant 1, Fort Worth, TX 76101. 817/280-2011. Contact Edward J. Evela, Manager of Technical Staffing. Engaged in the manufacturer of a variety of commercial and civilian helicopters, as well as extensive research and development activities. International: Australia, Belgium, Canada, England, France, Germany, Mexico, Singapore, Spain, Switzerland.

HOBART CORPORATION
4407 Alpha Road, Farmers Branch TX 75244. 214/233-7781. Contact Jean Ettli, Administrative Assistant. Manufactures food equipment for restaurants and supermarkets such as: slicers, mixers, scales, fryers, food cutters, toasters. Parent Company: Dart and Kraft. Common positions include: Accountant; Electrical and Mechanical Technician; Sales Representative. International: Australia, Belgium, Canada, France, Italy, Mexico, Netherlands, Switzerland.

HUNT OIL COMPANY
1401 Elm Street, Dallas TX 75202. 214/744-6991. Contact Paula J. Smith, Recruiter. A petroleum and natural gas refinery and distributor. Common positions include: Accountant; Computer Programmer; Petroleum Engineer; Geologist; Geophysicist; Purchasing Agent. Principal educational backgrounds sought include: Accounting; Engineer-

ing; Geology. Company benefits include: medical, dental and life insurance; pension plan; tuition assistance; disability coverage; employee discounts; savings plan. Corporate headquartersa location. Operations at this facility include: research and development; administration; services; sales. International: England.

M.W. KELLOGG COMPANY

Three Greenway Plaza East, Houston TX 77046. 713/690-2222. Contact Mr. Jim Wilhite, Manager of Personnel. A full service design, engineering, procurement, and construction management firm. Company serves the process and energy industries worldwide. Primarily involved in hydrocarbon-processing plants, including oil refining units, petrochemical manufacturing plants, ammonia and fertilizer plants, and gas processing units. Employs approximately 3,200 persons. A Signal Company. International: Argentina, Canada, Chile, England, Hong Kong, Indonesia, Saudi Arabia, Singapore, Spain, United Arab Emirates.

SIMMONS COMPANY

8600 Harry Hines Boulevard, Dallas TX 75235. 214/637-0460. Contact Alison Mathis, Personnel Director. Manufactures a wide range of home furnishings and caskets in 15 countries worldwide. Home furnishings segment manufactures and markets a broad range of furniture and accessories for the home, hospitals, nursing homes, hotels and motels. It produces a wide range of matresses and box springs in the United States, Puerto Rico, and 11 foreign countries, as well as upholstered furniture (primarily sofas) and a broad line of other furnishings including wood and metal tables and chairs, fabrics, drapes, pillows, wall coverings, lamps, and sculpture (including this facility). Casket segment manufactures and distributes wood and metal caskets to other distributors and funeral homes. Corporate headquarters location: Atlanta, GA. International: Australia, Brazil, Canada, England, France, Italy, Japan, Mexico, Morocco, Venezuela.

TENNECO INC.

1010 Milam, Houston, TX 77002. 713/757-2131. Contact Debbie Hanvel, Director, Human Resources. For information on professional hiring contact Howard Spiegel, Director, Human Resources at P.O. Box 2511, Houston, TX 77252. A diversified, multi-national corporation engaged in a wide range of industries, including oil, natural gas pipelines, construction, and farm equipment, shipbuilding, agriculture and land management, automotive, packaging, and insurance. Operates through the following groups: Tenneco Oil, Tennessee Gas Transmissions, J.I. Case, Newport News Shipbuilding, Tenneco West, Tenneco Automotive, Packaging Corporation of America, Philadelphia Life Insurance Company, Southwestern Life Insurance Company, and Southern General Life Insurance Company. Corporate headquarters location. New York Stock Exchange. International: Brazil, England, France, Malagasy, Spain.

ZALE CORPORATION

901 West Walnut Hill Lane, Irving, TX 75038. 214/580-4000. Contact Terry C. Boles, Personnel Manager. Corporate offices for one of the nation's largest specialty retailing firms and the world's largest retailer of fine jewelry, operating more than 1100 stores worldwide. Operating divisions: Fine Jewelers Guild Division, which operates carriage trade jewelry stores; Diamond Park Division, which operates leased departments. Company manages its operations in 48 states, and in international locations. Corporate headquarters location: Dallas, TX. Common positions include: Accountant; Buyer; Computer Programmer; Management Trainee; Marketing Specialist; Sales Representative; Store Manager. Principal educational backgrounds sought: Accounting, Business Administration; Computer Science; Marketing; Retail Management. Company benefits include: medical; dental; life insurance; pension plan; tuition assistance; disability coverage; profit sharing; employee discounts; savings plan. Corporate headquarter location. Divisional headquarters. Operations at this facility include: administration. International: Belgium, England, Japan, Switzerland.

UTAH

AMSCO

P.O. Box 25368, Salt Lake City UT 84125. 801/972-6444. Contact Howard Smith, Office Manager. Produces a broad range of building products. Corporate headquarters location. International: Canada, Hong Kong.

THE COLEMAN COMPANY

597 North 1500 West, Cedar City UT 84720. 801/586-9437. Contact Personnel Director. Manufactures a broad range of sleeping bags and tents. Nationally, the company manufactures the following classes of products: Outing Sports Products; 'Hobie Cat' and 'O'Brien' Marine Products; 'Coleman' Camping Trailers; 'Crosman' Airguns; Home Heating and Air Conditioning Products; and Recreational Vehicle Products. Operates internationally through Coleman Canadian Sales and Coleman Foreign Sales. Specific products include lanterns, camp stoves, sleeping bags, tents, sailboats, waterskis, camping trailers, air rifles, and air conditioners. Corporate headquarters location: Wichita, KS. International: Australia, Canada, England, Germany, Japan, Netherlands.

GEORGIA-PACIFIC CORPORATION

2875 South 300 West, Salt Lake City UT 84115. 801/486-9281. Contact Manager. Nationally, a leading manufacturer and distributor of a wide range of forest products, operating over 200 manufacturing and production facilities located throughout the United States and Canada, and internationally. One of the top producers of softwood, plywood, pulp, paper and paperboard. Also manufactures ammonia, methanol, cumene, acetone, and chlorine. Conducts extensive research and development. Corporate headquarters location: Atlanta, GA. International facilities. New York Stock Exchange. International: Brazil, Canada, Indonesia.

VARIAN EIMAC

1678 South Pioneer Road, Salt Lake City UT 84104. 801/972-5000. Contact John Gray, Personnel Manager. Produces electron tubes for use in company products. Nationally, company is engaged in the research, development, manufacture, and marketing of various products and services in the fields of communications, industrial equipment, medicine, scientific research, and defense. Operates in four industry segments: Electron Devices, Analytical Instruments, Industrial Equipment, and

Medical Equipment. Corporate headquarters location: Palo Alto, CA. New York Stock Exchange. International: Australia, Belgium, Brazil, Canada, England, France, Germany, Ireland, Israel, Italy, Japan, Mexico, The Netherlands, Sweden, Switzerland.

VERMONT

BOISE CASCADE CORPORATION/SPECIALTY PAPERBOARD DIVISION/PRESSBOARD PRODUCTS

Brudie Road, P.O. Box 498, Brattleboro VT 05301. 802/257-0365. Contact Jim Barker, Personnel Director. A manufacturer of types I, II, and III genuine and imitation pressboard, pattern board, jacquard board, electrical insulating paper and board, guide stock, tube stock, trunk board, and cover stock. Trade names include: Guidex, Norval, Fiberlec, Press-Guard, Press-Mate, Genuine Pressboard. Home office: One Jefferson Square, Boise, ID 83728. International: Austria, Canada, France, Germany.

KRAFT INC./MIDDLEBURY

500 Exchange Street, Middlebury VT 05753. 802/388-6731. Contact Douglas R. Marsden, Plant Manager. Produces Swiss cheese. Corporate headquarters location: Glenview, IL. International: Australia, Belgium, Denmark, England, Germany, Ireland, Italy, Mexico, Panama, Philippines, Spain, Switzerland, Venezuela.

VIRGINIA

FLOW GENERAL INC./FLOW LABRATORIES

7655 Old Springhouse Road, McLean, VA 22102. 703/893-5915. Contact Director of Corporate Affairs. Designs, manufactures, and markets biomedical and communications testing products, as well as preforming a variety of technological research and analysis services. Operates in two major divisions: Biomedical and Applied Sciences. Biomedical products are used in medical, veterinary, and biological research, vaccine production, testing, and clinical analysis. International: Australia, Belgium, Canada, England, Finland, France, Germany, Italy, Japan, Netherland, Scotland, Sweden, Switzerland.

INLAND MOTOR/KOLLMORGEN CORPORATION

501 First Street, Radford, VA 22102. 703/639-9045. Contact John Clark, Personnel Director. Manufacturers DC torque motors, amplifiers, electromechanical actuators and controllers, magnetic bearings, and other advanced motion control products. Divisional headquarters location. Operations include: manufacturing. Corporate headquarters location: Hartford, CT. New York Stock Exchange. Common positions include: Accountant; Buyer; Computer Programer; Draftsperson; Engineer; Electrical Engineer; Industrial Engineer; Mechanical Engineer; Department Manager; General Manager; Operations/Production Manager; Personnel & Labor Relations Specialist; Purchasing Agent; Quality Control Supervisor. Principal educational backgrounds sought; Engineering. Company benefits include: medical insurance; dental insurance; pension plan; life insurance; tuition assistance; disability coverage; profit sharing; saving plan. International: Ireland.

PITNEY BOWES, INC.

6100 Lincolnia Road, Alexandria, VA 22312. 703/750-1200. Contact Mark Cassanda, Sales Manager. Commercial sales and service facility for the world's largest producer of postage meters and other mailing equipment products, including mailing machines, postage scales, modular mailroom furniture, collators, addresser-printers, embossing machines, folding and inserting equipment, mail openers, counting and imprinting machines, and tax stamping equipment. Also a leading producer of copiers and copier supplies, retail price-marking equipment, and customer identification systems. Corporate headquarters location: Stamford, CT. New York Stock Exchange. International: Australia, Brazil, Canada, England, France, Germany, Switzerland.

WASHINGTON

OLIN DEFENSE SYSTEMS GROUP

11441 Willows Road, Redmond, WA 98052. 206/885-5000. Contact John Knapp, Employment Manager. A division of a major corporation engaged in manufacturing of rocket engines and gas generators, aviation power supplies and avionics. Also involved in high energy pulse power systems and their use in nuclear weapons effect testing. Common positions include: Electrical Engineer; Mechanical Engineer; Physicist. Principal educational backgrounds sought: Engineering, Physics. International: Australia, Belgium, Colombia, England, France, Germany, Ireland, Japan, Mexico, New Zealand, Singapore, Spain, Taiwan, Venezuela.

SUNDSTRAND DATA CONTROL, INC.
15001 Northeast 36th Street, P.O. Box 97001, Redmond, WA 98073. 206/885-3711. Contact Joe Luce, Manager/Employee Relations. Engaged in the production of aircraft equipment and parts including temperature control components, digital recorders, and an variety of instrumentation systems. Employs over 1000 people. Group headquarters location. Operations at this facility include: manufacturing, administration; service; sales. Common positions include: Accountant; Administrator; Computer Programmer; Customer Service Representative; Engineer; Aerospace Engineer; Electrical Engineer; Industrial Engineer; Mechanical Engineer; Financial Analyst; Manager; Department Manager; General Manager; Operations/Production Manager; Personnel & Labor Relations Specialist; Programmer; Purchasing Agent; Quality Control Supervisor Systems Analyst, Technical Writer/Editor. Principal educational backgrounds sought: Accounting, Business Administration; Computer Science; Engineering; Finance; Mathematics. Company benefits include: medical insurance; dental insurance; pension plan; life insurance; tuition assistance; savings plan. International: Belgium, France, Japan, Singapore, Switzerland.

WEYERHAEUSER COMPANY
College Relations & Recruiting, WTC-TR1, Tacoma, WA 98477. Mailed inquiries only. Contact Personnel. Send resume with cover letter. One of the world's largest forest products companies. Products include lumber, plywood, pulp, shipping, and milk cartons, speciality papers, and panel products. Also engaged in real estate development and the management of nurseries and ornamentals. Corporate headquarters location. Operations at this facility include: manufacturing; research/development; administration; service; sales. New York Stock Exchange. Common positons include: Accountant, Computer Programmer;

Economist; Engineer; Chemical Engineer; Electrical Engineer; Industrial Engineer; Mechanical Engineer; Financial Analyst; Forester; Management Trainee; Sales Representative. Principal educational backgrounds sought; Accounting; Biology; Computer Science; Engineering; Finance; Marketing. Company benefits include: medical insurance; dental insurance; pension plan; life insurance; tuition assistance; disability coverage. International: Australia, Belgium, Canada, Hong Kong, Japan, Switzerland.

WEST VIRGINIA

FMC CORPORATION SPRING HILL PLANT
3200 MacCorkle Avenue, South Charleston WV 25303. 304/746-1500. Contact Frank Powell, Personnel Director. Produces hydrogen peroxide for use in the pulp & paper, textile, semiconductor, and food industries. Corporate headquarters location: Chicago, IL. Common positions include: Chemist; Chemical Engineer. Principal educational backgrounds sought: Chemistry; Engineering. Company benefits include: medical insurance; pension plan; dental insurance; tuition assistance; life insurance; disability coverage; savings plan. Operations at this facility include: manufacturing. New York Stock Exchange. International: Australia, Austria, Brazil, Colombia, Costa Rica, Germany, Greece, Hong Kong, Ireland, Italy, Korea, Netherlands, Philippines, Singapore, Spain, Switzerland.

MANVILLE SALES
2905 3rd Avenue, P.O. Box 5130, Vienna WV 26105. 304/295-9361. Contact Tom Anderson, Manager/Employee Relations. Manufactures glass and fiberglass for automotive and commercial industries. Operations include: manufacturing. Corporate headquarters location: Denver, CO. New York Stock Exchange. Common positions include: Accountant; Computer Programmer; Customer Service Representative; Draftsperson; Ceramics Engineer; Electrical Engineer; Industrial Engineer; Mechanical Engineer; Department Manager; Personnel & Labor Relations Specialist; Quality Control Supervisor; Department Manager; Operations/Production Manager. Principal educational backgrounds sought: Accounting; Business Administration; Engineering; Finance; In-

dustrial/Labor Relations, Organizational Development. Company benefits include: medical insurance; dental insurance; pension plan; life insurance; tuition assistance; disability coverage; employee discounts; savings plan; prescription plan, accident insurance. Corporate headquarters location: Denver, CO. Operations at this facility includes: Manufacaturing. New York Stock Exchange. International: Australia, Austria, Belgium, Canada, England, France, Germany, Italy, Japan, Mexico, Saudi Arabia, Singapore, Spain, United Arab Emirates, Venezuela, Zaire.

PPG INDUSTRIES

P.O. Box 191, New Martinsville WV 26155. Mailed inquiries only. Contact C.K. Willis, Employment Manager. Major manufacturer of industrial and specialty chemicals. Common positions include: Chemical Engineer; Mechanical Engineer. Principal educational backgrounds sought: Chemistry; Computer Science; Engineering. Company benefits include: medical insurance; dental insurance; pension plan; life insurance; tuition assistance; disability coverage; profit sharing; employee discounts; savings plan. Parent Company: PPG Industries Inc. (Pittsburgh, PA). Operations at this facility include: manufacturing. New York Stock Exchange. International: Canada, France, Israel, Japan, Mexico, Switzerland, Taiwan, Venezuela.

WISCONSIN

BRIGGS & STRATTON CORPORATION

P.O. Box 702, Milwaukee, WI 53201. 414/259-5540. Contact Barbara Swarthout, Employment Manager. Briggs & Stratton is best known as the world's largest manufacturer of small air-cooled gasoline engines, powering equipment in more than 85 countries on all seven continents. In addition, the company is a major producer of automotive locking devices. Common positions include: Accountant; Blue-Collar Worker Supervisor; Buyer; Chemist; Computer Programmer; Customer Service Representative; Draftsperson; Electrical Engineer; Industrial Engineer; Mechanical Engineer; Metallurgical Engineer; Personnel and Labor Relations Specialist; Purchasing Agent; Qu ality Control Supervisor; Sales Representative; Statistician; Systems Analyst; Technical

Writer/Editor. Principal educational backgrounds sought: Accounting; Business Administration; communications; Engineering. Company benefits include: medical insurance; dental insurance; pension plan; life insurance; tuition assistance; disability coverage; profit sharing; savings pland. Coprporate headquarters location. Operations at this facility include: regional and divisional headquarters; manufacturing; research/development; administration; service; sales. New York Stock Exchange. International: Germany.

HARLEY DAVIDSON MOTOR COMPANY, INC.

P.O. Box 653, Milwaukee, WI 53201. 414/342-4680. Contact Bob Walters, Manager/Staffing & Development. A motorcycle manufacturer. Corporate headquarters location. Operations include: manufacturing; research/development; administration; service; sales. Common positions include: Accountant; Buyer; Claim Representative; Computer Programmer; Customer Service Representative; Draftsperson; Mechanical Engineer; Electrical Engineer; Financial Analyst; Department Manager; General Manager; Marketing Specialist; Personnel & Labor Relations Specialist; Sales Representative; Technical Writer/Editor. Principal educational backgrounds sought: Accounting; Business Administration; Engineering; Finance; Marketing. Company benefits include: medical, dental, and life insurance; pension plan; tuition assistance; disability coverage; employee discounts; savings plan. International: Germany.

OSCAR MAYER FOODS CORPORATION

910 Mayer Avenue, Madison, WI 53704. 608/241-6853. Contact Mr. Kwame S. Salter, Manager, Human Resources. Primarily involved in the manufacturer and distribution of processed meat and poultry products. A subsidiary of General Foods Corporation. Employs approxiamately 12,500. Corporate headquarters location. Operations include: Accountant; Computer Programmer; Biochemist; Chemist; Chemical Engineer; Civil Engineer; Electrical Engineer; Industrial Engineer; Mechanical Engineer; Food Technologist. Principal educational backgrounds sought: Accounting; Biology; Business Administration; Chemistry; Computer Science; Economics; Engineering; Finance; Marketing; Liber Arts. Company benefits include: medical, dental, and life insurance;

pension plan; tuition assistance; disability coverage; profit sharing; savings plan. corporate headquarters location. Operations at this facility include: regional headquarters, divisional headquarters, research/development, administration. International: Japan, Switzerland, Venezuela.

RAYOVAC CORPORATION

601 Rayovac Drive, Madison, WI 53711. 608/275-3340. Contact John Miller, Personnel Manager. Manufacturers primary batteries and battery-operated lighting devices. Corporate headquarters location. Common positions include: Accountant; Buyer; Chemist; Computer Programmer; Draftsperson; Engineer; Chemical Engineer; Mechanical Engineer; Financial Analyst; Marketing Specialist; Sales Representative; Systems Analyst. Principal educational backgrounds sought: Accounting; Business Administration; Chemistry; Computer Science; Engineering; Finance; Marketing. Company benefits include: medical, dental, and life insurance; tuition assistance; pension plan; disability coverage; profit sharing; employee discounts; savings plan. International: Brazil, Canada, England, Hong Kong, Japan, Mexico, Netherlands, Peru.

WYOMING

AMAX COAL COMPANY

P.O. Box 3005, Gillette WY 82717. 307/687-3200. Contact Personnel Specialist. Plant for the major coal company. Common positions include: Blue-Collar Worker Supervisor; Draftsperson; Agricultural Engineer; Electrical Engineer; Mechanical Engineer; Mining Engineer; Geologist; Operations/Production Manager; Environmental Specialists; Craftworkers; Operatives; laborers make-up 75% of our Gillette workforce. Principal education backgrounds sought: Biology; Business Administration; Engineering; Liberal Arts. Company benefits include: medical insuurance; dental insurance; pension plan; life insurance; tuition assistance; disability coverage; profit sharing; employee discounts; savings plan. Corporate headquarters location: Indianapolis, IN. International: Canada, England, Netherlands.

MARATHON OIL

P.O. Box 2690, Cody WY 82414. 307/587-4961. Contact Gregg A. Larson, Employee Relations Manager. Production and exploration office for the Rocky Mountain region. Common positions include: Accountant; Draftsperson; Petroleum Engineer; Geologist; Geophysicist. Principal educational backgrounds sought: Accounting; Business Administration; Engineering; Geology. Company benefits include: medical insurance; dental insurance; pension plan; life insurance; tuition assistance; disability coverage; savings plan. Corporate headquarters location: Findlay, OH. Regional headquarters location. International: Brazil, Egypt, England, Germany, Indonesia, Ireland, Nigeria, Scotland, Singapore, Syria, Tunisia.

SAFEWAY STORES

6106 Yellowstone, Suite E, Cheyenne WY 82009. 307/634-3591. Contact District Manager. District office for the major supermarket chain. Corporate headquarters location: Denver, CO. International: Australia, Canada, England, Germany.

Selected Foreign-based Companies with U.S. Offices

The following companies, taken together, employ well over four million people worldwide and have offices in more than 100 countries. As might be expected from such corporate giants, virtually every occupation is represented, ranging from secretaries to assemblers to accountants to sales people. To inquire about current international employment possibilities, write to the company's U.S. office, as listed.

BASF
Based in Ludwigshafen, West Germany.
Major product lines: paints, inks, chemicals, industrial products
Write to: BASF Corp.
200 Park Ave.
New York, NY 10166
(212) 682-1784

Bayer
Based in Leverkusen, West Germany
Major product lines: industrial and scientific chemicals,
   herbicides, pesticides, photographic chemicals and equipment
Write to: Bayer USA

500 Grant St.
Pittsburgh, PA 15219-2502
(412) 394-5554

Bridgestone
Based in Tokyo, Japan
Major product lines: bicycles, tires, rubber products
Write to: Bridgestone
2000 W. 190th St.
Torrance, CA 90504
(213) 320-6020

Casio
Based in Tokyo, Japan
Major product lines: electronic calculators, computers, watches,
  measurement devices
Write to: Casio, Inc.
15 Gardner Rd.
Fairfield, NJ 07006
(201) 575-7400

Club Mediterranee
Based in Paris, France
Major business line: hotels, tourist industry promotions
Write to: Club Mediterranee
40 West 57th St.
New York, NY 10019
(212) 944-2100

Daimler-Benz
Based in Stuttgart, West Germany
Major product lines: diesel engines and products, trucks, buses,
  automobiles, defense industry contracting
Write to: Mercedes-Benz of North America
1 Mercedes Dr., Montvale, NJ 07645
(201) 573-0600

Fiat
Based in Turin, Italy
Major product lines: automobiles and automobile parts, trucks,
   tractors
Write to: Fiat USA
375 Park Ave.
New York, NY 10152
(212) 486-3300

Heineken
Based in Amsterdam, The Netherlands
Major product lines: soft drinks, beer
Write to: Van Munching & Company
1270 Avenue of the Americas
New York, NY 10020
(212) 265-2685

Hitachi
Based in Tokyo, Japan
Major product lines: computer chips, consumer electronics,
   computers, TVs, construction, and chemicals
Write to: Hitachi America Ltd.
50 Prospect Ave.
Tarrytown, NY 10591
(914) 332-5800

F. Hoffmann-La Roche
Based in Basel, Switzerland
Major product lines: perfume, pharmaceuticals, vitamins,
   chemical laboratories and laboratory products
Write to: F. Hoffmann-La Roche
840 Kingsland St.
Nutley, NJ 07110
(201) 235-5000

Hyundai
Based in Seoul, Korea
Major product lines: ships, automobiles, construction, computer
    products, musical instruments, furniture
Write to: Hyundai
1 Bridge Plaza North
Fort Lee, NJ 07024
(201) 592-7766

Kikkoman
Based in Noda, Japan
Major product lines: food condiments, wine, soy products
Write to: Kikkoman International
50 California St.
San Francisco, CA 94111
(415) 956-7550

Matsushita
Based in Osaka, Japan
Major product lines: consumer electronics, TVs, VCRs, laser
    products, FAX, copiers
Write to: Matsushita
1 Panasonic Way
Seacaucau, NJ 07904
(201) 348-7000

Michelin
Based in Paris, France
Major product lines: tires, rubber products, tourist guides
Write to: Michelin
Patewood Industrial Park
P.O. Box 19001
Greensville, SC 29602

NEC

Based in Tokyo, Japan
Major product lines: telecommunication equipment, satellite
  components, computers, consumer electronics, monitors
Write to: NEC America
8 Old Farm Rd.
Melville, NY 11747
(516) 753-7060

Nestle

Based in Vevey, Switzerland
Major product lines: coffee, chocolate, infant formula, food
  products
Write to: Nestle
100 Blommingdale Rd.
White Plains, NY 10605
(914) 251-3000

Pearson

Based in London, England
Major product lines: magazines, newspapers, dishes, food
  products, textbooks
Write to: Pearson
c/o Lazard Freres
1 Rockefeller Plaza
New York, NY 10020
(212) 489-6600

Perrier

Based in Paris, France
Major product lines: bottled water, fitness systems
Write to: Perrier
Great Waters of France
777 W. Putnam Ave.
Greenwich, CN 06830
(203) 531-4100

Philips
Based in Eindhoven, The Netherlands
Major product lines: general industrial products, consumer
  electronics, light bulbs, TVs, medical equipment
Write to: North American Philips
100 E. 42nd St.
New York, NY 10017
(212) 697-3600

Siemens
Based in Munich, West Germany
Major product lines: medical equipment, telecommunications,
  dental equipment, lighting products
Write to: Siemens
767 Fifth Ave.
New York, NY 10153
(212) 832-6601

Sony
Based in Tokyo, Japan
Major product lines: radio, TV, consumer electronics, compact
  discs, motion pictures
Write to: Sony Corporation of America
9 West 57th St.
New York, NY 10019
(212) 371-5800

Thyssen
Based in Duisberg, West Germany
Major product lines: steel, heavy industrial products, shipping,
  pipes
Write to: Thyssen, c/o Budd Company
3155 W. Bay Beaver Road
Troy, Michigan 48084
(313) 643-3520

Toshiba
Based in Tokyo, Japan
Major product lines: nuclear products, lighting, computer
  products, TVs
Write to: Toshiba America
82 Totowa Ave.
Wayne, NJ 07470

Unilever
Based in London, England and Rotterdam, The Netherlands
Major products lines: food products, soaps, hygiene products
Write to: Unilever
10 East 53rd St.
New York, NY 10022
(212) 688-6000

Yamaha
Based in Hamamatsu, Japan
Major product lines: consumer electronics, musical instruments,
  recreational vehicles, boats, sports equipment, computers
Write to: Yamaha International
P.O. Box 6600
Buena Park, CA 90622
(714) 522-9011

Using a World Trade Center
in the Job Search

The World Trade Centers Association is an organization comprised of 115 member groups in 45 nations. Founded in 1968, the purpose of the association is to encourage the expansion of world trade and to promote international business relationships.

You can use a World Trade Center to receive information about business opportunities, meet influential foreign business people, and broaden your horizons with regard to the kind of career possibilities available internationally. For a job candidate beginning to build foreign contacts and acquire useful information about international trade, a visit to a World Trade Center is an extremely worthwhile investment of time.

AUSTRALIA

Melbourne
World Trade Center Melbourne
Cnr Flinoers and Spencer Streets
P.O. Box 4721
Melbourne, Victoria, Australia 3001
Tel. 611 1999

BAHRAIN

Bahrain
World Trade Center Bahrain
P.O. Box 669
Bahrain, Arabian Gulf
Tel. 243425

BELGIUM

Antwerp
N.V. The World Trade Center of
Belgium
Braderijstreat 12-14-16
B-2000 Antwerpen, Belgium
Tel. 031/31-80-71 and 72

Brugge
De Brugse Henze
Internationale Club of West
Flanders
Steenstraat 96
800 Brugge, Belgium
Tel. 050/33.47.99

Brussels
World Trade Center Association
Brussels
162 Boulevard Emile Jacqmain
1000 Brussels, Belgium
Tel. 018-05-49

Ghent
International Club of Flanders
Sint-Pietersplein 11
9000 Ghent, Belgium
Tel. 091.22.96.68

Luxemburg
World Trade Center Luxemburg
3 Square Baron Bouvier
Brussels 1060, Belgium
Tel. 02537.71.56

BRAZIL

Rio de Janeiro
World Trade Center do Rio de
Janeiro
Rua Mexico, 111/Gr.1504—15
andar
Rio de Janeiro, Brazil 20031
Tel. (021) 224-3065

Sao Paulo
World Trade Center de Sao Paulo
Serviease S.A.
Rua Estado Unido, 1093
01427 Sao Paulo—SP—Brazil
Tel. (011) 280.4811

BULGARIA

Sofia
Bulgarian Chamber of Commerce
and Industry
11A, Stambolilski Blvd.
Sofia, Bulgaria
Tel. 87 26 31

CANADA

Calgary
World Trade Centre Calgary
Suite 1900
Stock Exchange Tower
609 Granville Street
Vancouver, B.C. Canada V7Y 1A7
Tel. (604) 688-0211

Edmonton
World Trade Center Edmonton
7300—116 Avenue
Box 1480
Edmonton, Alberta, Canada T5J
2N5
Tel. (403) 471-7283

Halifax
World Trade and Convention
Center—Halifax
1800 Argyle Street
P.O. Box 955
Halifax, Nova Scotia, Canada B3J
2V9
Tel. (902) 421-8686

Montreal
World Trade Centre Montreal
Montreal Chamber of Commerce
772 West Sherbrooke St.
Montreal, Quebec, Canada H3A
1G1
Tel. (514) 288-9090

Ottawa
World Trade Centre Ottawa
W.T.C. World Trade Centres of
Canada Ltd.
1191 Mountain St.
Montreal, Quebec, Canada H3Q
1Z2
Tel. (514) 866-1352

Quebec
Centre de Commerce International
de l'Est du Quebec
17 rue St. Louis
Quebec City, Quebec, Canada GIR
3Y8
Tel. (481) 692-3853

Toronto
World Trade Centre Toronto
Toronto Harbour Commissioners
60 Harbour St.
Toronto, Ontario, Canada M5J 1B7
Tel. (416) 863-2154

Vancouver
World Trade Center Vancouver
The Vancouver Board of Trade
1177 W. Hastings St., Suite 500
Vancouver, B.C. Canada V6E 2K3
Tel. (604) 681-2111

Winnipeg
World Trade Center Winnipeg
c/o W.T.C. World Trade Centers of
Canada Ltd.
1191 Mountain St.
Montreal, Que, Canada H3Q 1Z2
Tel. (514) 866-1352

COLOMBIA

Bogota
World Trade Center Bogota
P.O. Box 6005
Bogota, Colombia
Tel. 2184411

CONGO

Pointe-Noire
Chamber of Commerce of
Pointe-Noire
3 Ave. du General de Gaulle
P.O. Box 665
Pointe-Noire, People's Republic of
Congo
Tel. 94-12-80

CUBA

Havana City
Chamber of Commerce of the
Republic of Cuba
661 21st St.
Vedado, Havana City, Cub
c/o Ramon Sanchez Parodi
Cuban Interests Section 2630 16 St.
N.W.
Washington, DC 20009 U.S.A.
Telex: 511752 CAMAR CU

CYPRUS

Cyprus Chamber of Commerce and
Industry
Evagoras Avenue
Hadjisavvas Bldg., 6th Floor
P.O. Box 1455
Nicosia, Cyprus
Tel. 63212/49500

DENMARK

Copenhagen
World Trade Center Copenhagen
International House
Bella Center A/S
Center Boulevard
DK-2300 Copenhagen S. Denmark
Tel. (01) 51 88 11

DUBAI
Dubai International Trade Centre
Trade Center Management Co., Ltd.
P.O. Box 9292
Dubai, United Arab Emirates
Tel. 472200

EGYPT

Cairo
Cairo World Trade Center
Arab International Bank
35 Abdel Khalek Sarwat Street
P.O. Box 1563
Cairo, Egypt
Tel. 926120 and 926233

Port Said
World Trade Center Port Said
Arab International Bank
35 Abdel Khalek Sarwat Street
P.O. Box 1563
Cairo, Egypt
Tel. 926233

FRANCE

Le Havre
World Trade Center Le Havre
Quai George V
76600 Le Havre, France
Tel. (35) 21.43.41

Marseille
Mediterranean World Trade Center
2, Rue Henri-Barbusse
13241 Marseille, Cedex 01, France
Tel. (91) 08.60.02

Nantes
Atlantic World Trade Center
Chamber of Commerce and
Industry
18X — 44040 Nantes, Cedex,
France
Tel. (40) 89.30.00

Paris
World Trade Center of Paris
Chamber of Commerce and
Industry
2 rue de Viarmes
75000 1 Paris, France
Tel. (1) 508.36.00

Strasbourg
Maison du Commerce International
de Strasbourg
Immeuble "Le Concorde"
4 Quai Kleber
F 67056 Strasbourg Cedex
France
Tel. (88) 32.48.90

HONG KONG

Hong Kong
World Trade Centre Hong Kong
c/o World Trade Centre Club Hong
Kong
2/M and 3/F World Trade Centre
Causeway Bay
Hong Kong
Tel. 5-779528

HUNGARY

Budapest
Hungarian Chamber of Commerce
Kossuth Lajos Ter 6-8
Budapest, Hungary 1389
Tel. 533-333

INDIA

Bombay
World Trade Center, Bombay
M. Vivesvaraya Industrial Research
and Development Centre
Cuffe Parade
Colaba, Bombay-5, India
Tel. 21 44 34/21 73 96

Chandigarh
World Trade Center Chandigarh
Bhatia and Associates
1532, Sector 34-D
Chandigarh—160 022
India Cable: "WORLDTRADE"
Chandigarh

New Delhi
Trade Development Authority
Bank of Baroda Building
16, Sansad Marg
P.O. Box 767
New Delhi, 110001, India
Tel. 312819

INDONESIA

Jakarta
World Trade Center of Indonesia
P.T. Jakarta Land
Level 10, Wisma Metropolitan
Jalan, Sudiman, Jakarta
P.O. Box 3164/JKT
Jakarta, Indonesia
Tel. 584801, 584801, 584803

ISRAEL

Tel-Aviv
World Trade Center Israel
Industry House
29 Hamered Street
P.O. Box 50029
Tel-Aviv, Israel
Tel. 03-65-01-20

ITALY

Genoa
Compagnia Sanbergnigno S.p.A.
Chamber of Commerce
Via Garibaldi, 4
16124 Genoa, Italy
Tel. (010) 20.941

Milan
World Trade Center Italy
Palazzo WTC
Centro Direzionale Milanofiori
20090 Asago (Milan) Italy
Tel. 8244086

JAPAN

Tokyo
The World Trade Center of Japan,
Inc.
P.O. Box 57
World Trade Center Building
No. 4-1, 2-chome, Hamamatsu-cho
Minato-ku, Tokyo, 105 Japan
Tel. (03) 435-5651

IVORY COAST

Abidjan
World Trade Center Abidjan
P.O. Box V.68
Abidjan, Ivory Coast
Tel. 32-38-69/32-37-87/32-38-74

MALAYSIA

Kuala Lumpur
Putra World Trade Centre
Rahim and Co., Chartered
Surveyors SDN BHD
International Real Estate Consultant
Wisma Jayanita
64 Jalan Raja Muda
P.O. Box 11215
Kuala Lumpur, Malaysia
Tel. 03-919922

THE NETHERLANDS

Amsterdam
World Trade Center Amsterdam
Prinses Irenestraat
P.O. Box 7030
1007 JA Amsterdam
The Netherlands
Tel. (01) 20-5759111

Eindhoven
World Trade Center Elecontronics
Fellenoord 51
P.O. Box 2085
5600 CB Eindhoven, The
Netherlands
Tel. (040) 442575

Leiden
World Flower Trade Center
P.O. Box 9324
2300 PH Leiden, The Netherlands
Tel. 31 (72) 31.2031

Rotterdam
World Trade Center Rotterdam
Meent 134
P.O. Box 30055
3001 DB Rotterdam
The Netherlands
Te. (010) 333611

NIGERIA

Lagos
World Trade Center of Nigeria, Ltd.
Western House, 8th Floor
8/10 Broad St.
P.O. Box 4466
Lagos, Nigeria
Tel. 635128

PEOPLE'S REPUBLIC OF CHINA

Beijing
World Trade Centre Beijing
Fua Hua Enterprises Ltd.
c/o World Trade Centre Club Hong
Kong
World Trade Centre
Causeway Bay
Hong Kong
Tel. 5-779528

Nanjing
Jiansu Provincial Travel and
Tourism Corp., P.R.C.
North Zhong Shan Road
Nanjing, P.R.C.
Tel. 34121, 44141

Shanghai
The Preparatory Office of Shanghai
World Trade Centre
c/o CCPIT Shanghai Sub-Council
33 Zhong Shan Dong yi Lu
Shanghai, P.R.C.
Tel. 232348

Shenzhen
Convention Center of Shenzhen
Parker Hill
Shenzhen, P.R.C.
Tel. 22834

PORTUGAL

Lisbon
World Trade Center Lisbon
Av. do Brasil, N.1
1700 Lisbon, Portugal
Tel. 733871-733571

Porto
World Trade Center Porto
Av. da Boavista N. 1203—5—sala 505
Porto, Portugal
Tel. (2) 62095

SAUDI ARABIA

Jeddah
Jeddah World Trade Center
Saudi Economic and Development Co., Ltd.
P.O. Box 4384
Jeddah, Kingdom of Saudi Arabia
Tel. (02) 644-0920-1

SINGAPORE

Singapore
World Trade Center Singapore
1 Maritime Square, No. 02-11
World Trade Centre
Singapore 0490
Republic of Singapore
Tel. 271221 Ext. 2791

SOUTH AFRICA

Johannesburg
The South African Froeign Trade Organization
P.O. Box 9039
Johannesburg, 2000
South Africa

SOUTH KOREA

Seoul
World Trade Center Korea
Korean Traders Association
10-1, 2-Ka Hoehyon-dong, Chung-Ku
C.P.O. Box 1117
Seoul, Korea
Tel. 771-41

SPAIN

Barcelona
Spanish Federation of Importers and Exporters
Trafalgar, 4, 4-A
06010 Barcelona, Spain
Tel. 317.95.86/317.95.90

Madrid
World Trade Center Madrid, S.A.
Jose Ortega Y Gasset 22,7
28006 Madrid, Spain
Tel. (1) 4359393

Valencia
World Trade Center Valencia S.A.
Eduarbo Bosca, 33
46023 Valencia, Spain
Tel. 6-360 46 77

SWEDEN

Gothenburg
Scandinavian World Trade Center AB
Storgatan 26
S-411 38 Goetborg, Sweden
Tel. 031/177660

SWITZERLAND

Basel
World Trade Center Basel
c/o Swiss Industries Fair, Basel

Isteinerstrasse 51
CH-4021 Basel, Switzerland
Tel. 061/26 2029

Geneva
World Trade Center Geneva
P.O. Box 306
CH 1215 Geneva—Airport 15
Switzerland
Tel. (022) 989 989

Zurich
FIATA
29 Brauerstrasse
POB 177
CH-8026 Zurich, Switzerland
Tel. 241.80.45

TAIWAN

Taipei
Taipei World Trade Center, Ltd.
Sung Shan Airport Terminal
340 Tun Hwa North Road
Taipei, Taiwan
Tel. (02) 715 1551

THAILAND

Bangkok
World Trade Center Bangkok Co.
Ltd.
8th Floor Sinthon Building
132 Wireless Road Patumwam
10500, Bangkok, Thailand
Tel. 2501801-7

TURKEY

Istanbul
Istanbul World Trade Center, Inc.
Istanbul Ticaret Odaai
Ragip Gumuspala Cad.
Eminomu, Istanbul
P.O. Box 377 Turkey
Tel. (00901) 526 62 15

UNION OF SOVIET SOCIALIST REPUBLICS

Moscow
World Trade Center Moscow
v/o SOVINCENTR
12, Krasnopresnenskaya nab.
123610 Moscow USSR
Tel. 256 63 03

UNITED KINGDOM

London
World Trade Centre London
International House
St. Katharine-by-the-Tower
London, E1 9UN
United Kingdom
Tel. 01-488 2400

Manchester
The Manchester Chamber of
Commerce and Industry
56 Oxford St.
King St.
Manchester, M60 7HJ
United Kingdom
Tel. 061 236-3210

UNITED STATES

Atlanta
World Trade Club of Atlanta, Inc.
240 Peachtree Street
Suite 2200
Atlanta, GA 30303 U.S.A.
Tel. (404) 525-4144

Baltimore
The World Trade Center Baltimore
Baltimore, MD 21202 U.S.A.
Tel. (301) 659-4544

Baltimore
The Merchants Club
206 Easte Redwood Street

Baltimore, MD 21202 U.S.A.
Tel. (301) 742-6467

Boston
International Business Center of New England
22 Batterymarch Street
Boston, MA 02210 U.S.A.
Tel. (617) 542-0426

Chicago
Club Internation
The Drake Hotel
140 East Walton Place
Chicago, IL 60611 U.S.A.
Tel. (312) 787-2200

Colorado Springs
Rocky Mountain World Trade Center
Red Rock Canyon Project
3221 W. Colorado Avenue
Colorado Springs, CO 80904 U.S.A.
Tel. (303) 633-9041

Columbus
World Trade and Technology Center of Columbus
10793 State Route 37 West
Sunbury, OH 43074 U.S.A.
Tel. (614) 965-2974

Des Moines
Iowa World Trade Center Des Moines
3200 Ruan Center
666 Grand Avenue
Des Moines, IA 50390 U.S.A.
Tel. (515) 245-2555

Ft. Lauderdale
World Trade Center Fort Lauderdale, Florida
P.O. Box 13066
1800 Eller Drive

Port Everglades, Florida 33316, U.S.A.
Tel. (305) 523-5307

Greensboro
World Trade Center—North Carolina
P.O. Box 19290 Greensboro, N.C. 27419
Tel. (929) 854-0078

Honolulu
Hawaii International Services Branch
Department of Planning and Economic Development
P.O. Box 2359
Honolulu, HI 96804 U.S.A.
Tel. (808) 548-3048

Houston
World Trade Center Houston
Suites 1D and 1E
1520 Texas Ave.
Houston, TX 77002 U.S.A.
Tel. (713) 225-0968

Jacksonville
Jacksonville International Trade Association
Jacksonville Chamber of Commerce
3 Independent Drive
P.O. Box 329
Jacksonville, Florida 32201 U.S.A.
Tel. (904) 353-0300

Long Beach
The Port of Long Beach
925 Harbor Plaza
P.O. Box 570
Long Beach, CA 92801 U.S.A.
Tel. (213) 437-0041

Miami
Execucentre International
Suite 650
444 Brickell Ave.
Miami, FL 33131 U.S.A.
Tel. (305) 374-8300

New Orleans
International House—WTC
611 Gravier Street
New Orleans, Louisiana 70230
U.S.A.
Tel. (504) 522-3591

New York
World Trade Center New York
The Port Authority of New York and
New Jersey
Suite 63 West, 1 World Trade Center
New York, NY 10048 U.S.A.
Tel. (212) 466-8380

Norfolk
World Trade Center Norfolk
600 World Trade Center
Norfolk, VA 23510 U.S.A.
Tel. (804) 623-8000

Orlando
World Trade Center Orlando
P.O. Box 1234
Orlando, Florida 32801 U.S.A.
Tel. (305) 425-1234

Pomona
Inland Pacific World Trade Institute
422 W. Seventh St., Suite 302
Los Angeles, CA 90014
Tel. (213) 627-6738

Portland
Columbia World Trade Center
Corp.
121 S.W. Salmon
Portland, OR 97204 U.S.A.
Tel. (503) 220-3067

San Francisco
World Trade Center of San
Francisco, Inc.
1170 Sacramento St.
Penthouse B
San Francisco, CA 92108 U.S.A.
Tel. (415) 928-3438

Santa Ana
World Trade Center Association of
Orange County
200 E. Sandpointe Ave.
Santa Ana, CA 92707 U.S.A.
Tel. (714) 549-8151

Sarasota
World Trade Council of Southwest
Florida
P.O. Box 911
Sarasota, Florida 33578 U.S.A.
Tel. (813) 366-4060

Seattle
Seattle World Trade Center Corp.
500 Union St.
Suite 840
Seattle, WA 96101
Tel. (206) 622-4121

St. Paul
Minnesota World Trade Center
1300 Conwed Tower
444 Cedar St.
St. Paul, Minnesota 55101 U.S.A.
Tel. (612) 297-1580

Tacoma
World Trade Center Tacoma
P.O. Box 1837
Tacoma, Washington 96401 U.S.A.
Tel. (206) 383-5841, Ext. 321

Tampa
Tampa Bay International Trade
Council
P.O. Box 420

Tampa Florida 33601
Tel. (813) 228-7777, Ext. 234

Toledo
Toledo World Trade Center
136 N. Summit St.
P.O. Box 2087
Toledo, OH 43603
Tel. (419) 255-7226

Washington, D.C.
World Trade Center Washington
1000 Connecticut Ave., NW
Suite 707
Washington, DC 20036
Tel. (202) 955-6164

WALES

Cardiff
World Trade Centre Cardiff
16 Cathedral Road
Cardiff, South Glamorgan, Wales
Tel. Cardiff 44191

WEST GERMANY

Ruhr Valley
World Trade Center Ruhrbebiet
Verein pro Ruhrgebiet e.V.
Kronprinzenstrasse 35
D 4300 Essen 1, W. Germany
Tel. 2069-318

YUGOSLAVIA

Ljubijana
Business Association MAGOS
Titova 118
6113 Ljubijana, Yugoslavia
Tel. 961/347-756

Embassies You Can Contact for Country Information

The Washington embassies of foreign countries are, collectively, a treasure house of information and potential contacts for international job seekers. Needless to say, embassies are not employment offices. They can, however, furnish you with detailed information about work permit procedures, types of business and industry in the country, and the culture and geography of the country.

To ask for this kind of information, simply write to the country's ambassador, as in this sample letter:

```
Date
Your Address
The Honorable Ambassador
Embassy of Sweden
600 New Hampshire Ave. NW
Washington, D.C. 20007
Dear Ambassador:
    I am planning a trip to Sweden in the near
future, and would deeply appreciate whatever
literature or information you can furnish on
[specify your interests here—visa informa-
```

```
tion, work permits, contact with trade or-
ganizations, general cultural information
about Sweden and its people]. By way of in-
troduction, I am [introduce yourself briefly—
what you do, what your background is, what
your goals are].

    I'm eager to learn as much as possible
about Sweden before beginning my trip. Thank
you for assisting me.
Sincerely,
(signature)
Your Name
```

Type this letter on quality stationery. The response you receive will be in direct relation to the professionalism of your letter.

When you receive a response from the ambassador, send a brief thank-you note. It's a contact you'll want to nurture.

Embassy of Afghanistan
2001 24th NW
Washington, D.C. 20008
Tel. (202) 234-3770

Embassy of Algeria
2118 Kalorama Rd. NW
Washington, D.C. 20008
Tel. (202) 265-2800

Embassy of Argentina
1600 New Hampshire Ave. NW
Washington, D.C. 20009
Tel. (202) 939-6400

Embassy of Australia
1601 Massachusetts Ave. NW
Washington, D.C. 20036
Tel. (202) 797-3000

Embassy of Austria
2343 Massachusetts Ave. NW
Washington, D.C. 20008
Tel. (202) 483-4474

Embassy of the Bahamas
600 New Hampshire Ave. NW
Washington, D.C. 20037
Tel. (202) 944-3390

Embassy of Bangladesh
2201 Wisconsin Ave. NW
Washington, D.C. 20007
Tel. (202) 342-8372

Embassy of Barbados
2144 Wyoming Ave. NW
Washington, D.C. 20008
Tel. (202) 939-9200

Embassy of Belgium
3330 Garfield St. NW
Washington, D.C. 20008
Tel. (202) 333-6900

Embassy of Belize
1575 I St. NW
Washington, D.C. 20008
Tel. (202) 363-4505

Embassy of The People's Republic of Benin
2737 Cathedral Ave. NW
Washington, D.C. 20008
Tel. (202) 232-6656

Embassy of Bolivia
3014 Massachusetts Ave. NW
Washington, D.C. 20008
Tel. (202) 483-4410

Embassy of Brazil
Madison Hotel
Washington, D.C. 20005
Tel. (202) 331-4374

Embassy of Brunei Darussalm
2600 Virginia Ave. NW
Washington, D.C. 20037
Tel. (202) 342-0159

Embassy of Burkina Fasco
2340 Massachusetts Ave. NW
Washington, D.C. 20008
Tel. (202) 332-5577

Embassy of the Union of Burma
2300 S St. NW
Washington, D.C. 20008
Tel. (202) 332-9044

Embassy of The United Republic of Cameroon
2349 Massachusetts Ave. NW
Washington, D.C. 20008
Tel. (202) 265-8790

Embassy of Canada
501 Penn Ave. NW
Washington, D.C. 20001
Tel. (202) 682-1740

Embassy of Cape Verde
3415 Massachusetts Ave. NW
Washington, D.C. 20007
Tel. (202) 965-6820

Embassy of Chad
2002 R St. NW
Washington, D.C. 20009
Tel. (202) 462-4009

Embassy of Chile
1732 Massachusetts Ave. NW
Washington, D.C. 20036
Tel. (202) 785-1746

Embassy of Colombia
2118 Leroy Place NW
Washington, D.C. 20008
Tel. (202) 387-8338

Embassy of Costa Rica
1825 Connecticut Ave. NW
Washington, D.C. 20009
Tel. (202) 234-2945

Embassy of Cyprus
2211 R St. NW
Washington, D.C. 20008
Tel. (202) 462-5772

Embassy of Czechoslovakia
3900 Linnean Ave. NW
Washington, D.C. 20008
Tel. (202) 363-6315

Embassy of Denmark
3200 Whitehaven Ave. NW
Washington, D.C. 20008
Tel. (202) 234-4300

Embassy of The Dominican Republic
1715 22nd St. NW
Washington, D.C. 20008
Tel. (202) 332-6280

Embassy of Ecuador
2535 15th St. NW
Washington, D.C. 20009
Tel. (202) 234-7200

Embassy of Egypt
2310 Decatur Pl. NW
Washington, D.C. 20008
Tel. (202) 232-5400

Embassy of El Salvador
2308 California St. NW
Washington, D.C. 20008
Tel. (202) 265-3480

Embassy of Ethiopia
2134 Kalorama Rd. NW
Washington, D.C. 20008
Tel. (202) 234-2281

Embassy of Fiji
2233 Wisconsin Ave. NW
Washington, D.C. 20007
Tel. (202) 337-8320

Embassy of Finland
3216 New Mexico Ave. NW
Washington, D.C. 20016
Tel. (202) 363-2430

Embassy of France
4101 Reservoir Rd. NW
Washington, D.C. 20007
Tel. (202) 944-6000

Embassy of The Republic of Gabon
2034 20th St. NW
Washington, D.C. 20009
Tel. (202) 797-1000

Embassy of German Democratic Republic
171 Massachusetts Ave. NW
Washington, D.C. 20001
Tel. (202) 232-3134

Embassy of German Federal Republic
4645 Reservoir Rd. NW
Washington, D.C. 20007
Tel. (202) 298-4000

Embassy of Greece
2221 Massachusetts Ave. NW
Washington, D.C. 20008
Tel. (202) 667-3168

Embassy of Grenada
1701 New Hampshire Ave.
Washington, D.C. 20009
Tel. (202) 265-2561

Embassy of Guatemala
2220 R St. NW
Washington, D.C. 20008
Tel. (202) 745-4952

Embassy of New Guinea
2112 Leroy Pl. NW
Washington, D.C. 20008
Tel. (202) 483-9420

Embassy of Guyana
3490 Tracy Pl. NW
Washington, D.C. 20008
Tel. (202) 265-6900

Embassy of Honduras
15 K St. NW
Washington, D.C. 20005
Tel. (202) 638-4348

Embassy of Hungary
3910 Shoemaker St. NW
Washington, D.C. 20008
Tel. (202) 362-6730

Embassy of Iceland
2022 Connecticut Ave. NW
Washington, D.C. 20008
Tel. (202) 265-6653

Embassy of India
2107 Massachusetts Ave. NW
Washington, D.C. 20008
Tel. (202) 939-7000

Embassy of The Republic of Indonesia
2020 Massachusetts Ave. NW
Washington, D.C. 20036
Tel. (202) 775-5200

Embassy of Iraq
1801 P St. NW
Washington, D.C. 20036
Tel. (202) 483-7500

Embassy of Ireland
2234 Massachusetts Ave.
Washington, D.C. 20008
Tel. (202) 462-3939

Embassy of Israel
3514 International Dr. NW
Washington, D.C. 20008
Tel. (202) 364-5500

Embassy of Italy
1601 Fuller St. NW
Washington, D.C. 20009
Tel. (202) 328-5500

Embassy of Jamaica
1850 K St. NW
Washington, D.C. 20006
Tel. (202) 452-0660

Embassy of Japan
2520 Massachusetts Ave.
Washington, D.C. 20008
Tel. (202) 939-6700

Embassy of Jordan
3504 International Dr. NW
Washington, D.C. 20008
Tel. (202) 966-2664

Embassy of Kenya
2249 R St. NW
Washington, D.C. 20008
Tel. (202) 387-6101

Embassy of Kuwait
3500 International Dr. NW
Washington, D.C. 20008
Tel. (202) 364-2100

Embassy of The Lao People's Democratic Republic
2222 S St. NW
Washington, D.C. 20008
Tel. (202) 332-6416

Embassy of Lebanon
2560 28th St. NW
Washington, D.C. 20008
Tel. (202) 939-6300

Embassy of Luxembourg
2200 Massachusetts Ave. NW
Washington, D.C. 20008
Tel. (202) 265-4171

Embassy of Madagascar
2374 Massachusetts Ave. NW
Washington, D.C. 20008
Tel. (202) 265-5525

Embassy of Malawi
1400 20th St. NW
Washington, D.C. 20036
Tel. (202) 223-4814

Embassy of Malaysia
2401 Massachusetts Ave. NW
Washington, D.C. 20008
Tel. (202) 328-2700

Embassy of The Republic of Mali
2130 R St. NW
Washington, D.C. 20008
Tel. (202) 332-2249

Embassy of Malta
2017 Connecticut Ave. NW
Washington, D.C. 20008
Tel. (202) 462-3611

Embassy of Mauritius
4301 Connecticut Ave. NW
Washington, D.C. 20008
Tel. (202) 244-1491

Embassy of Mexico
2829 16th St. NW
Washington, D.C. 20009
Tel. (202) 234-6000

Embassy of Morocco
2601 21st St. NW
Washington, D.C. 20009
Tel. (202) 462-7979

Embassy of Mozambique
1990 M St. NW
Washington, D.C. 20036
Tel. (202) 293-7146

Embassy of Nepal
2131 Leroy Pl. NW
Washington, D.C. 20008
Tel. (202) 667-4550

Embassy of The Netherlands
4200 Linnean Ave. NW
Washington, D.C. 20008
Tel. (202) 244-5300

Embassy of Nicaragua
1627 New Hampshire Ave. NW
Washington, D.C. 20009
Tel. (202) 939-6570

Embassy of Niger
2204 R St. NW
Washington, D.C. 20008
Tel. (202) 483-4224

Embassy of Nigeria
2201 M St. NW
Washington, D.C. 20037
Tel. (202) 822-1500

Embassy of Norway
2720 34th St. NW
Washington, D.C. 20008
Tel. (202) 333-6000

Embassy of Oman
1717 Massachusetts Ave.
Washington, D.C. 20036
Tel. (202) 387-2014

Embassy of Pakistan
2315 Massachusetts Ave. NW
Washington, D.C. 20008
Tel. (202) 939-6200

Embassy of Panama
2868 McGill Terrace NW
Washington, D.C. 20008
Tel. (202) 483-1407

Embassy of Papua New Guinea
1330 Connecticut Ave. NW
Washington, D.C. 20036
Tel. (202) 659-0856

Embassy of Paraguay
2400 Massachusetts Ave. NW
Washington, D.C. 20008
Tel. (202) 483-6960

Embassy of the Peoples Republic of China
2300 Connecticut Ave. NW
Washington, D.C. 20008
Tel. (202) 328-2500

Embassy of Peru
1700 Massachusetts Ave. NW
Washington, D.C. 20036
Tel. (202) 833-9860

Embassy of Portugal
2125 Kalorama Road NW
Washington, D.C. 20008
Tel. (202) 328-8610

Embassy of Qatar
600 New Hampshire Ave. NW
Washington, D.C. 20037
Tel. (202) 338-0111

Embassy of Romania
1607 23rd St. NW
Washington, D.C. 20008
Tel. (202) 232-4747

Embassy of Rwanda
1714 New Hampshire Ave. NW
Washington, D.C. 20009
Tel. (202) 232-2882

Embassy of Saudi Arabia
601 New Hampshire Ave. NW
Washington, D.C. 20037
Tel. (202) 342-3800

Embassy of Senegal
2112 Wyoming Ave. NW
Washington, D.C. 20008
Tel. (202) 234-0540

Embassy of Sierra Leone
1701 19th St. NW
Washington, D.C. 20009
Tel. (202) 939-9261

Embassy of Singapore
1824 R St. NW
Washington, D.C. 20009
Tel. (202) 667-7555

Embassy of Somali Democratic Republic
600 New Hampshire Ave. NW
Washington, D.C. 20037
Tel. (202) 342-1575

Embassy of South Africa
3051 Massachusetts Ave. NW
Washington, D.C. 20008
Tel. (202) 232-4400

Embassy of Spain
2700 15th St. NW
Washington, D.C. 20009
Tel. (202) 265-0190

Embassy of Sri Lanka
2148 Wyoming Ave. NW
Washington, D.C. 20008
Tel. (202) 483-4025

Embassy of St. Kitts Nevis
2100 M St. NW, Suite 608
Washington, D.C. 20037
Tel. (202) 833-3550

Embassy of St. Lucia
2100 M St. NW, Suite 309
Washington, D.C. 20037
Tel. (202) 463-7378

Embassy of Sudan
2210 Massachusetts Ave. NW
Washington, D.C. 20008
Tel. (202) 466-6280

Embassy of The Kingdom of Swaziland
4301 Connecticut Ave. NW
Washington, D.C. 20008
Tel. (202) 362-6683

Embassy of Sweden
600 New Hampshire Ave. NW
Washington, D.C. 20037
Tel. (202) 944-5600

Embassy of Switzerland
2900 Cathedral Ave. NW
Washington, D.C. 20008
Tel. (202) 745-7900

Embassy of Syria
2215 Wyoming Ave. NW
Washington, D.C. 20008
Tel. (202) 232-6313

Embassy of Tanzania
2139 R St. NW
Washington, D.C. 20008
Tel. (202) 939-6125

Embassy of Togo
2208 Massachusetts Ave. NW
Washington, D.C. 20008
Tel. (202) 234-4212

Embassy of Trinidad and Tobago
1708 Massachusetts Ave. NW
Washington, D.C. 20036
Tel. (202) 467-6490

Embassy of Tunisia
1515 Massachusetts Ave.
Washington, D.C. 20005
Tel. (202) 862-1850

Embassy of Turkey
2523 Massachusetts Ave.
Washington, D.C. 20008
Tel. (202) 483-5366

Embassy of Uganda
2909 16th St. NW
Washington, D.C. 20009
Tel. (202) 726-7100

Embassy of Uruguay
1918 F St. NW
Washington, D.C. 20004
Tel. (202) 331-1313

Embassy of the Union of Soviet Socialist Republics
1125 16th St. NW
Washington, D.C. 20036
Tel. (202) 618-7551

Embassy of The United Arab Emirates
600 New Hampshire Ave. NW
Washington, D.C. 20037
Tel. (202) 338-6500

Embassy of Venezuela
2445 Massachusetts Ave. NW
Washington, D.C. 20008
Tel. (202) 797-3800

Embassy of the SFR of Yugoslavia
2410 California St.
Washington, D.C. 20008
Tel. (202) 462-6566

Embassy of The Republic of Zaire
1800 New Hampshire Ave. NW
Washington, D.C. 20009
Tel. (202) 234-7690

Embassy of The Republic of Zambia
2419 Massachusetts Ave. NW
Washington, D.C. 20008
Tel. (202) 265-9717

Embassy of Zimbabwe
2851 McGill Terrace NW
Washington, D.C. 20008
Tel. (202) 332-7100

Councils, Associations, and Government Agencies with International Employment Possibilities

Each of the following organizations will provide you with information about its mission, geographical scope, and staffing. It's a good idea to write for general information before pursuing specific career possibilities. The presence of an organization in this list does not imply that it currently advertises international job openings.

AFL-CIO
Department of International Affairs
815 16th St. NW
Washington, D.C. 20006

Agency for International Development
International Development Intern Recruitment
Office of Personnel and Management
320 21st St. NW
Washington, D.C. 20523

Agricultural Development Council
1290 Ave. of the Americas
New York, NY 10020

AIESEC-US (Association internationale des etudiants en sciences economiques et commericiales)
14 West 23rd St.
New York, NY 10010

American Council on Education
1 Dupont Circle NW
Washington, D.C. 20036

American Field Service
313 East 43rd St.
New York, NY 10017

**American Graduate School of
International Management**
Glendale, AZ 85306

Asian Development Bank
2330 Roxas Boulevard
Pasay City, Philippines

**Association for International
Practical Training**
American City Building, Suite 217
Columbia, MD 21044

**Association of Teachers of
English as a Second Language
(TESOL)**
1860 19th St. N.W.
Washington, D.C. 20009

**Bureau of International
Aviation**
Civil Aeronautics Board
1825 Connecticut Ave. NW
Washington, D.C. 20428

**Bureau of International Labor
Affairs**
Department of Labor
200 Constitution Ave. NW
Washington, D.C. 20210

**Business Council for
International Understanding**
420 Lexington Ave.
New York, NY 10170

**Carnegie Endowment for
International Peace**
30 Rockefeller Plaza
New York, NY 10020

Central Intelligence Agency
Washington, D.C. 20505

**Chamber of Commerce of the
United States**
1615 H Street N.W.
Washington, D.C. 20006-4902

**Committee for Economic
Development**
477 Madison Ave.
New York, NY 10022

Congressional Budget Office
National Security and International
Affairs Division
Washington, D.C. 20515

Congressional Research Service
Library of Congress
10 1st St. SE
Washington, D.C. 20540

**Council on International
Educational Exchange**
205 E. 42nd St.
New York, NY 10017

Ford Foundation
320 E. 43rd St.
New York, NY 10017

Foreign Agriculture Service
Personnel Division
U.S. Department of Agriculture
Washington, D.C. 20007

Foreign Commercial Service
Commerce Department Building
Washington, D.C. 20230

**Foster Parents Plan
International**
Box 400
Warwick, RI 02887

**General Accounting Office
(GAO)**
International Division
441 G St. NW
Washington, D.C. 20548

**General Services
Administration (GSA)**
18th and F Streets NW
Washington, D.C. 20405

**Institute of International
Education**
809 United Nations Plaza
New York, NY 10017

**Inter-American Development
Bank**
808 17th St. NW
Washington, D.C. 20577

**International Atomic Energy
Agency**
P.O. Box 100
A-1400 Vienna, Austria

**International Association for
the Exchange of Students for
Technical Experience**
American City Building
Columbia, MD 21044

**International Development
Cooperation Agency**
320 21st St. NW
Washington, D.C. 20523

**International Fund for
Agricultural Development**
Via del Serafico 107
EUR 00142 Rome, Italy

**International Institute for
Studies and Training**
15-3 Kamiide
Fujinomiya-shi
Shizuoka-ken, Japan

**International League for
Human Rights**
236 E. 46th St.
New York, NY 10017

**International Schools
Association**
CTC Case 20
CH-1211 Geneva 20, Switzerland

International Schools Services
P.O. Box 5910
Princeton, NJ 08540

International Monetary Fund
Economists Program
700 19th St. NW
Washington, D.C. 20431

**International Trade
Administration**
Commerce Dept. Building
Washington, D.C. 20230-0002

Maritime Administration
U.S. Department of Transportation
400 7th St. SW
Washington, D.C. 20590

Modern Language Association
62 5th Ave.
New York, NY 10011

**National Association for
Foreign Student Affairs**
1860 19th St. N.W.
Washington, D.C. 20009

**National Association of Foreign
Trade Zones**
Commerce Tower, Suite 1020
911 Main St.
Kansas City, MO 64105

National Foreign Trade Council
100 E. 42nd St.
New York, NY 10017

National Geographic Society
17th and M Sts. NW
Washington, D.C. 20036

National Science Foundation
Division of International Programs
1800 G St. NW
Washington, D.C. 20550

Office of International Health
Department of Health and Human
Services
200 Independence Ave. SW
Washington, D.C. 20201

Operation Crossroads Africa
150 Fifth Ave.
New York, NY 10011

Organization of American States
Constitution Ave. and 17th Street NW
Washington, D.C. 20006

Overseas Education Association
1201 16th St. NW
Washington, D.C. 20036

Peace Corps
806 Connecticut Ave. NW
Washington, D.C. 20526

Rockefeller Foundation
1133 Ave. of the Americas
New York, NY 10020

Save the Children
50 Wilton Road
Westport, CT 06880

Sister Cities International
1625 I St. NW, Suite 424
Washington, D.C. 20006

Society for International Development
777 UN Plaza
New York, NY 10017

Teacher of English to Speakers of Other Languages (TESOL)
202 D.C. Transit Building
Georgetown University
Washington, D.C. 20057

United Board for Christian Higher Education in Asia
475 Riverside Drive
New York, NY 10027

United Nations
Recruitment Programmes Section
New York, NY 10017

United Nations Children's Fund
866 UN Plaza
New York, NY 10017

U.S. Civil Service Commission
1900 E St. NW
Washington, D.C. 20415

U.S. Department of Commerce
14th and E St., NW
Washington, D.C. 20230

U.S. Committee for UNICEF
331 E. 38th St.
New York, NY 10016

U.S. Customs Service
1301 Consitution Ave NW
Washington, D.C. 20002-6419

U.S. Department of Agriculture
14th St. and Independence Ave. SW
Washington, D.C. 20250

U.S. Department of Defense
The Pentagon
Washington, D.C. 20301-0999

U.S. Department of State
Bureau of Economic and Business
Affairs
Office of Business and Export
Affairs
2201 C St. NW
Washington, D.C. 20520

**U.S. Department of
Transportation**
Assistant Secretary for Policy and
International Affairs
400 7th St. SW
Washington, D.C. 20590

**United States Information
Agency**
301 4th St. SW
Washington, D.C. 20547

**U.S. Immigration and
Naturalization Service**
425 I St. NW
Washington, D.C. 20001-2542

**U.S. International Trade
Commission**
Office of Administration
701 E St. NW
Washington, D.C. 20436

U.S. Student Travel Service
801 2nd Ave.
New York, NY 10017

Voice of America
Office of Personnel and
Recruitment
3300 Independence Ave. SW
Washington, D.C. 20547

World Health Organization
20 Ave. APPIA
CH-1211 Geneva 27, Switzerland

World Tourism Organization
Calle Capitan Haya 42
E-Madrid 20, Spain

**World Trade Centers
Association**
One World Trade Center, 63W
New York, NY 10048

Where to Get Information on Federal Jobs Involving International Contacts or Travel

Alabama
Federal Job Information Center
806 Governors Dr. SW
Hunstsville, AL 35801

Alaska
Federal Job Information Center
P.O. Box 22
Anchorage, Alaska 99513

Arizona
Federal Job Information Center
522 N. Central Ave.
Phoenix, AZ 85004

Arkansas
Federal Job Information Center
700 W. Capitol Ave.
Little Rock, AR 72201

California
Federal Job Information Center
845 S. Figueroa
Los Angeles, CA 90017
Federal Job Information Center
880 Front St.
San Diego, CA 92188
Federal Job Information Center
1029 J St. Room 202
Sacramento, CA 91028
Federal Job Information Center
450 Golden Ave.
San Francisco, CA 94102

Colorado
Federal Job Information Center
1845 Sherman St.
Denver, CO 80298

Connecticut
Federal Job Information Center
450 Main St.
Hartford, CN 06103

Delaware
Federal Job Information Center
844 King St.
Wilmington, DE 19801

District of Columbia
Federal Job Information Center
1900 E St. NW
Washington, DC 20415

Florida
Federal Job Information Center
80 N. Hughey Ave.
Orlando, FL 32801

Georgia
Federal Job Information Center
75 Spring St. SW
Atlanta, GA 30303
Hawaii
Federal Job Information Center
300 Ala Moana Blvd.
Honolulu, HA 96850

Illinois
Federal Job Information Center
219 S. Dearborn St.
Chicago, IL 60604

Indiana
Federal Job Information Center
46 E. Ohio St. Rm. 123
Indianapolis, IN 46204

Iowa
Federal Job Information Center
210 Walnut St., Rm. 191
Des Moines, IA 50309

Kansas
Federal Job Information Center
230 S. Market St.
Wichita, KS 67202

Kentucky
Federal Job Information Center
600 Federal Pl.
Louisville, KN 40202

Louisiana
Federal Job Information Center
610 South St., Rm. 103
New Orleans, LA 70130

Maine
Federal Job Information Center
Federal Bldg, Rm. 611
Sewall St. & Western Ave.
Augusta, Maine 04330

Maryland
Federal Job Information Center
101 W. Lombard St.
Baltimore, MD 21201

Massachusetts
Federal Job Information Center
3 Center Plaza
Boston, MA 02108

Michigan
Federal Job Information Center
477 Michigan Ave, Rm. 595
Detroit, MI 48226

Minnesota
Federal Job Information Center
Ft. Snelling
Twin Cities, MN 55111

Mississippi
Federal Job Information Center
100 W. Capitol St.
Jackson, MS 39201

Missouri
Federal Job Information Center
601 E 12th St.
Kansas City, MO 64106

Montana
Federal Job Information Center
301 S. Park, Rm. 153
Helena, MT 59626

Nebraska
Federal Job Information Center
215 N. 17th St.
Omaha, NE 68102

Nevada
Federal Job Information Center
P.O. Box 3296
Reno, NV 89505

New Hampshire
Federal Job Information Center
Daniel and Penhallow Streets
Portsmouth, NH 07102

New Mexico
Federal Job Information Center
421 Gold Ave. SW
Albuquerque, NM 87102

New York
Federal Job Information Center
590 Grand Concourse
Bronx, NY 10451

North Carolina
Federal Job Information Center
310 New Bern Ave.
Raleigh, NC 27611

North Dakota
Federal Job Information Center
657 Second Ave. N.
Fargo, ND 58102

Ohio
Federal Job Information Center
1240 E. 9th St.
Cleveland, OH 44199

Oklahoma
Federal Job Information Center
200 NW Fifth St.
Oklahoma City, OK 73102

Oregon
Federal Job Information Center
1220 SW Third St.
Portland, OR 97204

Pennsylvania
Federal Job Information Center
600 Arch St.
Philadelphia, PA 19106

Rhode Island
Federal Job Information Center
Federal and Post Office Building
Providence, RI 02903

South Carolina
Federal Job Information Center
334 Meeting St.
Charleston, SC 29403

South Dakota
Federal Job Information Center
515 9th St.
Rapid City, SD 57701

Tennessee
Federal Job Information Center
167 N. Main St.
Memphis, TN 38103

Texas
Federal Job Information Center
1100 Commerce St.
Dallas, TX 75202

Utah
Federal Job Information Center
1234 S. Main St.
Salt Lake City, UT 84101

Vermont
Federal Job Information Center
P.O. Box 489
Burlington, VT 05402

Virginia
Federal Job Information Center
200 Granby Mall
Norfolk, VA 23510

Washington
Federal Job Information Center
915 Second Ave.
Seattle, WA 98174

Wisconsin
Federal Job Information Center
161 W. Wisconsin Ave.
Milwaukee, WI 53203

Wyoming
Federal Job Information Center
2120 Capital Ave.
Cheyenne, WY 82001

Selected Employment Agencies Handling International Placement

The following employment agencies advertise international placement services. No recommendation or endorsement is implied by the selection of employment firms in this list. If you are interested in the assistance of an employment agency, you may want to talk to these firms or others about your career goals. Make sure you understand what they can and cannot do for you, and any fees involved.

Atlanta
International Career Network Corp.
1645 Tullie Circle NE
Atlanta, GA
(404) 687-0612

Chicago
Dunhill Employment Agency
230 N. Michigan Ave.
Chicago, IL 60603
(312) 346-0933

Cincinnati
Professions, Inc.
4665 Cornell St., Ste. 204
Cincinnati, OH 45241
(513) 530-0909

Indianapolis
Century Personnel
3737 N. Meridian St., Ste. 500
Indianapolis, IN 46208
(317) 924-1216

Irvine (Orange County), California
TRS—Total Recruiting Service, Inc.
3333 Michelson Dr., A1-30
Irvine, CA 92730
(714) 975-3630

Los Angeles
Robert Half Employment Agency
3600 Wilshire Blvd.
Los Angeles, CA 90010
(213) 386-6805

Miami
Hamilton Personnel
3655 NW 87 Ave.
Miami, FL 33137
(305) 576-1802

Milwaukee
International Placement and Recruiting
7207 W. Greenfield Ave.
Milwaukee, WI 53225
(414) 257-3959

Minneapolis
LCW Group
6750 France Ave. S., Ste. 144
Edina, MN 55435
(612) 922-7879

New Orleans
Global Job Search Local
1605 Ridgelake Drive
Metaire, LA 70001
(504) 831-2885

New York
Snelling and Snelling Agency
25 Victory Blvd.
Staten Island, NY
(212) 273-1222

Pittsburgh
International Business Associates
Frick Bldg.
Pittsburgh, PA 15220
(412) 281-6263

Portland, Oregon
D. Brown and Associates
610 SW Alder, St. 1111
Portland, OR 97205
(503) 224-6860

San Diego
Robert Half Employment Agency
409 Camino Del Rio South
Suite 305
San Diego, CA 92111
(619) 291-7990

San Francisco
Pacific Rim Human Resources Service
690 Market St., Ste. 625
San Francisco, CA
(415) 956-6250

Washington, D.C.
Professional Search Personnel
4900 Leesburg Pike, Ste. 402
Alexandria, VA 22302
(708) 671-0010

Key American Officers in Foreign Service Posts

The U.S. Department of State and Department of Commerce maintian business representatives at over 100 embassies, consulates, and missions abroad. Many of these men and women, particularly the commerce officers, are charged specifically with assisting U.S. citizens seeking information about or contact with foreign business interests.

The Department of State provides these "job descriptions" of the officers listed by category in this appendix:

At the head of each U.S. diplomatic mission are the Chief of Mission (with the title of Ambassador, Minister, or Charge d'Affaires) and the Deputy Chief of Mission. These officers are responsible for all components of the U.S. Mission within a country, including consular posts.

At larger posts, Commercial Officers represent U.S. commercial interests within their country of assignment. Specializing in U.S. export promotion, Commercial Officers (COM) assist American businesses through arranging appointments with local businesses and government officials, providing counsel on local trade regulations, laws, and customs; identifying importers, buyers, agents, distributors, and joint venture partners for U.S. firms; and other business assistance.

At smaller posts, U.S. commercial interests are represented by Economic/Commercial Officers (ECO), who also have economic responsibilities.

Political Officers (POL) analyze and report on political developments and the potential impact on U.S. interests.

Labor Officers (LAB) follow the activities of labor organizations and can supply information on wages, non-wage costs, social security regulations, labor attitudes toward American investments, and so on.

Consular Officers (CON) extend to U.S. citizens and their property abroad the protection of the U.S. government. They maintain lists of local attorneys, act as liaison with police and other officials and have the authority to notarize documents. The Department recommends that business representatives residing overseas register with the consular officer; in troubled areas, even travelers are advised to register.

The Administrative Officer (ADM) is responsible for the normal business operations of the post, including purchasing for the post and its commissary.

Regional Security Officers (RSO) are responsible for providing physical, procedural, and personnel security services to U.S. diplomatic facilities and personnel; their responsibilities extend to providing in-country security briefings and threat assessments to business executives.

Scientific Attaches (SCI) follow scientific and technological developments in the country.

Agricultural Officers (AGR) promote the export of U.S. agricultural products and report on agricultural production and market developments in their area.

The AID Mission Director (AMD) is responsible for AID programs, including dollar and local currency loans, grants, and technical assistance.

The Public Affairs Officer (PAO) is the post's press and cultural affairs specialist and maintains close contact with the local press.

The government advises that business representatives planning a trip overseas include in their preparations a visit or telephone call to the nearest U.S. Department of Commerce District Office. The District Office can provide extensive information and assistance as well as a current list of legal holidays in the countries to be visited. If desired, the District Officer can also provide advance notice to posts abroad of the representative's visit.

The Department of State, Bureau of Diplomatic Security, can also provide current data on the security situation to interested persons planning trips abroad. Contact the Diplomatic Security Service, Overseas Support Programs Division, at (202) 647-3122.

HOW TO ADDRESS MAIL TO THESE LOCATIONS

Posts with APO/FPO Numbers:

APO/FPO Address*
Commercial Section
American Embassy
FPO New York 09526

International Address**
Commercial Section
American Embassy
P.O. Box 26431***
Manama, Bahrain

*Use domestic postage.
**Use international postage.
***Use Street Address only when P.O. Box is not supplied.

Posts without APO/FPO Numbers:

Diplomatic Pouch Address
Commercial Section
Bern
Department of State
Washington, D.C. 20521-5110
International Address
Commercial Section American Embassy Jubilaeumstras se 93
3005 Bern, Switzerland

NOTE: Do not combine any of the above forms (e.g., international plus APO/FPO addresses). This will only result in confusion and possible delays in delivery. Mail sent to the Department for delivery through its pouch system for posts with APO/FPO addresses cannot be accepted and will be returned to the sender.

ALGERIA
ALGIERS (E), 4 Chemin Cheikh
Bachir Ibrahimi; B.P. Box 549 1
(Alger-Gare) 6000
Tel [213](2)601-425/255/186
Telex 66047
Foreign Commercial Service
FAX [213](2)601863
Workweek: Saturday-Wednesday
  AMB: Christopher W.S. Ross
  DCM: Charles H. Brayshaw
  POL: Joseph D. Stafford, III
  ECO: David R. Burnett
  COM: Terence Flannery
  CON: Linda C. Turner
  ADM: Walter Greenfield
  RSO: Robert J. Recca
  ATO: Besa Kotati
  PAO: C. Edward Bernier
  ODA: Col. Allan Ingalls USA

ORAN (C), 14 Square de Bamako
Tel [213](6)334509 and 335499
Telex 22310 ACORN
Workweek: Saturday-Wednesday

PO: George S. Dragnich
CON: Diane W. Shelby

ANTIGUA AND BARBUDA
ST. JOHNS (E), FPO Miami
34054
Tel (809) 462-3505/06
Telex 2140 USEMB
FAX (809) 461-4771
  AMB: (Vacant)
  CHG: R. James McHugh
  ECO: Eric Sandberg
  CON: Ann Syrette
  COM: Stephen Helgesen (resident
    in Port-of-Spain)
  LAB: Charles R. Hare (resident in
    Bridgetown)
  ADM: Annette J. Moore
  RSO: George W. Goodrich III
    (resident in Bridgetown)
  PAO: Frank Chiancone (resident in
    Bridgetown)
  IRS: Tom R. Edward (resident in
    Caracas)
  AID: James S. Holtaway (resident
    in Bridgetown)

ARGENTINA

BUENOS AIRES (E), 4300
Colombia, 1425
APO Miami 34034
Tel [54](1)774-7611/8811/9911
Telex 18156 AMEMBAR
  AMB: Terence A. Todman
  DCM: Thomas A. Forbord
  POL: James D. Walsh
  ECO: Emil Castro
  COM: Rafael Fermoselle
  LAB: Donald R. Knight
  CON: Thomas L. Holladay
  ADM: Sandor Johnson
  RSO: Edward F. Gaffney
  SCI: Robert G. Morris
  AGR: Marvin L. Lehrer
  PAO: Frederic A. Coffey
  ODA: Col. Kenneth J. Monroe
    USAF
  MILGP: Col. George A. Carpenter
    USA
  IRS: Vincent Gambino (resident in
    Sao Paulo)

AUSTRALIA

CANBERRA (E), Moonah Pl.,
Canberra, A.C.T. 2600
APO San Fran 96404
Tel [61](62) 705000
Telex 62104 USAEMB
  AMB: (Vacant)
  CHG: E. Gibson Lanpher
  POL: John E. Kelley
  ECO: Tain P. Tompkins
  LAB: Robert E. Snyder
  CON: Elizabeth A. Schoppe
  ADM: Herbert W. Schulz
  MNL: James M. McGlinchey
  RSO: David R. Haag
  SCI: Donald R. Cleveland
  AGR: James V. Parker
  PAO: Lewis R. Luchs
  ODA: Col. R. Dean Stickell USAF

MELBOURNE (CG), 24 Albert
Rd., South Melbourne, Victoria
3205
APO San Fran 96405
Tel [61](3) 697-7900
FAX CG [61](3) 699-2608, FAX
USIS 690-2585
  CG: J. Richard Bock
  COM: (Vacant)
  CON: Sandra A. Stevens
  ADM: Cecilia B. Elizondo
  BPAO: John M. Keller

SYDNEY (CG), 36th Fl.,
Electricity House Cnr. Park and
Elizabeth Sts., Sydney N.S.W.
2000
APO San Fran 96209
Tel [61](2) 261-9200
Telex 74223 FCSSYD
FAX Admin [61](2) 264-9908,
FAX FCS 261-8148, FAX USIS
264-1719
  CG: Philip T. Lincoln, Jr.
  COM: Robert Taft
  CON: Robert J. Chevez
  ADM: Edward M. Harkness
  BPAO: Margaret Eubank
  IRS: William Voyzey

PERTH (CG), 13th Fl., 16 St.
Georges Terr.
Mail: P.O. Box 6044, East Perth
WA 6004
APO San Fran 96211
Tel [61](9) 221-1177
FAX [61](9) 325-3569
  CG: William H. Itoh
  COM: Charles M. Reese
  CON: Louis A. McCall
  BPAO: John F. Cannon
  COMSEVENTHFLT REPWA:
    Cdr. J.J. Gorman, Jr.

BRISBANE (C), 383 Wickham
Ter., Brisbane, Queensland 4000
APO San Fran 96211
Tel [61](7) 839-8955
Telex 145695 AMCON B
  PO: Frontis B. Wiggins

AUSTRIA

VIENNA (E), Boltzmanngasse
16, A-1091, Vienna
APO NY 09108
Tel [43](222) 31-55-11
Telex 114634
FAX [43](222) 330-8486/7
Consular Section:
Gartenbaupromenade 2, 4th
Floor, 1010 Vienna
Tel [43](222) 51451
  AMB: Henry A. Grunwald
  DCM: Michael J. Habib
  POL: Joseph C. Snyder III
  ECO: Charles G. Billo
  COM: Arthur J. Reichenbach
  LAB: Francis T. Scanlon
  CON: Thomas J. Rice
  ADM: Warren P. Nixon
  RSO: Timothy W. Fountain
  AGR: Robert J. Svec
  PAO: Thomas E. O'Connor
  ODA: Col. James L. Ford USA
  CUS: Roger M. Urbanski
  INS: Robert V. Looney

US MISSION TO
INTERNATIONAL
ORGANIZATIONS IN VIENNA
(UNVIE), obersteinergasse 11,
A-1190 Vienna
Tel [43](222) 36-31-52
FAX [43](222) 369-1585
  US REP: Michael H. Newlin
  DCM: John A. Buche
  IAEA: Frederick F. McGoldrick
  UNIDO: Lucy Tamlyn
  IAEA: Maurice J. Katz
  POL ADV: Richard Hoover
  NARC ADV: Gregory B. Sprow
  CFE REP: Stephen J. Ledogar
  CSBM REP: John J. Maresca
  SR SCI ADV: Theodore S. Sherr

SALZBURG (CG), Gisalakai 51,
A-5020 Salzburg
Tel [43] (662) 28-6-01
Telex 63-31-64
  CG: John K. Bowman

BAHAMAS

NASSAU (E), Mosmar Bldg.,
Queen St.
P.O. Box N-8107
Tel [809] 322-1181 and 328-2206
Telex 20-138 AMEMB NS138
FAX (809)328-7838
  AMB: Chic Hecht
  DCM: Martin L. Cheshes
  POL: Bruce E. Thomas
  ECO/COM: William A. Kolb
  CON: James H. Lassiter
  LAB: Bob Meagher (resident in
    Washington)
  ADM: Jacquelyn O. Briggs
  RSO: Darwin Cadogan
  PAO: Mary K. Reeber
  IRS: Louis Hobbie
  NAU: James Picard
  NLO: Cdr. Glen Eckley USN
  CGLO: LCdr. James Meisner

BAHRAIN

MANAMA (E), Shaikh Isa Rd.
P.O. Box 26431
FPO NY 09526
Tel [973] 714151
Telex 9398 USATO BN
Workweek: Saturday-Wednesday
  AMB: Charles W. Hostler
  DCM: Leonard J. Lange
  POL: Tatiana Gfoeller-Volkoff
  POL/MIL: Ronald L. Faucher
  ECO: Michael Gfoeller
  COM: Richard Para
  CON: Catherine Drucker
  ADM: Bernardo Segura-Giron
  RSO: David R. Bettis
  ATO: Pitamber Devgon
  PAO: John F. Burgess
  FIN: Kevin Taecker (resident in
    Riyadh)
  SAO: Col. Larry R. Crumrine
    USAF
  IRS: W. Denis Melton (resident in
    Riyadh)
  FBO: Peter H. Dettmer

BANGLADESH

DHAKA (E), Diplomatic
Enclave, Madani AVe., Baridhara
Model Town, G.P.O. Box 323
Dhaka 1212
Tel (88)(2) 608170-79, 610091-9
Telex 642319 AEDKA BJ
FAX [880](2) 411648
Workweek: Sunday-Thursday
  AMB: Willard A. De Pree
  DCM: Charles A. Mast
  POL: Stephen R. Snow
  ECO/COM: William R. Falkner
  CON: Ruth E. Bright
  ADM: Kenneth W. Parent
  AGR: Lyle V. Sebranek (resident in
    New Delhi)
  AID: Priscilla M. Boughton
  PAO: Ray Peppers
  ODA: Maj. James A. Dunn USA
  RSO: Robert M. Brittian

BARBADOS

BRIDGETOWN (E), P.O. Box
302
Box B, FPO Miami 34054
Tel [809] 436-4950 thru 7
Telex 2259 USEMB BG1 WB
FAX (809) 429-5246
Canadian Imperial Bank of
Commerce Bldg., Broad Street,
Bridgetown, Barbados
  AMB: (Vacant)
  CHG: John E. Clark
  POL/ECO: Robert W. Beckham
  ECO: Anthony C. Newton
  CON: Luciano Mangiafico
  COM: Stephen Helgesen (resident
    in Port-of-Spain)
  LAB: (Vacant)
  ADM: Ross Cook
  RSO: George W. Goodrich III
  AGR: Lloyd Fleck (resident in
    Caracas)
  AID: Aaron Williams
  PAO: Katherine Lee
  ODA: Ltc. Armand P. Haynes USA
  MLO: Cdr. Dean W. Schopp USN

BELGIUM

BRUSSELS (E), 27 Boulevard
du Regent
B-1000 Brussels
APO NY 09667-1000
Tel [32] (2) 513-3830
Telex 846-21336
FAX [32] (2) 511-2725
  AMB: Maynard W. Glitman
  DCM: Donald J. McConnell
  POL: Thomas H. Gewecke
  ECO: Arnold J. Croddy, Jr.
  COM: James E. Winkelman
  LAB: Paul W. Hilburn, Jr.
  CON: John M. Jones
  ADM: Nicholas S. Baskey, Jr.
  RSO: Richard M. Gannon
  AGR: John M. Beshoar
  PAO: John P. Harrod
  DAO: Col. Raymond K. Bluhm, Jr.
    USA
  ODC: Col. Alfred K. Muelhoefer
    USAF
  FAA: Benjamin Demps, Jr.

US MISSION TO THE NORTH
ATLANTIC TREATY
ORGANIZATION (USNATO),
Autoroute de Zaventem
B-1110 Brussels
APO NY 09667-5028
Tel [32] (2) 242-5280
FAX (2) 242-0696, FAX USIS
(2) 242-7768
US PERM REP: Amb. William
H. Taft, IV
  DEP PERM REP/DCM: John C.
    Kornblum
  DEF ADV: David R. Nichols
  POL ADV: Craig G. Dunkerly
  ECO ADV: E. Mark Linton
  PUB AFF ADV: Barry Fulton
  ADM ADV: Col. Henry M. Reed II

US MISSION TO THE
EUROPEAN COMMUNITIES
(USEC), 40 Blvd. du Regent
B-1000 Brussels

APO NY 09667-1030
Tel [32] (2) 513-4450
Telex 21336
FAX (2) 511-2092
  AMB: Thomas M.T. Niles
  DCM: Michael E.C. Ely
  POL COUNS: Joanna W. Martin
  ECO COUNS: Joel S. Spiro
  PUB AFF COUNS: David M.
    Wilson
  AGR MIN COUNS: Edmund L.
    Nichols
  CUSTOMS ATT: Alice M. Rigdon
  TRADE POL OFF: Christopher P.
    Marcich
  INDUST OFF: Alan R. Tousignant
  LAB: Dan E. Turnquist
  SCI/TECH AFF: Patricia A. Haigh

ANTWERP (CG), Rubens
Center, Nationalestraat 5, B-2000
Antwerp
APO NY 09667-1040
Tel [32] (03) 225-0071
Telex 31966
FAX (3) 234-3698
  CG: Sheldon I. Krebs
  POL: Alison Pentz
  ECO/COM: Jerome B. Neal
  CON: Lois A. Price
  BPAO: (Vacant)

EUROPEAN LOGISTICAL
SUPPORT OFFICE (ELSO -
Antwerp), Noorderlaan
147, Bus 12A, B-2030 Antwerp
APO New York 09667-1046
Tel [32] (3) 542-4775
Telex 34964
FAX [32] (3) 542-6567
  DIR: Clifford W. Mecklenburg
  DEP DIR: James O. Mazingo

SHAPE (POLAD) B-7010
SHAPE, Belgium
APO NY 09088
Tel [32] (65) 445-000
POLAD: Herbert D. Gelber

BELIZE
BELIZE CITY (E), Gabourel
Lane and Hutson St.
P.O. Box 286
Tel [501] (2) 77161
FAX [501] (2) 30802
  AMB: Robert G. Rich, Jr.
  DCM: Joseph E. Hayes
  POL: Alexander Featherstone
  ECO/COM: Katherine Christensen
  CON: Rudolph F. Boone
  ADM: Charles H. Grover
  AID: Mosina Jordan
  ODA: Maj. Randall R. Parish USA
  MLO: Maj. Jerry R. Croghan USA
  VOA: Frederick Haney
  AGR: John Jacobs (resident in
    Guatemala City)
  RSO: Jerry Wilson (resident in
    Guatemala City)

BENIN
COTONOU (E), Rue Caporal
Anani Bernard
B.P. 2012
Tel [229] 30-06-50
  AMB: Walter E. Stadtler
  ECO/COM: Michele J. Sison
  CON: Michael I. Dane
  ADM: James H. Webb
  RSO: Kevin O'Neil (resident in
    Lome)
  PAO: Herman W. Henning
  AID: Mark Wentling (resident in
    Lome)
  ATO: Alan Hemphill (resident in
    Lagos)
  ODA: Col. Roby M. Mauk USA
    (resident in Abidjan)

BERMUDA
HAMILTON (CG), Vallis Bldg.,
Front St.
P.O. Box 325, Hamilton HMBX
AMCON FPO NY 09560
Tel (809) 295-1342
  CG: James M. Medas
  CON: Lili Ming

LAB: Charles R. Hare (resident in
  Bridgetown)
POL/ECO: David A. Denny
ADM: Herbert T. Mitchell, Jr.
IRS: James Rideoutte (resident in
  Nassau)
RSO: Steven Cox (resident in
  Ottawa)

BOLIVIA

LA PAZ (E), Banco Popular Del
Peru Bldg., Corner of Calles
Mercado and Colon
P.O. Box 425 La Paz
APO Miami 34032
Tel [591] (2) 350251, 350120
Telex AMEMB BV 3268
FAX [591] (2) 359875
  AMB: Robert S. Gelbard
  DCM: David N. Greenlee
  POL: James C. Cason
  ECO/COM: Leslie Sternberg
  LAB: Gregory L. Berry
  CON: Roger J. Daley
  ADM: Russell R. King
  IRS: Vincent Gambino (resident in
    Sao Paulo)
  RSO: Dale A. Karlen
  AGR: Gary C. Groves (resident in
    Lima)
  AID: Reginald Van Raalte
  PAO: James T.L. Dandridge
  NAU: Brian R. Stickney
  IAGS: Charles Klimicek
  DAO: Col. Charles Hogan USAF
  MILGP: Col. George Allport II
    USA

BOTSWANA

GABORONE (E), P.O. Box 90
Tel [267] 353-982
Telex 2554 AMEMB BD
FAX [267] 353-982, x313
after hours: Tel [267] 312-960
  AMB: John F. Kordek
  DCM: Johnnie Carson
  POL/ECO: Douglas R. Kramer
  CON/COM: Ken McGee

LAB: Raymond J. Pardon (resident
  in Johannesburg)
MNL: Robert McSwain (resident
  in Johannesburg)
ADM: Frederick B. Cook
RSO: Kim T. Starke
AGR: Roger F. Puterbaugh
  (resident in Pretoria)
AID: John P. Hummon
PAO: Betty Ann Felthousen
OMC: Maj. Gary Walker
ODA: Ltc. Kim J. Henningsen
  USA (resident in Harare)

BRAZIL

BRASILIA (E), Avenida das
Nacoes, Lote 3
APO Miami 34030
Tel [55] (61) 321-7272
Telex 061-1091
FAX [55] (61) 225-9136
  AMB: (Vacant)
  CHG: James Ferrer, Jr.
  POL: John F. Keane
  ECO: Gordon Jones
  FIN: Matthew P. Hennesey
  COM: Kevin C. Brennan
  CON: Edward L. Beffel
  ADM: Jeremy Nice
  RSO: Thomas C. Allsbury
  SCI: Barbara J. Tobias
  AGR: Robert J. Wicks
  PAO: Robert F. Jordan
  ODA: Bg. Joseph S. Stringham
    USA
  MLO: Col. Vibert L. Strock USAF
  AID: Howard B. Helman
  NAU: John W. Corris, Jr.

RIO DE JANEIRO (CG),
Avenida Presidente Wilson, 147
APO Miami 34030
Tel [55] (21) 292-7117
Telex AMCONSUL 21-22831
USIS Telex 21-21466
FAX [55] (21) 533-3455
  CG: Louis Schwartz, Jr.
  POL: Daniel A. Strasser
  ECO: Edward Olson

COM: W. Kelly Joyce, Jr.
CON: Clyde Bishop
MLO: Cdr. Guy W. Wicks
DAO: Cdr. Bruce E. Holdt
RES: Gil Johnson
ADM: Manuel F. Acosta
AGR: Marcus E. Lower
BPAO: David Wagner
FAA: Raymond Ybarra
RSO: Craig P. Decampli

SAO PAULO (CG), Rua Padre
Joao Manoel, 933, 01411
P.O. Box 8063
APO Miami 34030
Tel [55] (11) 881-6511
Telex 11-31574
USIS Telex 21-21466
FAX [55] (11) 852-9949
  CG: Myles R. Frechette
  POL: Donald B. Harrington
  ECO: Ralph M. Buck
  COM: Albert Alexander
  LAB: James J. Ehrman
  CON: Joan E. Garner
  ADM: Edmund E. Atkins
  AGR: Joseph F. Somers
  BPAO: C. Sigrid Maitrejean
  IRS: Vincent Gambino

U.S. TRADE CENTER, Edificio
Eloy Chaves Avenida Paulista,
2439, Sao Paulo
APO Miami 34030
Tel (11) 853-2011/2411/2778
Telex 011-25274
  DIR: Arthur Trezise
  AGR: Joseph F. Somers

PORTO ALEGRE (C), Rua
Coronel Genuino, 421 (9th Fl.)
APO Miami 34030
Tel [55] (512) 26-4288/4697
Telex 051-2292 CGEU BR
  PO: Marianne M. Kunkel
  CON: Bennett Y. Lowenthal
  BPAO: Merrie D. Blocker

RECIFE (C), Rua Goncalves
Maia, 163
APO Miami 34030
Tel [55] (81) 221-1412
Telex 081-1190
  PO: Leslie V. Rowe
  CON: Richard G. Rosenman
  BPAO: Martin E. Adler

BRUNEI
BANDAR SERI BEGAWAN (E),
P.O. Box 2991
Tel [673] (2) 29670
Telex BU 2609 AMEMB
  AMB: Thomas C. Ferguson
  ECO/COM: James P. Wojtasiewicz
  CON/ADM: Dennis A. Droney
  AGR: Geoffrey W. Wiggins
    (resident in Singapore)
  PAO: James Pollock (resident in
    Singapore)
  ODA: Capt. George W. Lundy, Jr.
    USN (resident in Singapore)
  RSO: John Chernyak (resident in
    Kuala Lumpur)

BULGARIA
SOFIA (E), 1A. Stamboliski Blvd.
APO NY 09213
Tel [359] (2) 88-48-01 to 05
Telex 22690 BG
  AMB: Sol Polansky
  DCM: William D. Montgomery
  POL/ECO: Douglas Ray Smith
  ECO/COM: Michael Gelner
  CON: Johathan J. Coyne
  ADM: Peter W. Bodde
  RSO: Kevin W. Bauer
  AGR: Steve Washenko (resident in
    Belgrade)
  PRESS/CULT: John Menzies
  ODA: Col. John M. Handley USA
  IRS: Frederick Pablo (resident in
    Rome)

BURKINA FASO

OUAGADOUGOU (E), B.P. 35
Tel [226] 30-67-23/24/25,
33-34-22
Telex AMEMB 5290 BF
USAID FAX [226] 30-89-03
  AMB: David H. Shinn
  DCM: Robert M. Beecroft
  POL/ECO/COM: David C. Becker
  ADM: Walter J. Wooline
  AID: Herbert N. Miller
  PAO: Cynthia B. Caples
  POL/MIL: Michael E. Dougherty
  LAB: Ollie P. Anderson, Jr.
    (resident in Washington)
  RSO: Anthony Richards (resident
    in Niamey)
  ODA: Col. Roby M. Mauk USA
    (resident in Abidjan)

BURMA

RANGOON (E), 581 Merchant
St. (GPO Box 521)
AMEMBASSY, Box B, APO San
Fran 96346
Tel 82055 or 82181
Telex 21230 AIDRGN BM
  AMB: Burton Levin
  DCM: Christopher J. Szymanski
  POL/ECO: Marshall P. Adair
  COM: Shirlie C. Pinkham
  CON: Shelley E. Johson
  ADM: Leonard J. Porter
  RSO: Michael T. Manegan
  AID: Earl J. Young
  PAO: John A. Fredenburg
  ODA: Col. John B. Haseman USA

BURANDI

BUJUMBURA (E), B.P. 1720,
Avenue Du Zaire
Tel 234-54 thru 56
  AMB: James Daniel Phillips
  DCM: David B. Dunn
  ECO: Cornelia P.J. Miller
  COM: Jean C. Kruse
  ADM: Herbert R. Brown
  CON: James M. Warrick

  RSO: Joseph Davidson
  AID: Donald F. Miller
  PAO: Lucy H. Hall
  ODA: Col. Paul J. Wenzel USA
    (resident in Kinshasa)

CAMEROON

YAOUNDE (E), Rue Nachtigal
B.P. 817
Tel [237] 234014
Telex 8223KN
  AMB: Mark L. Edelman
  DCM: Edward P. Brynn
  POL: Roger J. Moran
  ECO/COM: Janet R. Malkemes
  CON: Mary Beth Leonard
  ADM: Harry E. Young, Jr.
  RSO: George Rodman, Jr.
  AGR: Thomas Pomeroy (resident
    in Lagos)
  AID: Jay P. Johnson
  PAO: James M. Haley
  ODA: Ltc. Steven A. Lovasz USA

DOUALA (C), 21 Avenue du
General De Gaulle
B.P. 4006
Tel [237] 425331, 423434
Telex 5233 KN
  PO: William R. Gaines
  BPAO: David R. Gilmour
  POL/ECO: Geeta Pasi

CANADA

OTTAWA, ONTARIO (E), 100
Wellington St., KIP 5T1
P.O. Box 5000, Ogdensburg, NY
13669-0430
Tel (613) 238-5335
FAX (613) 233-8511
  AMB: Edward N. Ney
  CHG: Dwight N. Mason
  POL: Robert J. Montgomery
  ECO: James R. Tarrant
  COM: James L. Blow
  LAB: Arlen R. Wilson
  FIN: Carl Lohmann
  CON: Leonard F. Willems

SCI: Francis M. Kinnelly
ADM: Eric J. Boswell
RSO: Steven Cox
AGR: Bryant H. Wadsworth
PAO: James P. Thurber
CUS: William Laverty
ODA: Col. George Manolis USAF
IRS: Joe D. Hook

CALGARY, ALBERTA (CG),
Suite 1000, 615 Macleod Trail,
S.E., Calgary, Alberta, Canada
T2G 4T8
Tel (403) 265-2116 or 266-8962
FAX (403) 264-6630
CG: Robert J. Kott
CON: Dennis W. Merz
ADM: Ann M. Evans
COM: Thomas K. Roesch
ECO: Patricia Foran

HALIFAX, NOVA SCOTIA
(CG), Suite 910, Cogswell Tower,
Scotia Sq., Halifax, NS, Canada
B3J 3K1
Tel (902) 429-2480-1
FAX (902) 423-6361
CG: James D. Walsh
CON: Barbara J. Baden

MONTREAL, QUEBEC (CG),
P.O. Box 65, Postal Station
Desjardins, H5B 1G1
P.O. Box 847, Champlain, NY
12919-0847
Tel (514) 281-1886
FAX (514) 281-1072
CG: Andrew F. Antippas
ECO: John P. Riley
COM: Geoffrey Walser
CON: David L. Boerigter
ADM: Melvin T. Spence
BPAO: Veda Wilson

US MISSION TO THE
INTERNATIONAL CIVIL
AVIATION ORGANIZATION
(ICAO), 1000 Sherbrooke, W.
Rm. 753, Montreal
Mailing address: Box 847,
Champlain, NY 12919
Tel (514) 285-8304
US REP: Edmund P.C. Stohr
ALT US REP: John S. Jamison
ALT FIC/JCS REP: David L.
Schiele

QUEBEC, QUEBEC (CG), 2
Place Terrasse, C.P. 939, G1R 4T9
Tel (418) 692-2095
Telex 051-2275
CG: Robert M. Maxim
CON: Douglas M. Griffiths

TORONTO, ONTARIO (CG),
360 University Ave., M5g 1S4
P.O. Box 135, Lewiston, NY
14092-0135
Tel (416) 595-5412
FAX (416) 595-5419
CG: John E. Hall
ECO: Leonard A. Hill
COM: Dale V. Slaght
CON: Ralph L. Nider
ADM: WIlliam N. Campbell
BPAO: John A. Quintus

VANCOUVER, BRITISH
COLUMBIA (CG), 1075 West
Georgia St., V6E 4E9
P.O. Box 5002, Point Roberts,
WA 98281-5002
Tel (604) 685-4311
FAX (604) 685-5285
CG: Samuel C. Fromowitz
ECO: Jack P. Orlando
COM: (Vacant)
CON: David P. Bocskor
BPAO: David F. Fitzgerald

REPUBLIC OF CAPE VERDE

PRAIA (E), Rua Hojl Ya Yenna 81
C.P. 201
Tel [238] 614-363 or 614-253
Telex 6068 AMEMB CV
  AMB: Vernon D. Penner, Jr.
  CON: Daniel M. Hirsch
  ADM: John Olson
  RSO: Michael LaFranchi (resident in Lisbon)
  AID: Thomas C. Luche
  LAB: Ollie P. Anderson, Jr. (resident in Washington)
  ODA: Cdr. Ronald Railsback USN (resident in Monrovia)

CENTRAL AFRICAN REPUBLIC

BANGUI (E), Avenue President Dacko
B.P. 924
Tel 61-02-00, 61-25-78, 61-43-33
Telex 5287 RC
FAX [190] (236) 61-44-94
  AMB: David C. Fields
  DCM: Mary B. Marshall
  POL: Eileen G. Swicker
  ECO/COM/CON: Willem H. Brakel
  GSO: Sarah F. Drew
  ADM: Christopher E. Wittmann
  RSO: Mark Kellinger
  PAO: Victoria A. Rose
  ODA: Col. Paul J. Wenzel USA (resident in Kinshasa)

CHAD

N'DJAMENA (E), Ave. Felix Eboue
B.P. 413
Tel [235] (51) 62-18, 40-09
Telex 5203 KD
  AMB: Robert L. Pugh
  DCM: Robert S. Ayling
  POL/CON: Louis J. Nigro
  POL/MIL: George S. Swicker

  ECO/COM: Richard J. Harvey
  ADM: Terrence P. McCulley
  RSO: Mark W. Caldwell
  AID: Bernard Wilder
  PAO: Christopher Fitzgerald
  ODA: Col. David G. Foulds USA

CHILE

SANTIAGO (E), Codina Bldg., 1343 Agustinas
APO Miami 34033
Tel [56] (2) 710133/90 and 710326/75
Telex 240062-USA-CL
FAX [56] (2) 699-1141
  AMB: Charles A. Gillespie, Jr.
  DCM: David N. Greenlee
  POL: Ronald D. Godard
  ECO: Glen R. Rase
  LAB: Nancy M. Mason
  CON: William H. Barkell
  ADM: Daniel A. Johnson
  COM: Richard R. Ades
  RSO: Lawrence H. Liptak
  AGR: Robert H. Curtis
  PAO: James T.L. Dandridge II
  ODA: Capt. Robert W. Peterson USN
  IRS: Vincent Gambino (resident in Sao Paulo)
  AID: Paul W. Fritz
  APHIS: Herbert L. Murphy

CHINA

BEIJING (E), Xiu Shui Bei Jie 3 100600, PRC. Box 50
FPO San Fran 96655-0001
Tel [86] (1) 532-3831
Telex AMEMB CN 22701
FAX [86] (1) 532-3178
  AMB: James R. Lilly
  DCM: B. Lynn Pascoe
  POL: Donald W. Keyser
  ECO: James A. Larocco
  COM: Timothy P. Stratford
  CON: Kathryn Dee Robinson
  ADM: Dorothy M. Sampas
  RSO: Frederic C. Brandt

SCI: William W. Thomas, Jr.
AGR: Edwin A. Bauer
ATO: Jonathan P. Gressel
PAO: McKinney H. Russell
ODA: Bg. John A. Leide USA

GUANGZHOU (CG), Dong
Fang Hotel, Liu Hua Road
Box 100, FPO San Fran
96655-0002
Tel [86] (20) 669900 (ext. 1000)
Telex GZDFHCN 44439
  CG: Mark S. Pratt
  POL: David J. Keegan
  ECO: John T. Tkacik, Jr.
  CON: Anthony Leggio
  COM: Todd N. Thurwachter
  ADM: Roberto Brady
  BPAO: Richard Stites
  ATO: Philip A. Shull

SHANGHAI (CG), 1469 Huai
Hai Middle Rd.
Box 200, FPO San Fran 96655
Tel [86] (21) 336-880
Telex 33383 USCG CN
  CG: Frank P. Wardlaw
  POL: Jonathan M. Aloisi
  COM: Nora Sun
  ECO: John J. Norris, Jr.
  CON: David C. Chang
  ADM: John B. Hitchcock
  BPAO: William R. Palmer III
  RSO/GSO: John A. Hurley III

SHENYANG (CG), 40 Lane 4,
Section 5, Sanjing St., Heping
District
Box 45, FPO San Fran
96655-0002
Tel [86] (24) 290000
Telex 80011 AMCS CN
  CG: C. Eugene Dorris
  ECO: Stephen R. Fox
  COM: Richard Mohr
  CON/POL: Laurent D. Charbonnet
  ADM: Robert Wilson
  BPAO: Nora Harris

CHENGDU (CG), Jinjiang Hotel,
180 Renmin Rd., Chengdu,
Sichuan, Box 85, FPO San Fran
96655-0002
Tel [86] (028) 24481, ext. 131,
135, 138, 141, 130, respectively
Telex 60128 ACGCH CN
FAX [86] (028) 583-520
  CG: Jan DeWilde
  POL: Kenneth H. Jarrett
  CON: Glen Carey
  ADM: Kenneth Cohen
  BPAO: A. Mark Crocker

COLUMBIA

BOGOTA (E), Calle 38, No. 8-61
P.O. Box A.A. 3831
APO Miami 34038
Tel [57] (1) 285-1300/1688
Telex 44843
FAX [571] 288-5687
  AMB: Thomnas E. McNamara
  DCM: J. Phillip McLean
  POL: Gerald C. McCulloch
  ECO: Robert B. McMullen
  COM: Peter T. Noble
  CON: David L. Hobbs
  LAB: Eduardo J. Baez
  ADM: Christopher H. Swenson
  RSO: Wallace R. Williams
  AGR: Larry M. Senger
  PAO: Howard A. Lane
  NAU: James V. Doane, Jr.
  ODA: Col. Eugene E. Bouley, Jr.
    USA
  AID: James F. Smith
  MAAG: Col. Manuel Torres USA

BARRANQUILLA (C), Calle 77
Carrera 68, Centro Comercial
Mayorista
P.O. Box A.A. 51565
APO Miami 34038
Tel [57] (5) 45-7088/7560
Telex 33482 AMCO CO
FAX [57] (58) 45964
  PO: Ross E. Benson
  ADM/CON: Anne Hall

COMOROS

MORONI (E), Boite Postale 1318
Tel 73-12-03
Telex 257 AMEMB KO
AMB: Harry K. Walker (resident in
Antananarivo)
CHG: Karl I. Danga
ADM/CON: William Carlson
DEF ATT: Cdr. William Feallock
(resident in Antananarivo)
RSO: Phil A. Whitney (resident in
Antananarivo)
PAO: Marilyn Hulbert (resident in
Antananarivo)

PEOPLE'S REPUBLIC OF CONGO

BRAZZAVILLE (E), Avenue
Amilcar Cabral
B.P. 1015
Box C, APO NY 09662-0006
Tel 80-20-72, 83-26-24
Telex 5367 KG
AMB: Leonard G. Shurtleff
DCM: Roger A. Meece
CON: Lynn Gutensohn
ECO: Alexander G. Andrews, Jr.
COM: James Strudwick
ADM: Elizabeth D. Thompson
RSO: Nanette Krieger (resident in
Kinshasa)
AID: Nell Diallo
PAO: Miriam Guichard
ODA: Maj. Karl Prinslow USA

COSTA RICA

SAN JOSE (E), Pavas, San Jose
APO Miami 34020
Tel [506] 20-39-39
FAX [506] 20-2305
AMB: Deane R. Hinton
DCM: J. Todd Stewart
POL: John R. Hamilton
ECO: John R. Dawson
Com: Judith Henderson
LAB: Frederick A. Becker
(resident in Panama)
CON: Donna J. Hamilton

RSO: Richard J. Watts
ADM: Robert L. Graninger
AGR: Lana Bennett
AID: Carl H. Leonard
PAO: Louise K. Crane
ODC: Ltc. Raul J. Colon USA

COTE D'IVOIRE (formerly Ivory Coast)

ABIDJAN (E), 5 Rue Jesse
Owens
01 B.P. 1712
Tel [225] 21-09-79 or 21-46-72
Telex 23660
FAX [225] 22-32-59
AMB: Dennis Kux
DCM: Hugh G. Hamilton, Jr.
ECO: Janice Price
POL: Thomas Price
COM: Gene Harris
CON: Vincent J. Rizzo
ADM: Elaine B. Schunter
RSO: Bernie M. Indahl
AGR: Richard J. Blabey
AID/REDSO: Arthur Fell
AID/RHUDO: Stephen Giddings
PAO: Robert Peterson
ODA: Col. Jerry R. Fry USA

AFRICAN DEVELOPMENT
BANK/FUND, Ave. Joseph
Anoma
01 B.P. 1387 Abidjan 01
Tel [225] 33-14-34
EXEC DIR: Mima S. Nedelcovych
ALT DIR: Stephen P. Donovan

CUBA

HAVANA (USINT), Swiss
Embassy, Calzada entre L Y M,
Vedado Seccion
2d Class Mailing Address:
USINT c/o International
Purchasing Group, 2052 NW93rd
Ave., Miami, FL 33172
Tel 320551, 320543
TELEX 512206

PO: John J. Taylor
DPO: L. Bradley Hittle
CON: William J. Brencick
ADM: Frank Rey, Jr.
RSO: Frederick A. Byron
PAO: David Evans

CYPRUS
NICOSIA (E), Therissos St. and
Dositheos St.
FPO NY 09530
Tel [357] (2) 465151
Telex 4160 AME CY
FAX [357] (2) 495-571
AMB: Bill K. Perrin
DCM: John U. Nix
POL: Eric Tunis
ECO/COM: Michael A. Meigs
CON: John Spiegel
ADM: Robert J. McAnneny
RSO: William Gaskill
PAO: Lane T. Cubstead
AGR: Mollie Iler (resident in
Athens)
ODA: Ltc. Stephen R. Norton USA
IRS: Frederick Pablo (resident in
Rome)

CZECHOSLOVAKIA
PRAGUE (E), Trziste 15-12548
Praha
Amembassy Prague, c/o
Amcongen (PRG), APO NY
09213 (PRG)
Tel [42] (2) 53 6641/9
Telex 121196 AMEMBC
AMB: Shirley Temple Black
DCM: Theodore E. Russell
POL: Clifford G. Bond
ECO: Harvey D. Lampert
COM: Janet G. Speck
CON: Richelle Keller
ADM: Steven J. White
RSO: Robert V. Daly
AGR: Robert J. Svec (resident in
Vienna)
PAO: Thomas Hull
ODA: Col. Edwin J. Motyka

DENMARK
COPENHAGEN (E), Dag
Hammarskjolds Alle 24
2100 Copenhagen O or APO NY
09170
Tel [45] (31) 42-31-44
Telex 22216 AMEMB DK
FAX (35) 43-02-23
AMB: Keith L. Brown
DCM: Ronald D. Flack
POL: Ward C. Thompson
ECO: Dennis A. Sandberg
COM: Robert Connan
LAB: Marc E. Northern
CON: Robert L. Fretz
ADM: Richard Smyth
RSO: Tony R. Bell
AGR: Anthony Cruit
PAO: Marry Ellen Connell
ODA: Capt. Michael C. Tiernan
USN
ODC: Col. Carl Lyday USAF
IRS: Robert Tobin (resident in
London)

REPUBLIC OF DJIBOUTI
DJIBOUTI (E), Plateau du
Serpent, Blvd. Marechal Joffre
B.P. 185
Tel [253] 35-39-95
FAX [253] 35-39-40
Workweek: Sunday-Thursday
AMB: Robert S. Barrett IV
DCM: John E. McAteer
POL: John H. Winant
ECO/COM: Thomas M. Murphy
LAB: Harry J. O'Hara (resident in
Nairobi)
ADM/CON: Sharon A. Lavorel
RSO: Steven Iverson
USLO: Maj. Reid Trummel
IRS: W. Dennis Melton (resident in
Riyadh)

DOMINICAN REPUBLIC
SANTO DOMINGO (E), Corner
of Calle Cesar Nicolas Penson &
Calle Leopoldo Navarro
APO Miami 34041-0008
Tel [809] 541-2171
  AMB: Paul D. Taylor
  DCM: Patricia A. Langford
  POL: David E. Randolph
  ECO: Robert J. Smolik
  COM: Lawrence Eisenberg
  CON: James L. Ward
  ADM: A. Lucille Thomas
  RSO: George Mitchell
  AGR: Forrest K. Geerken
  AID: Thomas W. Stukel
  PAO: Sheldon H. Avenius
  ODA: Ltc. Lynn J. Kimball USN
  MAAG: Col. Ramon Quijano, Jr.
    USA

ECUADOR
QUITO (E), Avenida 12 de
Octubre y Avenida Patria
P.O. Box 538
APO Miami 34039
Tel [593] (2) 562-890
FAX [593] (2) 502-052
  AMB: Richard H. Holwill
  DCM: Adolph H. Eisner
  POL: Hugh Simon, Jr.
  ECO: John R. Savage
  COM: Peter B. Alois
  LAB: Laurie Tracy
  CON: Carmen Maria Martinez
  ADM: J. Richard Mason
  RSO: Linda K. Fleetwood-Kincer
  AGR: Elizabeth B. Berry
  AID: Frank Almaguer
  PAO: Gregory Lagana
  ODA: Col. Michael E. Ryan USA
  MILGP: Col. James Proctor USA
  NAU: Yvonne F. Thayer

GUAYAQUIL (CG), 9 de
Octubre y Garcia Moreno
APO Miami 34039
Tel [593] (4) 323-570

Telex: 04-3452 USICAG ED
  CG: Ralph T. Jones
  CON: Nick Hahn
  ADM: Charles E. Nichols

EGYPT (ARAB REPUBLIC OF)
CAIRO (E), Lazougi St., Garden
City
FPO NY 09527
Tel [20] (2) 355-7371
Telex 93773 AMEMB
FAX [20] 355-7375
Workweek: Sunday-Thursday
  AMB: Frank G. Wisner
  DCM: Mark Johnson
  POL: Ryan C. Crocker
  ECO: G. Paul Balabanis
  COM: Frederic Gaynor
  LAB: Gina Abercrombie- Winstanley
  CON: Vincent M. Battle
  ADM: James McGunnigle
  RSO: Peter Bergin
  AID: Marshall D. Brown
  PAO: Kenton Keith
  AGR: Franklin D. Lee
  ODA: Col. David L. Lemon USA
  OMC: Mg. William A. Fitzgerald,
    Jr. USA
  IRS: W. Dennis Melton (resident in
    Riyadh)
  FBO: Kegham Shiranian

ALEXANDRIA (CG), 110 Ave.
Horreya
FPO NY 09527
Tel [20](3) 482-1911, 825607
Workweek: Sunday-Thursday
  CG: Robert M. Maxim
  CON/POL: Daniel Goodspeed
  ADM: Stephen Cromwell
  BPAO: Nabeel Khoury
  AID: Paul Rusby

EL SALVADOR
SAN SALVADOR (E), 25
Avenida Norte No. 1230
APO Miami 34023

Tel [503] 26-7100
FAX [503] 265839
  AMB: William G. Walker
  DCM: William J. Dieterich
  POL: Stephen G. McFarland
  ECO/COM: Richard Bash
  LAB: Leslie Ann Bassett
  CON: Nicholas J. Ricciuti
  ADM: Guido Del Prado
  RSO: Anthony Walters
  AGR: John Jacobs (resident in
    Guatemala)
  AID: Henry H. Bassford
  PAO: Barry Jacobs
  ODA: Col. Wayne R. Wheeler USA
  MILGP: Col. Milton R. Menjivar
    USA

EQUATORIAL GUINEA
MALABO (E), Calle de Los
Ministros
P.O. Box 597
Tel 2406, 2507
Workweek: Monday-Friday
  AMB: Chester E. Norris, Jr.
  POL/ECO: Carl F. Troy
  ADM/CON: Jose Latour
  RSO: George Rodman, Jr. (resident
    in Yaounde)
  PAO: James M. Haley (resident in
    Yaounde)
  AID: Jay P. Johnson (resident in
    Yaounde)
  ODA: Ltc. Scott L. Hayes USA
    (resident in Yaounde)
  AGR: Thomas Pomeroy (resident
    in Lagos)

ETHIOPIA
ADDIS ABABA (E), Entoto St.
P.O. Box 1014
Tel [251] (01) 551002
Telex 21282
  CHG: Robert G. Houdek
  DCM: Robert C. Frasure
  ECO/POL: Mark C. Eaton
  POL: Ken Foster
  ADM: Gregory W. Engle
  CON: Richard J. Adams

PAO: James Haley
AID: Willard J. Pearson
RSO/GSO: Timothy O'Brien
LAB: Harry J. O'Hara (resident in
  Nairobi)
IRS: W. Dennis Melton (resident in
  Riyadh)

FIJI
SUVA (E), 31 Loftus St.
P.O. Box 218
Tel [679] 3114-466 314069
Telex 2255 AMEMBASY FJ
AMB: Leonard Rochwarger
  DCM: Michael P. Owens
  POL: Robert A. Benzinger
  ECO: Glen B. Miller
  CON: Patricia A. Murphy
  ADM: Craig S. Tymeson
  RSO: David R. Haag (resident in
    Canberra)
  AID: John B. Woods
  PAO: Robert B. Laing
  ODA: Ltc. Craig L. Mayer USMC

FINLAND
HELSINKI (E), Itainen Puistotie
14A, SF-00140
APO NY 09664
Tel [358] (0) 171931
Telex 121644 USEMB SF
Commercial Section Telex 125541
FAX [3580] 174681
  AMB: Rockwell A. Schnabel
  DCM: Michael L. Durkee
  POL: William J. Kushlis
  ECO: Lawrence E. Butler
  COM: Tapan Banerjee
  LAB: John P. Fernandez
  CON: Robert O. Tatge
  ADM: William J. Burke, Jr.
  RSO: James W. Holt
  AGR: Gordon S. Nicks (resident in
    Stockholm)
  PAO: William P. Kiehl
  ODA: Col. William A.J. Mackie
    USAF

FRANCE
PARIS (E), 2 Avenue Gabriel,
75382 Paris Cedex 08
APO NY 09777
Tel [33] (1) 42-96-12-02,
42-61-80-75
Telex 650221 AMEMB
  AMB: Walter J.P. Curley
  DCM: Mark C. Lissfelt
  POL: Miles S. Pendelton, Jr.
  ECO: William H. Edgar
  FIN: T. Whittier Warthin
  COM: James A. Moorhouse
  LAB: John J. Muth
  CON: Donald K. Parsons
  ADM: Bruce W. Clark
  RSO: William D. Clarke
  SCI: Allen L. Sessons
  AGR: Herbert F. Rudd
  PAO: Robert J. Korengold
  CUS: George C. Corcoran, Jr.
  ODA: Radm. Norman Campbell
    USN
  ODC: Col. Richard J. Beauregard
    USAF
  FAA: Robert T. Francis II
  IRS: William Connett

US MISSION TO THE
ORGANIZATION FOR
ECONOMIC COOPERATION
AND DEVELOPMENT
(USOECD), 19 Rue de
Franqueville, 75016 Paris
APO New York 09777
Tel [33] (1) 45-24-74-77
Telex 643964 F
  US REP: Amb. Denis Lamb
  DCM: Richard E. Hecklinger
  ECON/FIN: John Lange
  INT ECO: John P. Spillane
  LAB/MANPOWER/AG: Robert C.
    Friel
  TRADE DIV: Ronnie C. Woody
  AMD OFF: Michael L. Milligan
  SCI/ENV/INDUST: Daniel L.
    Dolan
  ENRG/SCI ADV: Frank J. Goldner
  US REP DAC: Martin V. Dagata

  DAC Chrmn: Joseph C. Wheeler
  IND/COM: Charles W. Wessner
  INVESTMENT ADV: James T.
    Heg
  ENERGY ADV: Charles D. Trotter
  PAO: Alfred Kennedy
  STC: Robert R. Brungart

US OBSERVER MISSION TO
THE UNITED NATIONS
EDUCATIONAL, SCIENTIFIC
AND CULTURAL
ORGANIZATION (UNESCO), 2
Avenue Gabriel, 75008 Paris
CEDEX 08
APO NY 09777
Tel [33] (1) 42-96-12-02,
42-61-80-75
Telex 650-221
  OBSERVER: Richard T. Miller

BORDEAUX (CG), 22 Cours du
Marechal Foch, 33080 Bordeaux
Cedex
APO NY 09777
Tel [33] (56) 52-65-95
Telex 540918 USCSUL
  CG: Judith M. Heimann
  CON: Pamela K. Roe

LYON (CG), 7 Quai General
Sarrail
69454 Lyon CEDEX3
Tel [33] (78) 246-849
Telex 380597 USCSUL
  CG: Ann L. Stanford
  CON: Peter Whaley

MARSEILLE (CG), 12
Boulevard Paul Peytral, 13286
Marseille Cedex
APO NY 09777
Tel (33) (91) 549-200
Telex 430597
  CG: R. Susan Wood
  CON: William R. Carlson
  ECO/COM: (Vacancy)

STRASBOURG (CG), 15 Ave. D'Alsace
67082 Strasbourg CEDEX or
APO NY 09777
Tel [33] [88] 35-31-04
Telex 870907 AMERCON
  CG: Ints M. Silins

FRENCH CARIBBEAN DEPARTMENT
MARTINIQUE (CG), 14 Rue Blenac
B.P. 561, Fort-de-France 97206
Tel [596] 63-13-03
Telex 912670
912315 MR
FAX [596] 60-20-80
  CG: Mary Dell Palazzolo
  CON: Patsy G. Stephens
  POL/ECO: (Vacant)
  LAB: Charles R. Hare (resident in Bridgetown)
  RSO: George Goodrich III (resident in Bridgetown)
  PAO: Frank A. Chiancone (resident in Bridgetown)
  ADM: (Vacant)

GABON

LIBREVILLE (E), Blvd. de la Mer
B.P. 4000
Tel [241] 762003/4, 743492
Telex 5250 GO
FAX [241] 745-507
  AMB: Warren Clark, Jr.
  DCM: Kenneth M. Scott, Jr.
  POL: William D. Barrett
  ECO/COM: Ronald K. McMullen
  CON: Mark R. Jensen
  ADM: Paul E. Rowe
  RSO: Melissa McPeak
  PAO: William F. Melvin
  ODA: Col. Paul J. Wenzel USA (resident in Kinshasa)

THE GAMBIA

BANJUL (E), Fajara, Kairaba Ave
P.M.B. No. 19, Banjul
Tel [220] 92856 or 92858, 91970, 91971
Telex 2300 GV
FAX [220] 92475
  AMB: Herbert E. Horowitz
  ADM: Mark M. Boulware
  POL/ECO/COM/CON: Linda Thomas-Greenfield
  RSO: Gregory B. Starr (resident in Dakar)
  AID: Jimmie Stone
  LAB: Anthony Kern (resident in Washington)
  ODA: Ltc. Michael J. Graf USMC (resident in Dakar)

GERMAN DEMOCRATIC REPUBLIC

BERLIN (E), 1080 Berlin, Neustaedtische Kirchstrasse 4-5
USBER Box E, APO NY 09742
Tel [37] (2) 2202741
Telex 112479 USEMB DD
  AMB: Richard C. Barkley
  DCM: J.D. Bindenagel
  POL: Jonathan G. Greenwald
  ECO/COM: Michael C. Mozur
  CON: Mary Rose Brandt
  ADM: Harry E. Young
  RSO: David B. Marshall
  AGR: Debra D. Henke
  PRESS/CULT: Jaroslav J. Verner

FEDERAL REPUBLIC OF GERMANY

BONN (E), Deichmanns Aue, 5300 Bonn 2
APO NY 09080
Tel [49] (228) 3391
Telex 885-452
  AMB: Vernon A. Walters
  DCM: George F. Ward, Jr.
  POL: Olaf Grobel
  ECO: Richard H. Imus

COM: John W. Bligh, Jr.
FIN: James G. Wallar
LAB: John A. Warnock
CON: Peter K. Murphy
ADM: Harold W.Geisel
RSO: Ronald A. Reams
SCI: Edward M. Malloy
AGR: Gerald W. Harvey
PAO: Terrence F. Catherman
CUS: Viktor Jacobson
ODA: Col. Roger Thomas Hilton USA
ODC: Col. Arthur A. Lovegren USAF
IRS: Larry J. LeGrand

BERLIN (M), Clayallee 170,
D-1000 Berlin 33 (Dahlem)
APO NY 09742
Tel [49] (30) 83240 87
Com. Unit: Tel [49] (30) 819-7561
Telex 183-701 USBER-D
  ADM: Harry J. Gilmore
  DEP: James A. Williams
  POL: Thomas H. Gerth
  ECO: David R. Pozorski
  COM: John P. Mondejar
  CON: Diane E. Henshaw
  ADM: Donald S. Hays
  RSO: Robert Brand
  BPAO: Caroline Osterling

US COMMERCIAL OFFICE
(DUSSELDORF),
Emmanuel-Leutze-Str.1B
4000 Duesseldorf 11
Tel 0211-596790
Telex 8584246 FCS

FRANKFURT AM MAIN (CG),
Siesmayerstrasse 21, 6000
Frankfurt
APO NY 09213
Tel [49] (69) 75305-0 or 75304-0
after hours: Tel [49] (69)
75305-500 or 56002-700
FAX [49] (69) 748-938

CG: Alexander L. Rattray
DPO: J. Brayton Redecker
COM: Thomas L. Boam
CON: Carl W. McCollum
ADM: Maurice N. Gralnek
RSO: Stephen Kruchko
BPAO: Craig B. Springer
POLAD: T. Patrick Killough
CINCUSAFE (resident in Ramstein)
INS: WIlliam Bryan

HAMBURG (CG), Alsterufer
27/28, 2000 Hamburg 36
APO NY 09215-0002
Tel [49] (40) 41171-0, after hours
[49] (40) 4117-1211
FAX FBU [49] (40) 443004
FAX FCS [49] (40) 4106598
FAX USIS [49] [40] 444705
US Agricultural Trade Office:
Grosse Theaterstrasse 42
Tel [49] (40) 341207
Telex 2163970 ATO D
FAX [49] [40] 341200
  CG: James C. Whitlock, Jr.
  COM: James L. Joy
  CON: Karl H. Sprick
  POL/ECON: Oliver W. Griffith
  ADM: Virginia I. Kurapka
  BPAO: Lynn M. Martin
  ATO: Dale L. Good
  RSO: James E. Dolan

MUNICH (CG), Koeniginstrasse
5, 8000 Muenchen 22
APO NY 09108
Tel [49] (89) 23011
Telex 5-22697 ACGM D
FAX [49] (89) 283-047, FCS
FAX [49] (89) 285-261
  CG: David J. Fischer
  POL: James F. Jeffrey
  COM: Edward E. Ruse III
  CON: Patricia L. Hall
  ADM: Eugene A. Trahan, Jr.
  RSO: John J. Stein, Jr.
  BPAO: Kathryn L. Koob

STUTTGART (CG),
Urbanstrasse 7, 7000 Stuttgart
APO NY 09154
Tel [49] (711) 210221
Telex 07-22945
FAX [49] (711) 241046
FAX FCS [49] (711) 234350
  CG: Douglas H. Jones
  COM: Catherine Houghton
  CON: Jane Whitney
  ADM: Robert B. Houston III
  BPAO: Samuel Westgate
  POL/ECON: Michael J.
    Springmann
  RSO: John J. Stein (resident in
    Munich)
  POLAD: Allen C. Davis
    USCINCEUR (resident in
    Vaihingen)
  POLAD: David A. Betts
    CINCUSAREUR (resident in
    Heidelberg)

GHANA
ACCRA (E), Ring Road East
P.O. Box 194
Tel Chancery 775347, 775297/8
Tel Annex 776601/2, 776008
Telex 2579
EMBUSA GH
  AMB: Raymond C. Ewing
  DCM: John C. Holzman
  POL/ECO: John L. Berntsen
  ECO/COM: Martha N. Kelley
  CON: Richard Gonzalez
  ADM: Thomas Cross
  RSO: James Marek
  AGR: Thomas Pomeroy (resident
    in Lagos)
  AID: F. Gary Towery
  PAO: Daniel McGaffie
  ODA: Col. Clarence Grant, Jr. USA

GREECE
ATHENS (E), 91 Vasilissis
Sophias Blvd., 10160 Athens or
APO NY 09255-0006
Tel [30] (1) 721-2951 or 721-8401

Telex 21-5548
FAX [30] (1) 722-6724
  AMB: Michael G. Sotirhos
  DCM: Edward M. Cohen
  POL: Gregory L. Mattson
  POL/MIL: Angel M. Rabasa
  ECO: Michael J. Cleverley
  COM: Jerry K. Mitchell
  LAB: John L. Klekas
  CON: James F. Myrick
  ADM: Peter S. Flynn
  RSO: David G. Bowyer
  AGR: Mollie J. Iler
  PAO: Arthur S. Giuliano
  ODA: Capt. Stanley C. Kozlowski
    USN
  IRS: Frederick Pablo (resident in
    Rome)
  ODC: Bg. Edmond S. Solymosy
    USA
  INS: Anthony Lascaris

REGIONAL TRADE
DEVELOPMENT OFFICE, 91
Vasilissis Sophias Blvd. (c/o
Embassy)
THESSALONIKI (CG), 59
Leogoros Nikis, GR-546-22
Thessaloniki
APO NY 09693
Tel [30] (31) 266-121
  CG: A. Donald Bramante
  POL/ECO: Donald M. Miller
  BPAO: Stephen B. Morisseau

GRENADA
ST. GEORGE'S (E), Ross Point Inn
P.O. Box 54, St. George's,
Grenada, W.I.
Tel [809] 440-1731/4
FAX [809] 444-4820
  CHG: James F. Cooper
  POL: John A. Butler
  ECO: Eugene Tuttle
  COM: Stephen J. Helgesen
    (resident in Trinidad)
  CON: Barry L. Mark
  ADM: Roy F. Sullivan

AID: (Vacant)
LAB: Charles R. Hare (resident in
　Bridgetown)
PAO: Katherine I. Lee (resident in
　Bridgetown)
RSO: George Goodrich III
　(resident in Bridgetown)

GUATEMALA
GUATEMALA CITY (E), 7-01
Avenida de la Reforma, Zone 10
APO Miami 34024
Tel [502] (2) 31-15-41
FAX [502] (2) 318885
　AMB: James H. Michel
　DCM: Philip B. Taylor III
　POL: Thomas M. Tonkin
　ECO: Rafael L. Marin
　COM: Charles A. Ford
　LAB: Joseph G. McLean
　CON: Sue H. Patterson
　ADM: Russell L. Keeton
　RSO: Seymour C. DeWitt
　AGR: John Jacobs
　AID: Anthony J. Cauterucci
　PAO: John Treacy
　ROCAP: Nadine M. Hogan
　ODA: Col. Allen C. Cornell USA
　MILGP: Col. Armando Lujan USA

GUINEA
CONAKRY (E), 2d Blvd. and 9th
Ave.
B.P. 603, Tel 44-15-20 thru 24
　AMB: Samuel E. Lupo
　DCM: Gregory T. Frost
　POL: Patrick McHugh
　ECO/COM: F. Mark Rondon
　CON: (Vacant)
　ADM: Gerald Hanisch
　RSO: Michael G. Considine
　PAO: Louise Bedichek
　AGR: Richard J. Blabey (resident
　　in Abidjan)
　LAB: Ollie P. Anderson, Jr.
　　(resident in Washington)
　ODA: Cdr. Donald C. Railsback
　　USN (resident in Monrovia)
　AID: Byron Bahl

GUINEA-BISSAU
BISSAU (E), Avenida Domingos
Ramos
C.P. 297
Mail: Apartado 97, 1021 Bissau
Codex, Guinea-Bissau
Tel [245] 21-2816/7, 21-3674
　AMB: John Dale Blacken
　ADM: Edmee H. Pastore
　POL/ECO/CON: Gary Oba
　LAB: Ollie P. Anderson, Jr.
　　(resident in Washington)
　RSO: Greg Starr (resident in Dakar)
　AID: Anne Williams

GUYANA
GEORGETOWN (E), 31 Main St.
Tel [592] (02) 54900-9
Telex 213 AMEMSY GY
FAX [592] (1) 58497
　AMB: Theresa A. Tull
　DCM: Dennis K. Hays
　POL: Donald G. Teitelbaum
　ECO/COM: James L. Dudley
　CON: Nicholas M. Williams
　LAB: (Vacant) (resident in
　　Bridgetown)
　ADM: Edward E. Anderson
　RSO: Joseph C. Vaccarino
　AGR: Lloyd Fleck (resident in
　　Caracas)
　PAO: James D. Burns
　ODA: Ltc. Ovidio Perez (resident
　　in Paramaribo)

HAITI
PORT-AU-PRINCE (E), Harry
Truman Blvd., P.O. Box 1761
Tel [509] (1) 20354, 20368,
20200, 20612
FAX [509] (1) 39007
　AMB: Brunson McKinley
　DCM: Douglas K. Watson
　POL: Jeffrey C. Gallup
　ECO/COM: J. Gordon Dugan
　CON: Robert E. Ezelle
　ADM: Adriaen M. Morse
　RSO: Abigail E. Smith

AGR: Forrest Geerken (resident in
  Santo Domingo)
AID: Gerald Zaar
PAO: Susan A. Clyde
ODA: Maj. Robert Goyette USA

THE HOLY SEE
VATICAN CITY (E), Villino
Pacelli, Via Aurelia 294, 00165
Rome
APO NY 09794
Tel [396] 639-0558
Telex 622322 AMBRMC
  AMB: Thomas P. Melady
  DCM: James F. Creagan
  POL: Deborah Graze
  ADM: Douglas B. Leonnig
  PAO: Frank Lattanzi
  RSO: Bernhard B. Collins, Jr.

HONDORAS
TEGUCIGALPA (E), Avenido La
Paz
APO Miami 34022
Tel [504] 32-3120
FAX [504] 32-0027
  AMB: (Vacant)
  CHG: John H. Penfold
  POL: Donald C. Johnson
  ECO: Ward D. Barmon
  COM: T. Porter Clary
  LAB: Kathleen W. Barmon
  CON: Richard R. LaRoche
  ADM: Robert D. Austin
  RSO: Robert E. Benker
  AGR: John D. Jacobs (resident in
    Guatemala)
  AID: John A. Sanbrailo
  PAO: Terrence Kneebone
  ODA: Ltc. Samuel M Jones USAF
  MILGP: Col. Jose R. Feliciano
    USA

HONG KONG
HONG KONG (CG),26 Garden Rd
Box 30, FPO San Fran
96659-0002

Tel [852](5)239011
Telex 63141 USDOC HX
FAX [852](5)845-1598
  CG: Donald M. Anderson
  DPO: David G. Brown
  POL/ECO: Gilbert J. Donahue
  COM: Ying Price
  CON: John H. Adams
  INS: Jerry W. Stuchiner
  ADM: J. Michael O'Brien
  RSO: John H. Kaufmann
  AGR: Phillip C. Holloway
  PAO: Lloyd W. Neighbors
  CUS: Thomas E. Gray
  ODA: Capt. John W. Athanson USN

HUNGARY
BUDAPEST (E), V. Szabadsag
Ter 12
Am. Embassy
APO NY 09213
Tel [36](1) 112-6450
Telex 18048 224-222
Commercial Devel Ctr: Telex
227136 USCDC H
FAX 132-8934, FBO FAX
175-5924
  AMB: Mark Palmer
  DCM: Donald B. Kursch
  POL: Thomas A. Lynch
  ECO: Sandra A. Dembski
  COM: Stephen Wasylko
  CON: Elizabeth Barnett
  PRESS/CULT: Robert McCarthy
  ADM: Wayne K. Logsdon
  RSO: Kenneth Kayatin
  AGR: Robert Svec (resident in
    Vienna)
  ODA: Col. Ruth Anderson USA
  SCI: Thomas A. Schlenker
  IRS: Frederick Pablo (resident in
    Rome)

ICELAND
REYKJAVIK (E), Laufasvegur 21
FPO NY 09571-0001
Tel [354](1) 29100
Telex USEMB IS3044

AMB: L. Nicholas Ruwe
DCM: David F. Rogus
POL: Richard P. Rogers
POL/MIL: Michael H. Schwartz
ECO/COM: Jay L. Dehmlow
CON: Long N. Lee
ADM: Joseph R. Manzanares
RSO: Tony R. Bell (resident in
  Copenhagen)
PAO: William G. Crowell

INDIA

NEW DELHI (E), Shanti Path,
Chanakyapuri 110021
Tel [91](11)600651
Telex 031-65269 USEM IN
USIS Tel 331-6841 or 4251
  CHG: John R. Hubbard
  POL: George F. Sherman
  ECO: Duane C. Butcher
  COM: Melvin W. Searls, Jr.
  LAB: William R. Salisbury
  CON: Leo Wollemborg
  ADM: Bert C. Moore
  INS: Jose Salazar
  RSO: Frank E. Juni
  SCI: Peter Hydemann
  AGR: Lyle J. Sebranek
  AID: Robert N. Bakley
  PAO: Leonard Baldyga
  ODA: Col. Leon T. Hunt
  ODC: Col. Scott Fisher USAF

BOMBAY (CG), Lincoln House,
78 Bhulabhi Desai Rd. 400026
Tel [91](022)822-3611
Telex 011-75425 ACON IN
FAX [91](22)822-0350
  CG: John J. Eddy
  POL: Andrew C. Mann
  ECO: David E. Thurman
  COM: Dorothy L. Lutter
  CON: John W. Vessey III
  ADM: James D. McGee
  BPAO: Roger C. Rasco

CALCUTTA (CG), 5/1 Ho Chi
Minh Sarani, Calcutta 700071
Tel [91](033)44-3611/6

Telex 021-5982
  CG: Ronald D. Lorton
  POL/ECO: (Vacant)
  ECO/COM: James C. Newman
  CON: Richard D. Haynes
  ADM: F. Stephen Malott
  BPAO: Bruce J. Kruetzer

MADRAS (CG), Mount Rd.
600006
Tel [91](44)473-040/477-542
  CG: Thomas M.F. Timberman
  POL/ECO: Lawrence E. Cohen
  COM: Rajendra K. Dheer
  CON: Gilbert J. Sperling
  ADM: Patricia N. Moller
  BPAO: John Challinor

INDONESIA

JAKARTA (E), Medan Merdeka
Selatan 5
APO San Fran 96356
Tel [62](21)360-360
Telex 44218 AMEMB JKT
  AMB: John C. Monjo
  DCM: Michael V. Connors
  POL: Timothy M. Carney
  ECO: Bruce F. Duncombe
  COM: Paul T. Walters
  LAB: Gail P. Scott
  CON: Richard P. Livingston
  ADM: David A. Roberts
  RSO: William A. Cole
  AID: David N. Merrill
  AGR: Kenneth L. Murray
  PAO: Michael Yaki
  ODA: Col. John D. Mussells USA
  OMADP: Col. Karl Piotrowski

MEDAN (C), Jalan Imam Bonjol
13
APO San Fran 96356
Tel [62](61)322200
Telex 51764
  PO: Donald K. Holm
  ECO/COM: Joseph Y. Yun
  COM: John W. Roberts
  ADM: Virginia I. Kurapka
  BPAO: Stanley J. Harsha

SURABAYA (C), Jalan Raya Dr.
Sutomo 33
APO San Frank 96356
Tel [62](31) 69287/8
Telex 031-334
  PO: Lee O. Coldren
  ADM/CON: Terrence J. Daru
  ECO/COM: John E. Roberts
  BPAO: Karl G. Nelson

IRAQ
BAGHDAD (E), Opp. For.
Ministry Club (Masbah Quarter)
P.O. Box 2447 Alwiyah Baghdad,
Iraq
Tel [964](1) 719-6138/9,
718-1840, 719-3791
Telex 212287 USINT IK, 213966
USFCS IK
Workweek: Sunday-Thursday
  AMB: April C. Glaspie
  DCM: Joseph C. Wilson, IV
  POL: Haywood Rankin
  ECO: Daniel A. Vernon
  COM: Russell Y. Smith
  CON: Daniel C. Stoll
  ADM: James R. VanLaningham
  RSO: John DiCarlo
  ATO: Larry L. Panasuk
  PAO: Jack R. McCreary
  ODA: Col. Gary W. Nelson USA
  IRS: W. Dennis Melton (resident in
    Riyadh)

IRELAND
DUBLIN (E), 42 Elgin Rd.,
Ballsbridge
Tel Dublin[353](1)687122
Telex 93684
FAX [353](1)689-946
  AMB: Richard A. Moore
  DCM: Brian D. Curran
  POL: George T. Dempsey
  COM: John W. Avard
  ECO: Curtis A. Stone
  CON: William H. Griffith
  ADM: Samual A. Rubino

PAO: Joe B. Johnson
ODA: Col. John K. Moon USA
AGR: James P. Rudbeck
IRS: William H. Connett (resident
  in London)
CUS: Paul W. O'Brien
RSO: Thomas W. Chace

ISRAEL
TEL AVIV (E), 71 Hayarkon St.
APO NY 09672
Tel [972](3)654338
Telex 33376 or 371386 USFCS IL
  AMB: William A. Brown
  DCM: Mark Parris
  POL: John P. Becker
  ECO: Henry Clarke
  COM: Michael J. Mercurio
  LAB: Charlotte Roe
  CON: Michael Metrinko
  ADM: Clarence E. Pegues, Jr.
  RSO: Alan O. Bigler
  SCI: Charles A. Lawson
  AGR: Mollie Iler (resident in
    Athens)
  PAO: Leonard Lefkow
  DAO: Col. Joseph P. Koz USAF
  IRS: Frederick Pablo (resident in
    Rome)

ITALY
ROME (E), Via Veneto 119/A,
00187-Rome
APO NY 09794
Tel [39](6)46741
Telex 622322 AMBRMA. USIS:
Via Boncompagni 2, 00187-Rome
Telex 625847 USISRM
FAX [39](6)4674-2356, FAX
FCS [39](6)4674-2113
  AMB: Peter F. Secchia
  DCM: John W. Holmes
  POL: John S. Brims
  ECO: Daniel P. Serwer
  FIN: Llewelyn Pascoe
  COM: Emilio Iodice
  POL/MIL: (Vacant)
  LAB: William B. Harbin

CON: Dudley Sipprelle
ADM: Donald R. Schoeb
RSO: Bernhard B. Collins, Jr.
SCI: Gerald J. Whitman
AGR: Frank J. Piason
PAO: Jodie Lewinsohn
CUS: Peter J. Dispenzirie
ODA: Capt. Lawrence E. Ewert
 USN
ODC: Col. Joel A. Gruell USA
FAA: James T. Murphy
IRS: Frederick Pablo
INS: Benedict J. Ferro

US MISSION TO THE UNITED NATIONS AGENCIES FOR FOOD AND AGRICULTURE (FODAG), c/o U.S. Embassy, Villino Pacelli, Via Aurelia 294, 00165 Rome
APO NY 09794-0007
Tel [39](6)639-0558, ext. 260, 262
Telex 622322 AMBRMA
FAX [39](6)638-2792
 US REP: Gerald J. Monroe
 AID: Richard M. Seifman
 AGR: J. Dawson Ahalt

GENOA (CG), Banca d'America e d'Italia Bldg., Piazza Portello, 6- 16124 GENOA
Tel [39](10)282-741 thru 5
Telex 270324 AMCOGEI
 CG: Richard J. Higgins
 BPAO: Corinne Heditsian
 RSO: Joseph Baxter (resident in Milan)

MILAN (CG), Via Principe Amedeo, 2/10, 20121 Milano
c/o U.S. Embassy, Box M, APO NY 09794-0007
Tel [39](2)655-7533 thru 6
Telex 330208. Commercial Section: Centro Cooperazione Internazionale, Piazzale Giulio Cesare, 20145 Milano
Tel [39](2)498-2241/2/3

FAX [39](2)653-251, FAX FCS [39](2)481-4161
 CG: John A. Boyle
 DPO/ECO: Alan W. Barr
 COM: Thomas C. Moore
 ECO: John F. Fogarty
 CON: Marilyn Jackson
 ADM: Robert I. Weisberg
 AGR: Stan Cohen
 RSO: Joseph Baxter

US INFORMATION SERVICE:
Via Bigli 11/A, 20121 Milano Tel 795051 thru 5
 BPAO: David Seal

NAPLES (CG), Piazza Della Repubblica 80122 Naples
Box 18, FPO
Tel [39](81)761-4303
FAX [39](81)761-1869, USIS
FAX (81)664-207
 CG: Emil P. Erickson
 POL/ECO/COM: Kenneth R. Audroue
 CON: Nancy Pelletreau
 ADM: Suneta Lyn Halliburton
 BPAO: Timothy Randall
 POLAD: Stephen Dawkins CINCAFSOUTH
 RSO: Bernhard B. Collins, Jr. (resident in Rome)

PALERMO (CG), Via Vaccarini 1, 90143
APO NY 09794-0007 (c/o AmEmbassy Rome-P)
Tel [39](91)343-532
Telex 910313 USACON I.
Commercial Section
Tel [39](91)346-036, 345-192
 CG: Katherine Shirley
 POL/ECO/COM: Donald Shemanski
 CON: Joseph B. Torres
 ADM: Jan N. Sittel
 BPAO: Douglas M. Barnes
 RSO: Bernhard B. Collins, Jr. (Resident in Rome)

FLORENCE (CG), Lungarno
Amerigo Vespucci 38
APO NY 09019
Tel [39](55)298-276
Telex 570577 AMCOFI I
FAX (55)284-088
Commercial Section
Tel (55)211-676
FAX (55)283-780
  CG: D. Stephen May
  CON: Virginia Morris
  ADM: Margaret Barnett
  BPAO: Robert K. Geis
  RSO: Joseph Baxter (resident in
    Milan)

IVORY COAST—See Cote d'Ivoire

JAMAICA
KINGSTON (E), Jamaica Mutual
Life Center, 2 Oxford Rd., 3d Fl.
Tel [809]929-4850
FAX (809)926-6743
  AMB: (Vacant)
  CHG: Stephen R. Gibson
  POL: James P. Nach
  ECO: Dorothy J. Black
  COM: Franklin J. Gilland
  CON: Lois J. Matteson
  ADM: George H. Haines III
  RSO: Mary K. Bauer
  AGR: Forrest Geerken (resident in
    Santo Domingo)
  AID: William R. Joslin
  LAB: (Vacant)
  PAO: Razvigor Bazala
  ODA: Ltc. Michael E. Lowe USMC
  MLO: Ltc. Samuel T. Smith USA

JAPAN
TOKYO (E), 10-1, Akasaka
1-chome, Minato-ku (107)
APO San Fran 96503
Tel [81](3)224-5000
Telex 2422118 AMEMB J

  AMB: Mihcale H. Armacost
  DCM: L. Desaix Anderson
  POL: Rust M. Deming
  ECO: Aurelia E. Brazeal
  FIN: Jon K. Hartzell
  COM: Keith R. Bovett
  LAB: John J. Lamazz
  CON: M. Patricia Wazer
  FAA: Edwin T. Kaneko
  ADM: Jose J. Cao-Garcia
  RSO: Bernd W. Schaumburg
  SCI: Richard W. Getzinger
  AGR: Laverne Brabant
  PAO: Robert L.M. Nevitt
  ATO: Laverne Brabant
  IRS: Dennis Tsujimoto
  CUS: Gary W. Waugh
  ODA: Capt. Scott A. Van Hoften
    USN

US EXPORT DEVELOPMENT
OFFICE, 7th Fl., World Import
Mart, 1-3 Higashi Likebukuro
3-chome, Toshima-ku, Tokyo 170
Tel [81](3)987-2441
Telex 27224468
  DIR: Edward Oliver, Jr.
NAHA, OKINAWA (CG), 2564
Nishihara, Urasoe City, Okinawa
901-21
Box 840, FPO Seattle, WA 98772
Tel [81](98)876-4211
  CG: Lawrence F. Farrar
  CON: Thomas W. Callow
  POL/MIL: Richard M. Gibson

OSAKA-KOBE (CG), 11-15,
Nishitenma 2-chome, Kita-Ku,
Osaka 530
APO San Fran 96503
Tel (81)(6)315-5900
Telex 5233037 AMCONJ
  CG: John R. Malott
  COM: Michael J. Benefiel
  POL/ECO: Robert S. Hyams
  ADM: David L. Shuler
  CON: Edward McKeon
  BPAO: Laurence D. Wohlers

SAPPORO (CG), Kita 1-Jo Nishi
28-chome, Chuo-ku, Sapporo 064
APO San Fran 96503
Tel [81](11)641-1115/7
Telex 935338 AMCONSJ
  CG: John R. Dinger
  CON: Mark J. Bezner
  BPAO: Timothy F. Smith

FAKUOKA (C), 5-26 Ohori
2-chome, Chuo-ku, Fukuoka-810
or Box 10, FPO Seattle 98766
Tel [81](92)751-9331/4
Telex 725679
  PO: Stephen W. Kennedy
  ECO/COM: William Weinstein
  CON: Alec Wilczynski
  BPAO: William M. Morgan

JERUSALEM (CG), 18 Agron
Rd., Jerusalem 94190
P.O. Box 290
APO NY 09672
Tel [972](2)234271 (via Israel)
Consular & Cultural Sections: 27
Nablus Rd
Tel [972](2)234271 (both offices
via Israel).
  CG: Philip C. Wilcox, Jr.
  DPO: David M. Winn
  POL: Mark M. Foulon
  ECO/COM: Jonathan R. Cohen
  CON: Catherine M. Barry
  ADM: Mark L. Jacobs
  RSO: Mark C. Boyett
  PAO: Gilbert K. Sherman

JORDON

AMMAN (E), Jabel Amman
P.O. Box 354 or APO NY 09892
Tel [962](6)644-371, USAID
Office Tel [962](6)660-4171
Comm. Off. Telex 24070
USCOMMJO
FAX Front Office/POL 659-720,
FAX ECO/COM/CON 659-767,

FAX ADM 646-301, FAX AID
604-858, FAX FAA 655-856,
FAX FBIS 654-824, FAX FBO
822-470, FAX USIS 649-925
Workweek: Sunday-Thursday
  AMB: Rosco S. Suddarth
  DCM: Patrick N. Theros
  POL: Pedro Martinez
  ECO/COM: Janet Sanderson
  CON: Allen J. Kepchar
  ADM: Anne M. Hackett
  RSO: Dennis Ravenscroft
  AGR: Larry L. Panasuk (resident
    in Baghdad)
  AID: Lewis P. Reade
  PAO: James E. Smith
  ODA: Col. Daniel Larned USA
  IRS: W. Dennis Melton (resident in
    Riyadh)
  FBO: Francis C. Schwab
  FAA: Donald Jones

KENYA

NAIROBI (E), Moi/Haile
Selassie Ave.
P.O. Box 30137
APO NY 09675
Tel [254](2)334141
Telex 22964
FAX [254](2)340838
  AMB: Elinor G. Constable
  DCM: George G.B. Griffin
  POL: Judith R. Johnson
  ECO: Paul E. Behnke
  COM: Richard Benson
  CON: Charles L. Stephan III
  LAB: Harry J. O'Hara
  ADM: Terrence M. Day
  RSO: Stephen H. Jacobs
  UNEP: John K. Atchley
  AGR: Susan R. Schayes
  AID: Steven W. SInding
  AID/REDSO: Satih Shah
  PAO: Laurence Garufi
  MLO: Ltc. Alden D. Ackels USA
  INS: Denise Blackburn

MOMBASA (C), Palli House,
Nyerere Avenue
P.O. Box 88079
Tel [254](11)315101
Telex 21063 AMCONS
  PO: Stephen Eisenbraun

KOREA
SEOUL (E), 82 Sejong-Ro
Chongro-ku
APO San Fran 96301
Tel [82](2)732-2601 thru 18
Telex AMEMB 23108
FAX [82](2)738-8845
US Agricultural Trade Office: 63,
1-KA, Ulchi-Ro, Choong-Ku
  AMB: Donald P. Gregg
  CHG: Thomas S. Brooks
  POL: Charles Kartman
  ECO: Kevin J. McGuire
  COM: Peter Frederick
  CON: Edward H. Wilkinson
  ADM: Robert G. Deason
  RSO: Paul D. Sorensen
  SCI: Kenneth D. Cohen
  INS: Donald Whitney
  AGR: George J. Pope
  ATO: Howard R. Wetzel
  PAO: John M. Reid
  CUS: Calvin G. White
  MAAG: Bg. Fred N. Halley USA
  ODA: Col. James V. Young USA
  DEA: David Surh
  IRS: Dennis Tsujimoto (resident in
    Tokyo)

US EXPORT DEVELOPMENT
OFFICE/USTRADE CENTER,
c/o US Embassy
FAX [82](2)739-1628
  DIR: William M. Yarmy
PUSAN (C), 24 2-Ka, Dacchung
Dong, Chung-ku
Tel 23-7791
  PO: Dennis P. Halpin
  BPAO: Ann E. Welden
  CON: Jeffrey M. Zaiser

KUWAIT
KUWAIT (E), P.O. Box 77
SAFAT, 13001 SAFAT, Kuwait
Tel [965]242-4151 thru 9
Workweek: Saturday-Wednesday
Telex 2039 HILTELS KT
FAX [965]240-7368
  AMB: W. Nathaniel Howell
  DCM: Barbara K. Bodine
  POL: David D. Pearce
  ECO: Emile M. Skodon
  FIN: Kevin Taecker (resident in
    Riyadh)
  COM: Paul Scogna
  CON: William A. Colwell
  ADM: Lawrence S. Blackburn
  RSO: Michael Bender
  ATO: Pitamber Devgon (resident in
    Manama)
  PAO: Alberto M. Fernandez
  MAAG: John D. Mooneyham
    USMC
  IRS: W. Dennis Melton (resident in
    Riyadh)

LAOS
VIENTIANE (E), Rue
Bartholonie
B.P. 114
Mail to: Box V, APO San Fran
96346
Tel 2220, 2357, 2384, or 3570
and 2357 after office hours,
weekends, and holidays
  CHG: Charles B. Salmon, Jr.
  DCM: D. Stephen May
  POL/ECO: Lisa Taylor
  COM/CON: E. James Steele

LEBANON
BEIRUT (E), Antelias, P.O. Box
70-840
FPO New York 09530
Tel [961]417774, 415802/3,
402200, 403300
  AMB: John T. McCarthy
  DCM: Charles H. Brayshaw

POL: David Satterfield
ECO/COM: James B. Magnor
CON: Jean Bradford
ADM: Harold T. Burgess
ATO: Allan Mustard (resident in
  Istanbul)
RSO: James McWhirter
AID: Frederick Machmar
ODA: Ltc. David J. Anthony USA
OMC: Maj. David Picard USA
IRS: W. Dennis Melton (resident in
  Riyadh)

LESOTHO

MASERU (E), P.O. Box 333,
Maseru 100
Tel [266]312666
Telex 4506 USAID
FAX [266]310-666, x102
  AMB: Robert M. Smalley
  DCM: Howard F. Jeter
  ECO/COM: Shaun F. Murphy
  ADM: Constance Hammond
  CON: Robert O. Morris
  RSO: Jeffrey W. Bowers (resident
    in Pretoria)
  LAB: John R. Dinger (resident in
    Johannesburg)
  AID: Jesse L. Snyder
  AGR: Roger F. Puterbaugh
    (resident in Pretoria)
  PAO: Richard O. Lankford

LIBERIA

MONROVIA (E), APO New
York 09155
111 United Nations Dr.
P.O. Box 98
Tel [231]222991 thru 4
FAX [23]222-450
  AMB: James K. Bishop
  DCM: Keith L. Wauchope
  POL: Simeon L. Moats
  ECO/COM: Herman J. Rossi III
  CON: Penny McMurtry
  RSO: Lawrence Hartnett
  ADM: Michael J. Adams
  AGR: Richard J. Blabey (resident
    in Abidjan)

AID: John F. Hicks
PAO: David Krecke
VOA: Wallace Freeman
LAB: Ollie P. Anderson, Jr.
  (resident in Washington)
ODA: Cdr. Donald C. Railsback
  USN
MAAG: Col. David H. Staley USA

LUXEMBOURG

LUXEMBOURG (E), 22 Blvd.
Emmanuel-Servais, 2535
Luxembourg
APO NY 09132
Tel [352]460123
Telex 46 14 01
  AMB: Jean B.S. Gerard
  DCM: David B. Dlouhy
  POL: Thomas C. Fosnacht
  ECO/COM: Kenneth B. Davis
  CON: Leroy O. Smith
  ADM: P. Albert Terry, Jr.
  RSO: Richard Gannon (resident in
    Brussels)
  AGR: John Beshoar (resident in
    Brussels)
  ODA: Col. Alan B. Phillips USA
    (resident in Brussels)
  ODC: Col. Alfred K. Muelhoefer
    USAF (resident in Brussels)

MADAGASCAR

ANTANANARIVO (E), 14 and
16 Rue Rainitovo, Antsahavola
B.P. 620
Tel 212-57, 209-567. 20-89,
207-18
Telex USA EMB MG 22202, 101
ANTANANARIVO
FAX 261-234-539
  AMB: Howard K. Walker
  DCM: Marilyn E. Hulbert
  ECO/COM: Alfred E. Smith
  ECO: Donald W. Koran
  POL: Liam Humphreys
  CON: Bette Jean Hammond
  ADM: Alexander T. Kirkpatrick
  RSO: Phil A. Whitney

PAO: Marilyn E. Hulbert
AID: Baudouin De Marcken
ODA: Cdr. William John Feallock
III USN

MALAWI
LILONGWE (E), P.O. Box 30016
Tel 730-166
Telex 44267
AMB: George A. Trail, III
DCM: George Dragnich
ECO/COM: Phillip Carter
POL: Horace Speed
LAB: Harry J. O'Hara (resident in
Nairobi)
ADM: Jerry L. Baker
RSO: Kevin Flanagan (resident in
Dar esSalaam)
PAO: Donald Creager
AID: Carol A. Peasley
ODA: Maj. Michael A. Via USA
AGR: Susan Schayes (resident in
Nairobi)

MALAYSIA
KUALA LUMPUR (E), 376
Jalan Tun Razak
50400 Kuala Lumpur
P.O. Box No. 10035, 50700
Kuala Lumpur
Tel [6](03)248-9011
Telex FCSKL MA 32956
FAX [60](3) 243-5207
AMB: (Vacant)
CHG: Thomas C. Hubbard
POL: Thomas P. Hamilton
ECO: Paul H. Blakeburn
COM: Jonathan Bensky
CON: Allen S.H. Kong
LAB: Gail Scott (resident in
Jakarta)
ADM: Patrick R. Hayes
RSO: John P. Chornyak
AGR: Jeffrey A. Hesse
PAO: James C. Pollock
ODA: Col. George P. McQuillen
USA

MALI
BAMAKO (E), Rue Testard and
Rue Mohamed V.
B.P. 34
Tel 225834
Telex 448 AMEMB
AMB: Robert M. Pringle
DCM: John Hargraves Lewis
POL: Frances R. Culpepper
ECO/COM: Jane B. Buchmiller
CON: James E. Dillon
LAB: Anthony M. Kern (resident
in Washington)
ADM: Stanley P. Jakubowski
RSO: John Frese
AID: Dennis J. Brennan
PAO: Linda A. Buggeln
ODA: Cdr. Donald C. Railsback
USN (resident in Dakar)

MALTA
VALETTA (E), 2d Fl.,
Development House, St. Anne
St., Floriana, Malta
P.O. Box 535, Valetta
Tel [356]623653, 620424, 623216
AMB: Peter R. Sommer
DCM: Eric A. Kunsman
ECO/COM: Damon V. LaBrie
POL/LAB: George H. Johnsom
CON: Jennifer A. Gregg
ADM: Ernest J. Parkin, Jr.
PAO: Yolande Veron-Sullivan
RSO: Bernhard B. Collins, Jr.
(resident in Rome)
AGR: Frank Piason (resident in
Rome)
IRS: Frederick Pablo (resident in
Rome)

MARSHALL ISLANDS
MAJURO (E), P.O. Box 680,
Republic of the Marshall Islands
96960
Tel 692-4011
CHG: Samuel B. Thomsen
POL/ECO/CON: Arnold Campbell

ADM: Martha Campbell
RSO: Philip Jornlin (resident in
Manila)
DOD: Maj. Michael Pettitt USA

MAURITANIA
NOUAKCHOTT (E), B.P. 222
Tel [2222]52660/3
Telex AMEMB 558 MTN
Workweek: Sunday-Thursday
AMB: William H. Twaddell
DCM: John W. Vincent
ECO/COM/CON: Catherine J.
Elkins
POL: Lucien Vandenbroucke
ADM: Gregory L. McLerran
RSO: David L. Lyons
AID: Glenn G. Slocum, Jr.
ODA: Ltc. Stefan Mytczynksy
(resident in Dakar)

MAURITIUS
PORT LOUIS (E), Rogers Bldg.
(4th Fl.), John Kennedy St.
Tel 082347
FAX [203]089534
AMB: Ronald D.F. Palmer
DCM: Robert C. Perry
POL: Robert J. Sise, Jr.
ECO/COM/CON: Francis H.
Bostock, Jr.
LAB: Harry O'Hara (resident in
Nairobi)
ADM/CON: Gerald J. Loftus
RSO: Phil A. Whitney (resident in
Antananarivo)
PAO: John Quintas
ODA: Cdr. William J. Feallock
USN (resident in Antananarivo)

MEXICO
MEXICO CITY, D.F. (E), Paseo
de la Reforma 305, Mexico
06500, Mexico D.F.
Mail: P.O. Box 3087, Laredo, TX
78044-3087
Tel [52](5)211-0042

Telex 017-73-091 and 017-75-685
FAX [52](5)511-9980
AMB: John D. Negroponte
DCM: Robert S. Pastorino
POL: Andrew G. Thomas, Jr.
ECO: Edmund M. Parsons
COM: John D. Perkins
LAB: John B. Gwynn
CON: Norman A. Singer
ADM: Jerome F. Tolson, Jr.
IRS: James E. Wright
FIN ATT: Jack Sweeney
CG: Jon G. Edensword
RSO: Michael W. Beckner
SCI: Roy C. Simpkins
AGR: William L. Davis
PAO: Robert L. Earle
NAU: John Crow
CUS: Roberto J. Fernandez
ODA: Bg. Edward N. Fletcher USA
AID: Samuel Taylor
MLO: Col. Robert G. Fullenkamp
USA
INS: Ernest M. Trominski
US EXPORT DEVELOPMENT
OFFICE, Liverpool 31, 06600
Mexico, D.F.
Tel [52](5)591-0155
Telex 01773471
DIR: Carol Murray Kim

CUIDAD JUAREZ (CG), CHIH
AVenue Lopez Mateos 924N
P.O. Box 10545, El Paso, TX
79995-0545
Tel [52](16)134048
Telex 033-840
FAX [52](161)34048/50 x210
CG: Louis P. Goelz
ADM: Trevor A. Snellgrove
CON: Michael J. Hogan
INS: Epifanio O. Miera
RSO: Mark G. Hoffman (resident
in Guadalajara)

GUADALAJARA (CG), JAL
Progreso 175
Mail: Box 3088, Laredo, TX
78044-3088

Tel [52](36)25-2998, 25-2700
Telex 068-2-860
ACDMC
FAX [52](36)26-6549
  CG: Irwin Rubenstein
  POL/ECO: Manfred G. Schweitzer
  CON: Elayne J. Urban
  COM: (Vacant)
  ADM: Ralph D. Chiocco
  AGR: Nathaniel Perry
  BPAO: John D. Roney
  INS: Victor W. Johnston
  RSO: Mark G. Hoffman

MONTERREY (CG), N.L.
Avenida Constitucion 411
Poniente 64000
Mail: Box 3098, Laredo, TX
78044-3098
Tel [52](83)45-2120
Telex 0382853 ACYMYME
FAX [52](83)42-0177
  CG: John E. Bennett
  ECO: Paul A. Trivelli
  CON: Ralph C. Walsh
  RSO: Edward A. Lennon
  INS: Olen R. Martin
  POL: Leo F. Cecchini
  COM: Robert M. Shipley
  ADM: M. Ann Kelleran
  BPAO: Robert L. Brown
  CUS: Kenneth J. Torres

TIJUANA (CG), B.C.N.
Tapachula 96
Mail: Box 1358, San Ysidro, CA
92073-1358
Tel [52](66)81-7700
Telex 0566836 ACTJMEX
FAX [52](66)81-8016
  CG: Larry Colbert
  CON: Thomas L. Randall, Jr.
  ADM: Joseph L. Warner
  INS: Robert A. Monets

HERMOSILLO (C), Son.
Monterrey 141
Mail: Box 3087, Laredo, TX
78044-3087

Tel [52](621)723-75
Telex 05889 ACHEME
FAX [52](62)172375 x49
  PO: J. Christian Kennedy
  CON: Ann K. Ganzer
  CUS: William T. Long

MATAMOROS (C), Tamps
Ave. Primera NO. 2002
Mail: Box 633, Brownsville, TX
78520-0633
Tel [52](891)2-52-50/1/2
Telex 035-827 ACMTME
FAX [52](89)138048
  PO: Donald E. Wells
  CON: Michael J. O'Keefe

MAZATLAN (C), Sin.
6 Circunvalacion 120, Centro
Mail: Box 2708, Laredo, TX
78044-2703
Tel [52](678)5-22-05
Telex 066-883 ACMZME
FAX
[52](678)2-1775
  PO: Steven P. Coffman
  CON: Lawrence P. Noyes
  RSO: Mark G. Hoffman (resident
    in Guadalajara)

MERIDA (C), Yuc.
Paseo Montejo 453
Mail: Box 3087, Laredo, TX
78044-3087
Tel [52](99)25-5011
Telex 0753885 ACMEME
FAX [52](99)25-6219
  PO: Bryant J. Salter
  CON: Christopher P. Henzel
  CUS: Andrew F. Soto

NUEVO LAREDO (C), Tamps.
Calle Allende 3330, Col. Jardin
88260 Nuevo Laredo, Tamps
Mail: Box 3089, Laredo, TX
78044-3089
Tel [52](871)4-0696, 4-9616

Telex 036-849 ACMLME
FAX [52](871)4-0696 x128
  PO: Manuel R. Guerra
  CON: Melinda Tabler-Stone

MICRONESIA
KOLONIA (E), P.O. Box 1286,
Pohnpei, Federated States of
Micronesia 96941
Tel 691-320-2187
  CHG: Michael G. Wygant
  ADM: Martha Campbell (resident
    in Majuro)
  POL/ECO/CON: Edward J. Michal
  RSO: Philip Jornlin (resident in
    Manila)

PEOPLE'S REPBULIC OF MONGOLIA
ULAANBAATAR (E), c/o
American Embassy Beijing
Tel 29095
Telex 253 TLX UB
  AMB: Richard L. Williams
  CHG: Steven Mann
  POL/ECO: Victoria Nuland
  RSO: Fred Brandt (resident in
    Beijing)

MOROCCO
RABAT (E), 2 Ave. de
Marrackech
P.O. Box 120
APO NY 09284
Tel [212](7)622-65
Telex 31005
  AMB: E. Michael Ussery
  DCM: Richard L. Jackson
  POL: Michael C. Lemmon
  ECO: David S. Robins
  CON: George W. Brazier III
  ADM: Alphonse Lopez
  RSO: Peter Stella
  AGR: Andrew A. Duymovic
  AID: Charles W. Johnson
  PAO: John E. Graves

ODA: Col. James E. Murphy
  USMC
MLO: Col. Thomas A. Burch
  USAF

CASABLANCA (CG), 8 Blvd.
Moulay Youssef
APO NY 09284 (CAS)
Tel [212]26-45-50
  CG: Timberlake Foster
  DPO/LAB: Lois Aroian
  POL: S. Phillips Amerman
  COM: Samuel D. Starrett
  ECO: Allen S. Greenberg
  CON: Suella Pipal
  ADM: J. Patrick Truhn
  BPAO: Elizabeth Thornhill

MARRAKECH (US Information
Service), Villa Saloua, Rue
Chouhada, L'Hivernage
Tel [212](4)327-58
  BPAO: Franklin Huffman

MOZAMBIQUE
MAPUTO (E), Avenida Kaunda
193
P.O. Box 783
Tel 74279, 743167, 744163
Telex: 6-143 AMEMB MO
FAX 743114 Int'l Op.
  AMB: Melissa F. Wells
  DCM: Michael E. Ranneberger
  POL/LAB: Aubrey V. Verdun
  ECO/COM/CON: Crayon C. Neil
    Efird
  LAB: John R. Dinger (resident in
    Johannesburg)
  ADM: Carol A. Hammond
  AID: Julius Schlotthauer
  PAO: Howard Leeb
  RSO: Robert Conrad
  DAO: Maj. Richard H. Fritz USA

NEPAL
KATHMANDU (E), Pani Pokhari
Tel [977]411179, 412718,
411601, 411604, 411613, 413890

Telex NP 2381 AEKTM
  AMB: Julia Chang Bloch
  DCM: Albert A. Thibault, Jr.
  POL/ECO: Hunt Janin
  ECO/COM: Carol T. Reynolds
  CON: Charles Parish, Jr.
  ADM: Norma L. Kleiber
  RSO: Mike Wanagel, Jr.
  AID: Kelly Kammerer
  PAO: William C. Dawson
  ODA: Ltc. Thomas A. Haase USA

NETHERLANDS
THE HAGUE (E), Lange
Voorhout 102
APO NY 09159
Tel [31](70)62-49-11
Telex (044) 31016
  AMB: C. Howard Wilkins, Jr.
  DCM: Thomas H. Gewecke
  POL: Lawrence G. Rossin
  ECO: David Rehfuss
  COM: Harrison B. Sherwood
  ADM: Timothy E. Roddy
  RSO: Robert J. Whigham
  AGR: Norval Francis
  PAO: C. William La Salle
  ODA: Capt. Roger E. Carlson USN
  ODC: Col. Charles W. Brewer
    USAF
  LAB: T. Jesse Clear
  CUS: Robert L. Gerber

AMSTERDAM (CG),
Museumplein 19
APO NY 09159
Tel [31](20)64-56-61 or 79-03-21
Telex 044-16176 CGUSA NL
  CG: Jake Dyels
  COM: George F. Ruffner
  CON: Walter Davenport

NETHERLANDS
ANTILLES
CURACAO (CG)St. Anna Blvd. 19
P.O. Box 158, Willemstad,
Curacao
Tel [599](9)613066

Telex 1062 AMCON NA
  CG: Sharon P. Wilkinson
  DPO: David Dreher
  CON: William L. Rada
  RSO: K. Scott McQuire (resident
    in Caracas)
  AGR: Lloyd J. Fleck (resident in
    Caracas)
  PAO: Margaret Westmoreland
    (resident in Paramaribo)

NEW ZEALAND
WELLINGTON (E), 29
Fitzherbert Ter., Thorndon,
Wellington
P.O. Box 1190
FPO San Fran 96690-0001
Tel [64](4)722-068
FAX [64](4)712-380
  AMB: (Vacant)
  CHG: Alphonse F. La Porta
  POL: Donald L. Jameson
  ECO: Verne R. Dickey
  LAB: Robert G. Loftis
  CON: Robert A. Callard
  ADM: Landon C. Carter
  RSO: David R. Haag (resident in
    Canberra)
  AGR: Evans Browne III
  PAO: William J.A. Barnes
  ODA: Capt. Linda J. Balink-White
    USN

AUCKLAND (CG), 4th Fl.,
Yorkshire General Bldg.
CNR Shortland and O'Connell
Sts., Auckland
Private Bag, Auckland
FPO San Fran 96690-0002
Tel [64](9)303-2724
Telex NZ 3305
FAX [64](9)366-0870
  CG: Edric Sherman
  COM: Bobette K. Orr
  CON: Alma F. Engel

NICARAGUA

MANAGUA (E), Km. 4-1/2
Carretera Sur.
APO Miami 34021
Tel [505](2)666010, 666013,
666015-18, 666026-27,
666032-34
FAX [505](2)666046
  AMB: (Vacant)
  CHG: John P. Leonard
  POL: John S. Boardman
  ECO: Joel F. Cassman
  CON: Wayne Griffith
  LAB: Joseph G. McLean (resident
    in Guatemala)
  ADM: John W. Fuhrer
  RSO: Daniel J. Pocus
  AGR: John Jacobs (resident in
    Guatemala)
  AID: (Vacant)
  PAO: Louis P. Falino
  ODA: Ltc. Dennis F. Quinn USA

NIGER

NIAMEY (E), (No street address)
B.P. 11201
Tel [227]72-26-61 thru 4
Telex EMB NIA 544NI
  AMB: Carl C. Cundiff
  DCM: Joseph A. Saloom III
  POL: Richard E. Blee
  ECO/CON: Douglas van Treeck
  ADM: Stephen H. King
  RSO: Anthony Richard
  AID: George T. Eaton
  PAO: Larry Moody
  SAO: Maj. Joe W. Parker USA
  ODA: Col. Roby M. Mauk USA
    (resident in Abidjan)

NIGERIA

LAGOS (E), 2 Eleke Crescent
P.O. Box 554
Tel [234](1) 610097
Telex 23616 EMLA NG and
21670 USATO NG
FAX [234](1)610257

  AMB: Princeton N. Lyman
  DCM: David L. Blakemore
  POL: John Campbell
  ECO: Constance Freeman
  COM: Norman D. Glick
  LAB: Thomas P. Doubleday, Jr.
  CON: Bobby L. Watson
  ADM: Gerald S. Rose
  RSO: Robert Franks
  AGR: Thomas A. Pomeroy
  ATO: Alan Hemphill
  AID: Henry Merrill
  PAO: Robert Lagamma
  ODA: Col. Douglas Mehle USA
  SAO: Maj. William Guglielmi

KADUNA (CG), 2 Maska Road,
P.O. Box 170
Tel [234](62)201070, 201071,
201072
Telex 71617 CG NG
  CG: Brooke C. Holmes
  POL/ECO: William E. Wilkin
  ADM: Ruben Alcantara
  CON: Andrew Passen
  BPAO: Brooks Robinson

NORWAY

OSLO (E), Drammensveien 18,
0244 Oslo 2, or APO NY 09085
Tel [47](2)44-85-50
Telex 78470
  AMB: Loret Miller Ruppe
  DCM: Donald J. Planty
  POL: James E. Thyden
  ECO: Weldon Burson
  COM: Robert C. Fraser
  LAB: Jonathan Benton
  CON: Elizabeth J. Berube
  ADM: David W. Mulenex
  RSO: Chris Andrews
  AGR: Anthony Cruit (resident in
    Copenhagen)
  PAO: David L. Arnett
  IO: John Matel
  ODA: Capt. Douglas D. Blaha USN
  ODC: Col. Daniel Konopatzke
    USAF

OMAN
MUSCAT (E), P.O. Box 50202
Madinat Qabos
Tel 698-989
Eco/Com Section: Tel
[968]703-287, 702-545
Telex 3785 AMEMBMUS ON
Defense Att. Telex 5457
USDAOMUS ON
ECA FAX 699-989, USIS FAX
699-771, COE FAX 601-510,
GSO FAX 699- 778
Workweek: Saturday-Wednesday,
7:30-4:00
  AMB: Richard W. Boehm
  DCM: Haywood Rankin
  POL/ECON: Anthony Benesch
  POL/MIL: John G. O'Connell
  ECO/COM: Henry S. Ensher
  CON: Douglas F. McCallum
  ADM: Louis N. Lemieux
  RSO: James T. Cronin
  ATO: Pitamber Devgon (resident in
    Manama)
  PAO: Leigh Colitre
  ODA: Col. James C. Lesseig USAF
  OMC: Col. George R. Mauldin
    USA
  IRS: W. Dennis Melton (resident in
    Riyadh)
  FBO: James Lederman

US REP TO THE
OMANI/AMERICAN JOINT
COMMISSION FOR
ECONOMIC AND TECHNICAL
COOPERATION, P.O. Box 6001,
Ruwi, Oman
Tel 703-000
FAX 797-778
Workweek: Saturday-Wednesday
  AID REP: Duncan R. Miller

PAKISTAN
ISLAMABAD (E), Diplomatic
Enclave, Ramna 5
P.O. Box 1048

APO New York 09614
Tel [92](51)826161 thru 79
Telex 82-5-864
FAX [92](51)822004
Workweek: Sunday-Thursday
  AMB: Robert B. Oakley
  DCM: A. Elizabeth Jones
  POL: Edward G. Abington
  ECO: Lawrence N. Benedict
  CON: Michael A. Gayle
  ADM: John C. Daniels
  RSO: Melvin L. Harrison
  AGR: Robin Tillsworth
  AID: James Norris
  PAO: William Lenderking
  NAU: Joseph A. Limprecht
  REF: Marisa R. Lino
  ODA: Col. Donald S. Jones USAF
  MAAG: Bg. James R. Ellis
  IRS: W. Dennis Melton (resident in
    Riyadh)

KARACCHI (CG), 8 Abdullah
Haroon Rd.
Tel [92](21)515081 thru 8
Telex 82-2-611
Workweek: Sunday-Thursday
  CG: Joseph H. Melrose, Jr.
  POL/ECO: A. Ellen Shippy
  COM: George A. Kachmar
  CON: Jean A. Louis
  ADM: Burton O. Allan
  BPAO: Gene R. Preston
  AID: Robert M. Traister
  RSO: ALfred L. Santos

LAHORE (CG), 50 Zafar Ali
Rd., Gulberg 5
APO NY 09614
Tel [92](42)870221 thru 5
Workweek: Sunday-Thursday
  CG: Richard K. McKee
  POL: Lynn A. Allison
  ECO/COM: Michael H. Howland
  CON: Susan E. Alexander
  ADM: David S. Wick
  BPAO: Kyra Eberle
  AID: Richard S. Stevenson

PESHAWAR (C), 11 Hospital
Road
APO NY 09614
Tel [92](521)79801, 79802, 79803
Telex 52-364
Workweek: Sunday-Thursday
  PO: Gerald M. Feinstein
  POL/CON: Dan J. Larsen
  BPAO: Helen L. Margiou
  ADM: Larry W. Paxton
  AID: Donald N. Melville
  FBO: William Robinson

PALAU, REPUBLIC OF
KOROR (USLO), P.O. Box
6028, Republic of Palau 96940
Tel 160-680-920/990
  USLO: Steven R. Pruett
  ADM: Martha Campbell (resident
    of Majuro)
  RSO: Philip Jornlin (resident in
    Manila)

PANAMA
PANAMA CITY (E), Apartado
6959, Panama 5, Rep. de Panama
Box E, APO Miami 34002
Tel [507]27-1777
FAX [507]03-9470
  AMB: Arthur H. Davis
  DCM: John F. Maisto
  POL: Michael C. Polt
  ECO: Edward B. O'Donnell, Jr.
  COM: Peter Noble
  LAB: Patricia E. Perrin
  CON: Gary S. Usrey
  ADM: John K. Ivie
  RSO: George J. Goldstein
  AGR: Lana Bennett (resident in
    San Jose)
  PAO: Terrence H. Kneebone
  CUS: John D. Fernandez
  ODA: Ltc. Layton G. Dunbar USA
  MAAG: Col. James M. Kelly USA
  INS: Raul Ozuna

PAPUA NEW GUINEA
PORT MORESBY (E), Armit St.
P.O. Box 1492
Tel [675]211-455/594/654
Telex 22189 USAEM
FAX [675]213-423
  AMB: Everett E. Bierman
  DCM: Dean L. Welty
  POL: Oscar W. Clyatt, Jr.
  ECO/COM: Robin K. McClellan
  CON: Lawrence G. Richter
  ADM: Richard B. Sorg
  AID: Louis H. Kuhn (resident in
    Suva)
  RSO: David R. Haag (resident in
    Canberra)
  PAO: Terence J. Spencer
  ODA: Col. Dean Stickell USAF
    (resident in Canberra)
  AGR: Geoffrey W. Wiggins
    (resident in Singapore)

PARAGUAY
ASUNCION (E), 1776 Mariscal
Lopez Ave.
Casilla Postal 402
APO Miami 34036-0001
Tel [595](21)201-041/9
FAX [595](21)205-018
  AMB: Timothy L. Towell
  DCM: Michael Ranneberger
  POL: Rose M. Likins
  ECO/COM: Jonathan D. Farrar
  CON: Clarence A. Hudson, Jr.
  ADM: Francine L. Bowman
  RSO: Daryl L. Rashkin
  AGR: Alan Hrapsky (resident in
    Brasilia)
  AID: Peter R. Orr (resident in
    Montevideo)
  PAO: Alan A. Rogers
  ODA: Ltc. Douglas C. McCary
    USA
  ODC: Col. Paul A. Scharf USA
  IRS: Vincent Gambino (resident in
    Sao Paulo)

PERU

LIMA (E), Corner Avenidas Inca
Garcilasode la Vega & Espana
P.O. Box 1995, Lima 100
APO Miami 34031
Tel [51](14)338-000
Telex 25212 PE (USEMBGSO)
FAX [51](14)316682
Consular Section: Grimaldo Del
Solar 346, Miraflores Lima 18
Tel [51](14)44-3621
Commercial Section: Larrabure Y
Unanue 110, Lima 1
Tel [51](41)33-3200
USAID Tel 20335 PE
(USAIDPR)
  AMB: Alexander F. Watson
  DCM: Douglas Langan
  POL: John Hamilton
  ECO: Russell Graham
  COM: Michael J. Hand
  CON: Donna Hamilton
  ADM: George Lowe, Jr.
  LAB: Maria Sanchez-Carlo
  IRS: Vincent Gambino (resident in
    Sao Paulo)
  RSO: Timothy Dixon
  AGR: Gary C. Groves
  AID: Donor Lion
  PAO: Charles Loveridge
  NAU: Ceasar P. Bernal
  ODA: Capt. John W. Shillingsburg
    USAF
  MAAG: Col. August Jannarone
  IAGS: Ltc. Raymond Becerril USA

PHILIPPINES

MANILA (E), 1201 Roxas Blvd.
APO San Fran 96528
Tel [63](2)521-7116
Telex 722-27366 AME PH
Com. Off.: 395 Buendia Ave.
Extension Makati
Tel [63](2)818-6674
Telex 22708 COSEC PH
  AMB: Nicholas Platt
  DCM: Kenneth M. Quinn

  POL: John D. Finney, Jr.
  ECO: John P. Modderno
  COM: Theodore J. Villinski
  ADM: Robert A. MacCallum
  CON: Bruce A. Beardsley
  LAB: James P. Dodd
  INS: Gregory Smith
  RSO: Philip E. Jornlin
  AGR: Lyle Moe
  AID: Malcolm H. Butler
  PAO: Robert F. Jordan
  ODA: Col. Terry C. Isaacson USAF
  JUSMAG: Mg. Thomas H. Harvey,
    Jr. USA
  IRS: Marilyn Dearsman

ASIAN DEVELOPMENT
BANK (Manila), 2330 Roxas
Blvd.
P.O. Box 789
Tel [63](2)807251
Telex 7425071
  U.S. EXEC DIR: Victor H. Frank,
    Jr.
  U.S. ALT EXEC DIR: (Vacancy)

CEBU (C), 3d Fl., PCI Bank,
Gorordo Avenue, Lahug
APO San Fran 96528
Tel [63](32)73486
Telex 712-6226 AMCON PU
  PO: Franklin P. Huddle, Jr.
  CON: Kathleen H. Manalo
  ECON/COM: George H. Johnson
  POL: Mary H. Amaral
  BPAO: James H. Sease

POLAND

WARSAW (E), Aleje
Ujazdowskle 29/31
AmEmbassy Warsaw, c/o
AmConGen (WAW), APO NY
09213
Tel [48](22)283041-9
Telex 813304 AMEMB PL
  AMB: John R. Davis, Jr.
  DCM: Darryl Johnson
  POL: Terry R. Snell

ECO: Howard H. Lange
COM: Edgar D. Fulton
CON: Phyllis Villegoureix-Ritaud
ADM: Mark J. Lijek
RSO: Thomas J. Comiskey
SCI: Gary R. Waxmansky
AGR: John Harrison
PRESS/CULT: Stephen M. Dubrow
ODA: Col. Glenn A. Bailey USA

US TRADE CENTER (Warsaw),
Ulica Wiejska 20
Tel [48](22)21-45-15
Telex 813934 USTDO PL
DIR: Edgar D. Fulton
KRAKOW (CG), Ulica Stolarska
9, 31043 Krakow
c/o AmConGen (KRK), APO NY
09213
Tel [48](12)229764, 221400,
226040,227793
Telex 0325350
  CG: Michael T. Barry
  POL/ECO: Steven L. Blake
  CON: Michael D. Kirby
  ADM: Daniel F. Romano
  BPAO: John H. Brown

POZNAN (C), Ulica Chopina 4
c/o AmConGen (POZ), APO NY
09213
Tel [48](61)529586, 529587,
529874
Telex 041-34-74 USA PL
  PO: Peter S. Perenyi
  CON: Robert O. Tatge
  BPAO: (Vacant)
  ADM: William A. Heidt

PORTUGAL
LISBON (E), Avenida das Forcas
Armadas, 1600 Lisbon
APO NY 09678-0002
Tel [351](1)726-6600, 726-6659,
726-8670, 726-8880
Telex 12528 AMEMB
FAX [351](1)726-8814

AMB: Edward M. Rowell
DCM: Wesley W. Egan
POL: Jeffrey Millington
ECO: David Miller
COM: Carlos Poza
LAB: Martin G. Brennan
CON: Arturo Macias
ADM: Thomas M. Widenhouse
RSO: Michael LaFranchi
AGR: Daniel K. Berman
AID: David C. Leibson
PAO: Richard A. Virden
ODA: Col. Van C. Sanders, Jr.
  USAF
MAAG: Col. Robert A. Young USA

OPORTO (C), Rua Julio Dinis
826, 3d Floor, 4000 Oporto
Tel [351](2)63094 and 690008
Telex 24905 AMCONP
FAX [351](2)62737
  PO: Herb Yarvin
  VC: John Alan Connerley
  CON: Bertram D. Braun
PONTA DELGADA, SAO
MIGUEL, AZORES (C), Avenida
D. Henrique
APO NY 09406-0002
Tel [351](96)22216/7
Telex 82126 AMCNPD P
  PO: Mahlon Henderson
  VC: Abigail S. Friedman
  CON: Russell J. Hanks

QATAR
DOHA (E), Fariq Bin Omran
(opp. TV Station)
P.O. Box 2399
Tel [974]864701/2/3
Commercial Section Tel
[974]867460
Telex 4847 AMEMB DH
FAX [974]861669
Workweek: Saturday-Wednesday
  AMB: (Vacant)
  POL/ECO: Donald A. Roberts
  CON: Michelle Bernier-Toth

ADM: Sandra Wenner
RSO: Frederick M. Krug (resident
   in Riyadh)
PAO: Martin Quinn
ATO: Pitamber Devgon (resident in
   Manama)
IRS: W. Dennis Melton (resident in
   Riyhadh)

ROMANIA

BUCHAREST (E), Strada Tudor
Arghezi 7-9, or
AmConGen(Buch), APO NY
09213
Tel [40](0)10-40-40
Telex 11416
   AMB: (Vacant)
   CHG: Larry C. Napper
   POL: Brian M. Flora
   ECO: Donald E. Booth
   COM: Kay R. Kuhlman
CON: Virginia C. Young
ADM: Anita S. Booth
   RSO: William J. Maher
   AGR: Steve Washenko (resident in
      Belgrade)
   PRESS/CULT: C. Miller Crouch
   ODA: Col. Branko B. Marinovich
      USA
   IRS: Frederick Pablo (resident in
      Rome)

RWANDA

KIGALI (E), Blvd. de la
Revolution, B.P. 28
Tel [205]75601/2/3 and 72126/7/8
   AMB: Leonard H.O. Spearman, Sr.
   DCM: Sue Ford Patrick
   ECO/COM/CON: Thomas Marten
   ADM: Joseph Cuadrado III
   RSO: Joseph Davidson (resident in
      Bujumbura)
   GSO: Robert F. Hannan, Jr.
   AID: James A. Graham
   PAO: David Ballard
   ODA: Col. Paul J. Wenzel USA
      (resident in Kinshasa)

SAUDI ARABIA

RIYADH (E), Collector Road M,
Riyadh Diplomatic Quarter
APO NY 09038
International Mail: P.O. Box
9041, Riyadh 11143
Tel [966](1)488-3800
Telex 406866 AMEMB SJ
USIS: P.O. Box 865
FCS Telex 401363 USFCS SJ
Workweek: Saturday-Wednesday
(all posts)
   AMB: (Vacant)
   CHG: David J. Dunford
   POL: Richard H. Jones
   ECO: Brian J. Mohler
   COM: Dirck Teller
   FIN: Kevin Taecker
   CON: Stephanie Smith
   ADM: Michael J. McLaughlin
   RSO: Frederick M. Krug
   PAO: Frank Stovras
   FBO: Alfred Leung
   ODA: Col. J.F. Fields USA
   USMTM: Mg. John R. Farrington
      USAF
   IRS: W. Dennis Melton
   POL/MIL: William A. Pierce

DHAHRAN (CG), Between
Aramco Hqrs and Dhahran Int'l
Airport
P.O. Box 81, Dhahran Airport
31932, or APO NY 09616
Tel [966](3)891-3200
Telex CONGEN: 801925
AMCON SJ
FAX [966](3)891-3296
FAX USIS [966](3)891-8212,
FAX FCS [966](3)291-8332
   CG: Brooks Wrampelmeier
   DCPL James P. Bell, Jr.
   ECO: Todd Schwartz
   CON: Leslie Hickman
   COM: Carmine D'Aloisio
   ADM: Eileen J. Quinn
   BPAO: Jonathan K. Rice

JEDDAH (CG), Palestine Rd.,
Ruwais
P.O. Box 149, Jeddah 21411 or
APO NY 09697-0002
Tel [966](2)667-0080
Telex 605175 USCONS SJ
Com. Off: Tel [966](2)667-0040
Telex 601459 USFCS SJ
US Agric. Trad Off.: Tel
[966](2)661-2408
Telex 604683 USATO SJ
  CG: Jay P. Freres
  COM: Michael R. Frisby
  CON: T. Dennis Reese
  ADM: Charles B. Angulo
  ATO: John A. Williams
  BPAO: Chris Eccel
  USGS: Paul Williams
  POL/ECO: Karen H. Sasahara
  FAA: Chester Chang

US REP TO THE SAUDI
ARABIAN US JOINT
COMMISSION ON
ECONOMIC COOPERATION
(USREP/JECOR), P.O. Box
5927, Riyadh
Tel [966](1)464-0433
Telex 201012
  DIR: William Griever
  DEP: Larry Bacon

SENEGAL
DAKAR (E), B.P. 49, Avenue
Jean XXIII
Tel [221]23-42-96 or 23-34-24
USIS Tel [221]23-59-28, 23-11-85
Telex 21793 AMEMB SG
FAX [221]23-92-86
  AMB: George E. Moose
  DCM: Prudence Bushnell
  POL: J. Michael Davis
  ECO: Alice A. Dress
  COM: Harold D. Foster
  CON: Ann B. Sides
  ADM: Ned W. Arcement
  RSO: Gregory B. Starr

AGR: Richard J. Blabey (resident
  in Abidjan)
AID: Julius Coles
PAO: Robert J. Palmeri
LAB: Ollie P. Anderson, Jr.
  (resident in Washington)
ODA: Maj. Stefan Mytczynsky
  USMC
FAA: Richard L. Hurst

SEYCHELLES
VICTORIA (E), Box 148
APO NY 09030-0006 or Victoria
House, Box 251, Victoria, Mahe,
Seychelles
Tel 23921/22
  AMB: James B. Moran
  POL/ECO: Gary E. Anderson
  CON: James D. Melville, Jr.
  LAB: Harry J. O'Hara (resident in
    Nairobi)
  ADM: Wayne J. Bush
  RSO: Stephen H. Jacobs (resident
    in Nairobi)
  AID/REDSO: (Vacant)

SIERRA LEONE
FREETOWN (E), Corner
Walpole and Siaka Stevens St.
Tel 26481
Telex (989)3509 USEMBSL
  AMB: Cynthia S. Perry
  DCM: Gregory M. Talcott
  CON: Barbara M. Johnson
  ECO/COM: James Dunn
  ADM: Larry L. Palmer
  RSO: Robert Weitzel
  LAB: Ollie P. Anderson, Jr.
    (resident in Washington)
  AGR: Richard J. Blabey (resident
    in Abidjan)
  AID: James W. Habron
  PAO: Michael T. Scanlin

SINGAPORE
SINGAPORE (E), 30 Hill St.
Singapore 0617
FPO San Fran 96699

Tel [65]338-0251
Telex RS 42289 AMEMB
  AMB: Robert D. Orr
  DCM: Kent M. Weidemann
  ECO/POL: Thomas H. Martin
  COM: George Ruffner
  CON: Joan V. Smith
  LAB: Gail P. Scott (resident in
    Jakarta)
  RSO/RSO: John F. Donato
  IRS: Jerome Rosenbaum
  ADM: Robert B. Courtney
  ATO: Geoffrey W. Wiggin
  PAO: Richard D. Gong
  ODA: Capt. George W. Lundy, Jr.
    USN
  INS: William J. Ring, Jr.

USIA, Tung Center Building, 20
Collyer Quay
Tel [65]224-5233.
COMMERCIAL SERVICES
AND LIBRARY, 111 N. Bridge
Rd. #15-05, Peninsula Plaza,
Singapore 0617
Tel [65]338-9722
Telex RS25079 (SINGTC)
US AGRICULTURAL OFFICE,
541 Orchard Road, 08-04, Liat
Towers Bldg., Singapore 0923
Tel [65]7371233
Telex RS55138 USDA

SOLOMON ISLANDS
HONIARA (E), Mud Alley
P.O. Box 561
Tel (677)23890
Telex 66461 HQ USACON
FAX (677)23488
  AMB: Everett Bierman (resident in
    Port Moresby)
  CHG: William Warren
  RSO: David R. Haag (resident in
    Canberra)

SOMALIA
MOGADISHU (E), Corso Primo
Luglio
P.O. Box 574
Tel [252](01)20811
Public Telex (999)789
AMEMBMOG
Workweek: Sunday-Thursday
  AMG: T. Frank Crigler
  DCM: Joseph J. Borich
  POL/ECON: Herbert S. Thomas, III
  POL: George Frederick
  ECO: David Fetter
  CON: John Francis McCarthy, III
  LAB: Harry J. O'Hara (resident in
    Nairobi)
  ADM: William Hoffman
  RSO: Kim T. Starke
  AID: Lois Richards
  PAO: William Harwood
  ODA: Col. Robert L. Bidwell USA
  OMC: Col. Walter C. Zaremba
    USA
  IRS: W. Dennis Melton (resident in
    Riyadh)

SOUTH AFRICA
PRETORIA (E), Thibault House,
225 Pretorius St.
Tel [27](12)28-4266
Telex 3-751
TAX [27](12)28-4266 x259,
USIS 266-495, 217-490
  AMB: William L. Swing
  CHG: Genta Hawkins Holmes
  POL: Robin L. Raphel
  ECO/COM: Stephen H. Rogers
  ADM: Andrew J. Winter
  RSO: Jeffrey W. Bowers
  AGR: Roger Puterbaugh
  PAO: Eugene Friedman
  ODA: (Vacant)
  AID: Dennis P. Barrett

CAPE TOWN (CG), Broadway
Industries Center, Heerengracht,
Foreshore
Tel [27](21)214-280/7

Telex 522387
FAX [27](21)214-280, x226
  CG: Charles R. Baquet III
  POL/ECO: Gillian A. Milovanovic
  ECO: Norman B. Imler
  ADM: Efraim A. Cohen
  CON: James B. Gray
  BPAO: Michael T. Scanlan

DURBAN (CG), Durban Bay
House, 29th Fl., 333 Smith St,
Durban 4001
Tel [27](31)304-4737/8
FAX [27](31)301-8206, USIS
FAX 304-2847
  CG: F. Allen Harris
  CON: Terrence P. McCulley
  BPAO: John S. Dickson

JOHANNESBURG (CG), 11th
Fl., Kine Center, Commissioner
and Krulis Sts.
P.O. Box 2155
Tel [27](11)331-1681
Telex 483780-SA
FAX [27](11)331-1681, x105
  CG: Peter R. Chaveas
  POL: Ronald A. Trigg
  ECO: John Driscol, Jr.
  COM: Benjamin N. Brown
  LAB: John R. Dinger
  MNL: Robert J. McSwain
  CON: Thomas P. Furey
  BPAO: Harvey I. Leifert

SPAIN

MADRID (E), Serrano 75, 28006
Madrid
or APO NY 09285
Tel [34](1)276-3400/3600
Telex 27763
FAX [34](1)564-1652
  AMB: (Vacant)
  CHG: Edward A. Casey
  POL: Gerald Desantillana
  ECO: Pierce Bullen
  COM: Robert Kohn
  POL/MIL: Donald Planty

  LAB: Frank R. Golino
  CON: Michael L. Hancock
  RSO: Stanley Bielinski, Jr.
  ADM: Perry W. Linder
  AGR: Richard T. McConnell
  SCI: Ishmael Lara
  PAO: Sally Grooms-Cowal
  ODA: Capt. Carmine Tortora USN
  MAAG: Radm. Gerald L. Riendeau
  FAA: Robert J. Bernard

BARCENLONA (CG), Via
Layetana 33
APO NY 09286
Tel [34](3)319-9550
Telex 52672
  CG: Ruth A. Davis
  COM: Ralph Griffin
  CON: Mark Davison
  ADM: Benjamin Castro
  BPAO: Guy Burton

BILBAO (C), Avenida Del
Ejercito, 11-3, 48014 Bilbao
APO NY 09285
Tel [34](4)435-8300
Telex 32589
  PO: Heather M. Hodges
  CON: Bradford H. Johnson

SRI LANKA

COLOMBO (E), 210 Galle Rd.,
Colombo 3
P.O. Box 106
Tel [94](1)548007
Telex 21305 AMEMB CE
USAID/USIS/VOA—44 Galle
Rd., Colombo 3
Tel [94](1)21271, 21520
FAX [94](1)549070
  AMB: James W. Spain
  DCM: Edward Marks
  POL: Ernestine S. Heck
  ECO: Bruce D. Strathearn
  COM: Colin Helmer
  ADM: Stephen A. Browning
  CON: Richard M. Sherman
  RSO: Joseph D. Morton

AGR: Lyle J. Sebranek (resident in
 New Delhi)
AID: Peter J. Bloom
PAO: Clathan M. Ross
ODA: Cdr. David A. Harry USN
LAB: Paul J. Mailhot

SUDAN
KHARTOUM (E), Sharia Ali
Abdul Latif
P.O. Box 699, APO NY 09668
Tel 74700, 74611
Telex 22619 AMEM SD
Workweek: Sunday-Thursday
 AMB: G. Norman Anderson
 DCM: Dane F. Smith, Jr.
 POL: Robert E. Downey
 ECO: Matthew P. Ward
 LAB: Harry J. O'Hara (resident in
  Nairobi)
 CON: Dennis B. Hankins
 ADM: Joseph T. Sikes
 RSO: W. Christopher Reilly
 AID: Frederick E. Gilbert
 AGR: Franklin D. Lee (resident in
  Cairo)
 PAO: Evelyn A. Early
 ODA: Maj. James P. Gerhard USA
 OMC: Col. Stephen Monsees
  USAF
 IRS: W. Dennis Melton (resident in
  Riyadh)
 REF: David E. Reuther

SURINAME
PARAMARIBO (E), Dr. Sophie
Redmondstraat 129
P.O. Box 1821
Tel [597]72900, 76459
USIS: Tel [597]75051
Telex 373 AMEMSU SN
FAX [597]10025
 AMB: Richard C. Howland
 DCM: Stanley T. Myles
 POL: Theodore H. Andrews
 COM/ECO: Lance Hopkins
 CON: Jacob DeRaat

RSO: Joseph C. Vaccarino
 (resident in Georgetown)
ADM: Benjamin R. Justesen II
AGR: Lloyd J. Fleck (resident in
 Caracas)
PAO: Carlos Bakota
LAB: (Vacant) (resident in
 Bridgetown)
ODA: Maj. David R. Coven USA

SWAZILAND
MBABANE (E), Central Bank
Bldg., Warner Street
P.O. Box 199
Tel 46441/5
USAID Telex 2016 WD
FAX [268]46446
 AMB: Mary A. Ryan
 DCM: Armajane Karaer
 POL/ECO/CON: Bruce A. Lowry
 LAB: John R. Dinger (resident in
  Johannesburg)
 ADM: Joseph B. Schreiber
 RSO: Jeff Bower (resident in
  Pretoria)
 AGR: Roger F. Puterbaugh
  (resident in Pretoria)
 AID: Roger D. Carlson
 PAO: J. Brooks Spector

SWEDEN
STOCKHOLM (E), Strandvagen
101, S-11527 Stockholm
Tel [46](8)7835300
Telex 12060 AMEMB S
FAX [46](8)661-1964
 AMB: Charles E. Redman
 DCM: Roland K. Kuchel
 POL: Thomas R. Hanson
 ECO: F. Brenne Bachmann
 COM: Robert S. Connan
 LAB: Robert J. Carroll
 CON: Justice B. Stevens
 ADM: Jeffrey S. White
 RSO: James A. Hush
 AGR: Gordon S. Nicks
 PAO: George F. Beasley
 ODA: Col. John L. Golden USAF

SWITZERLAND

BERN (E), Jubilaeumstrasse 93, 3005 Bern
Tel [41](31)437-011
Telex (845)912603
FAX [41](31)437-344
AMB: Joseph B. Gildenhorn
DCM: Frederick H. Hassett
POL/ECO: Joan Corbett
COM: Daniel Taher
CON: William Muller
ADM: Theodore A. Dawson
AGR: Robert S. Simpson
FIN: William Quinn
PAO: J. Michael Korff
ODA: Col. Leo J. Weeks USAF
RSO: Henry Jenkins

GENEVA (BO), 11, Route de Pregny, 1292 Chambesy/Geneva
1-3 Ave de la Paix, 1201 Geneva
Tel [41](22)738-76-13, 738-50-95
Telex 22103 USMIO CH (This office offers no commercial services.)
CON: S. Jean Melvin

US MISSION TO THE EUROPEAN OFFICE OF THE UN AND OTHER INTERNATIONAL ORGANIZATIONS (GENEVA), Mission Permanente Des Etats-Unis, Route de Pregny 11, 1292 Chambesy-Geneva, Switzerland
Tel [41](22)799-02-11
Telex 22103 USMIO CH
CM: Amb. Morris B. Abram
DCM: William H. Marsh
ECO: Roderick M. Wright
REFUGEE/MIGRATION AFF: Michael Carpenter
LEGAL AFF: Thomas A. Johnson
ADM: Franklin D. English
LAB: Richard T. Booth
SPEC. AGENCY AFF: Anne W. Patterson

RSO: Jerry P. Wilson
PAO: John D. Garner
IRM: (Vacant)
AGR: James A. Truran

UNITED STATES TRADE REPRESENTATIVE, Botanic Bldg., 103 Avenue de la Paix, Geneva
Tel [41](22)320970
CM: Amb. Rufus H. Yerxa
DCM: Andrew L. Stoler
AGR: James A. Truran
COM: Stephen Arlinghaus

ZURICH (CG) Zollikerstrasse 141, 8008, Zurich
Tel [41](1)552566
Telex 0045-816830
CG: Ruth N. Van Heuvan
CON: Joseph O. Streicher

SYRIA

DAMASCUS (E), Abu Rumaneh, Al Mansur St. No. 2
P.O Box 29
Tel [963](11)333052, 332557, 330416, 332315
Telex 411919
USDAMA SY
AMB: Edward P. Djerejian
DCM: John B. Craig
POL: David C. Litt
ECO/COM: Barbara L. Schell
CON: Lisa A. Piascik
ADM: Charles R. Allegrone
RSO: Walter B. Deering
AGR: W. Garth Thorburn (resident in Ankara)
ATO: Allan P. Mustard (resident in Istanbul)
PAO: Darryl L. Penner
ODA: Ltc. Robert C. Allen USA

TANZANIA

DAR ES SALAAM (E), 36 Laibon Rd. (off Bagamoyo Rd.)

P.O. Box 9123
Tel [255(51) 37501-4
Telex 41250 USA TZ
FAX [255](51)37408
  AMB: Donald K. Petterson
  DCM: Joseph M. Segars
  POL: Stevenson McIlvaine
  ECO/COM: Gayleatha B. Brown
  CON: Barbara M. Johnson
  ADM: Robert L. Kile
  RSO: Kevin F. Flanagan
  AGR: Susan R. Schayes (resident
    in Nairobi)
  AID: Joseph F. Stepanek
  PAO: Michael L. Braxton
  LAB: Harry J. O'Hara (resident in
    Nairobi)

THAILAND
BANGKOK (E), 95 Wireless Rd.
APO San Fran 96346
Tel [66](2)252-5040
Com. Off. and Library: "R" Fl.,
Kian Gwan Bldg., 140 Wireless
Rd.
Tel [66](2)253-4920/2
(Commercial Section) Telex
20966 FCSBKK
FAX [66](2)254-2990,
Procurement FAX 254-2994
  AMB: Daniel A. O'Donohue
  DCM: Victor L. Tomseth
  POL: Ralph L. Boyce
  ECO: Robert B. Duncan
  COM: Herbert A. Cochran
  LAB: R. Niels Marquardt
  CON: David L. Lyon
  ADM: Gerald E. Manderscheid
  RSO: William H. O'Rourke
  AGR: Weyland Beeghly
  AID: John R. Erikkson
  PAO: Donna Marie Oglesby
  NAU: Albert L. Bryant
  REF/ODP: Bruce A. Beardsley
  CUS: James L. Cable
  INS: James B. Foster
  ODA: Col. Vernon D. Ellis USAF
  JUSMAG: Bg. Peter W. Lash USA

CHIANG MAI (CG),
Vidhayanond Rd.
Box C, APO San Fran 96346
Tel [66](53)252-639
  PO: Richard M. Gibson
  POL/CON: Jeffrey A. Moon
  ADM: Charles A. Ray
  BPAO: Pendleton C. Agnew

SONGKHLA (C), 9 Sadao Rd.
Box S, APO San Fran 96346
Tel [66](2)311-589
PO: Donald B. Coleman
UDORN (C), 35/6 Supakitjanya
Rd.
Box UD, APO San Fran 96346
Tel [66](42)244-270
FAX [66](42)244-273
  PO: Dewey R. Pendergrass
  CON: Michael A. Glancy

TOGO
LOME (E), Rue Pelletier
Caventou & Rue Vauban
B.P. 852
Tel [228]21-29-91 thru 94 and
21-36-09
FAX [228]217952
  AMB: Rush W. Taylor, Jr.
  DCM: Tibor P. Nagy, Jr.
  POL: Victor C. Eissler
  CON/ECON: Bryan G. Lowe
  ECON/COM: Louis Mazel
  ADM: Joseph Huggins
  RSO: Kevin P. O'Neal
  AID: Mark G. Wentling
  ODA: Col. Roby M. Mauk
    (resident in Abidjan)
  PAO: Dudley O. Sims
  LAB: Thomas P. Doubleday, Jr.
    (resident in Lagos)

TRINIDAD AND TOBAGO
PORT-OF-SPAIN (E), 15
Queen's Park West
P.O. Box 752
Tel [809]622-6372/6, 6176

FAX (809)622-9583
  AMB: Charles A. Gargano
  DCM: Lacy A. Wright, Jr.
  POL: Gordon Stirling
  LAB: (Vacant) (resident in
    Bridgetown)
  ECO: Judson L. Bruns
  CON: Bruce McKenzie
  ADM: John P. Markey
  COM: Stephen J. Helgesen
  RSO: Tony Jones
  AGR: Lloyd J. Fleck (resident in
    Caracas)
  PAO: Mark A. Glago
  ODA: Ltc. Armand P. Haynes
    (resident in Bridgetown)

TUNISIA

TUNIS (E), 144 Ave. de la
Liberte, 1002 Tunis-Belvedere
Tel [216](1)782-566
Telex 13379 AMTUN TN
FAX [216](1)789-719
  AMB: Robert H. Pelletreau, Jr.
  DCM: Shaun E. Donnelly
  POL: Edmund J. Hull
  ECO/COM: Jay R. Grahame
  LAB: Eric H. Madison
  CON: Jon L. Noyes
  ADM: Stephen T. Smith
  RSO: Arthur W. Jones
  ATO: Abdullah A. Saleh
  AID: George Carner
  PAO: Richard Undeland
  ODA: Col. Marc B. Powe USA
  USLOT: Col. Laney K. Cormney
    USA
  IRS: Frederick Pablo (resident in
    Rome)

TURKEY

ANKARA (E), 110 Ataturk Blvd.
APO NY 09257-0006
Tel [90](4) 126 54 70
  AMB: Morton I. Abramowitz
  DCM: William F. Rope
  POL: Michael I. Austrian
  ECO: G. Clay Nettles
  COM: Dan A. Wilson

  POL/MIL: Regina M. Eltz
  LAB: Carl S. Matthews
  SCI: N. John MacGaffin
  CON: Robert E. Sorenson
  ADM: Katherine L. Kemp
  RSO: Gerald Kilgore
  AGR: W. Garth Thorburn
  PAO: Frank Scotton
  ODA: Col. Carlton L. Betts USAF
  MAAG: Mg. Fred E. Elam USA
  IRS: Frederick Pablo (resident in
    Rome)

ISTANBUL (CG), 104-108
Mesrutiyet Caddesi, Tepebasl
APO NY 09380
Tel [90](1) 151 36 02
Telex 24077 ATOT-TR
  CG: Thomas J. Carolan, Jr.
  POL: Timothy Collins
  ECO: Elizabeth W. Shelton
  COM: E. Scott Bozek
  CON: Roger D. Pierce
  ADM: William A. Eaton
  RSO: John B. McKennan
  BPAO: John T. Ohta
  ATO: Allan P. Mustard

IZMIR (CG), 92 Ataturk Caddesi
(3d Fl.)
APO NY 09224
Tel [90](51)149426, 131369
  CG: Albert N. Williams
  POL/ECON: Stephen H. Klemp
  CON/COM: Lauren M. Heuber
  ADM: Karen D. Klemp
  BPAO: Edith Russo

ADANA (C), Ataturk Caddesi
APO NY 09289
Tel [90](71)139106, 142145,
143774
  PO: Harry E. Cole, Jr.
  POL/ECO: Sheldon J. Rapoport
  ADM/CON: Paul G. Gilmer

UGANDA

KAMPALA (E), Parliament Ave.
P.O. Box 7007

Tel [256](41)259791/2/3/5
  AMB: John A. Burroughs, Jr.
  DCM: Robert E. Gribbin
  CON: David R. Salazar
  POL: Colin Cleary
  LAB: Harry J. O'Hara (resident in
    Nairobi)
  ADM: Roger C. Nottingham
  RSO: Walter Huscilowitc
  AID: Richard Podol
  PAO: Ramona Harper
  ECO/COM: Robert Finneran

UNION OF SOVIET SOCIALIST REPUBLICS

MOSCOW (E), Ulitsa
Chaykovskogo 19/21/23, or APO
NY 09862
Telex 413160 USGSO SU
Tel 252-2451 thru 59
  AMB: Jack F. Matlock, Jr.
  DCM: John M Joyce
  POL: Mark Ramee
  ECO: Mary Ann Peters
  COM: James May
  CON: Max N. Robinson
  ADM: William C. Kelly
  RSO: Mark Sanna
  SCI: John K. Ward
  AGR: William P. Huth
  ODA: Bg. Ervin J. Rokke USAF
  PAO: Philip C. Brown

US COMMERCIAL OFFICE
(MOSCOW)
Ulitsa Chaykovskogo 15
Tel [7](096)255-48-48, 255-46-60
Telex 413-205 USCO SU
  DIR: James May

LENINGRAD (CG), Ulitsa, Petra
Lavrova St. 15
Box L, APO NY 09664
Tel [7](812)274-8235
Telex 64-121527 AMCONSUL
SU
  CG: Richard M. Miles
  DPO: Jon R. Purnell

CON: Paul N. Timmer
POL/ECO: Douglas B. Wake
ADM: Robert E. Patterson
RSO: Raymond V. Jarek
BPAO: James Hutcheson

UNITED ARAB EMIRATES

ABU DHABI (E), Al-Sudan St.
P.O. Box 4009
Tel [971](2)336691
Telex 23513 AMEMBY EM
Com. Sec: Blue Tower Bldg., 8th
Floor, Shaikh Khalifa
Bin Zayed St.
Tel [971](2)345545
Telex 22229 AMEMBY EM
FAX [971](2)213771
FAX COM [971](2)331374
Workweek: Saturday-Wednesday
  AMB: David L. Mack
  DCM: Ronald E. Neumann
  POL: Dennis A. Foster
  ECO: William T. Fleming, Jr.
  COM: John L. Priamou
  CON: Charles E. Robertson
  ADM: Robert A. Essington, Sr.
  RSO: Paul J. Vogel
  PAO: James R. Moore
  USLO: Col. William K.S. Olds USA
  IRS: W. Dennis Melton (resident in
    Riyadh)

DUBAI (CG), Dubai
International Trade Center
P.O. Box 9343
Tel [971](4)371115
Telex 46031 BACCUS EM
FAX [971](4)379043, FAX COM
[971](4)375121
Workweek: Saturday-Wednesday
  CG: John W. Limbert
  ECO: Robert W. Richards
  COM: John L. Priamou (resident in
    Abu Dhabi)
  CON: Harry A. Nunnemacher
  ATO: Pitamber Devgon (resident in
    Manama)
  RSO: Louis M. Possanza

UNITED KINGDOM

LONDON, ENGLAND (E),
24/31 Grosvenor Sq., W.1A 1AE
or Box 40, FPO NY 09509
Tel [44](01)499-9000
Telex 266777
FAX 409-1637
  AMB: Henry E. Catto
  DCM: Ronald E. Woods
  POL: Bruce Burton
  ECO: Richard M. Ogden
  FIN: John M. Abbott
  COM: David A. Diebold
  LAB: Lester P. Slezak
  CON: Norbert Krieg
  ADM: John Condayan
  RSO: Robert O'Brien
  IRS: Robert Tobin
  SCI: James B. Devine
  AGR: James P. Rudbeck
  ATO: Robert D. Fondahn
  PAO: Charles Courtney
  CUS: John A. Hurley
  POLAD: David Kruse USNAVEUR
  ODA: Col. Chester P. Garrison
    USAF
  FAA: Patrick Poe
  SAO: (Vacant)
  INS: Anne Arries

BELFAST, NORTHERN
IRELAND (CG), Queen's House,
14 Queen St., BT1 6EQ
Tel [44](232)328239
Telex 747512
  CG: Douglas Archard
  AGR: Rolland E. Anderson, Jr.
    (resident in London)
  CON: Hilarion Martinez
  RSO: Robert O'Brien (resident in
    London)

EDINBURGH, SCOTLAND
(CG), 3 Regent Ter. Eh 75BW
Tel [44](31)556-8315
Telex 727303
  CG: Donald Holm
  AGR: Rolland E. Anderson, Jr.
    (resident in London)

  CON: Elizabeth Leighton
  RSO: Robert O'Brien (resident in
    London)

UNITED STATES

US MISSION TO THE UNITED
NATIONS (USUN), 799 United
Nations Plaza, New York, NY
10017
Tel (212)415-4050
After hours: Tel (212) 415-4444
FAX (212) 415-4443
  US REP: Amb. Thomas R.
    Pickering
  DEP US REP: Amb. Alexander F.
    Watson
  DEP US REP in the Security
    Council: Amb. James Wilkinson
  US REP to ECOSOC: (Vacant)
  ALT US REP for Special Political
    Affairs in the UN: Amb.
    Jonathan Moore
  DEP US REP to ECOSOC:
    (Vacant)
  POL: Robert T. Grey
  UN RES MGT: (Vacant)
  PAO: Frederick B. Negem, Jr.
  ADM: Linda S. Shenwick
  RSO: George McCauley
  INT LEGAL: Robert B. Rosenstock
  HOST COUNTRY: George J.
    O'Donnell
  MSC: Col. Robert R. Anderson
    USAF

US MISSION TO THE
ORGANIZATION OF
AMERICAN STATES (USOAS),
Department of State, Washington,
D.C. 20520
Tel (202) 647-9376
  US REP: Amb. Richard T.
    McCormack
  DEP US REP: William T. Pryce
  SEN POL ADV: Richard Hines
  ECO: James C. Todd
  BUD: Owen B. Lee
  PAO: Russell Wapensky
  INT ORG: Donald E.J. Stewart

EDUC SCI & CULT: Margarita
Riva-Geoghegan
AMD/HOSTSHIP: Eliska Coolidge

URUGUAY

MONTEVIDEO (E), Lauro
Muller 1776
APO Miami 34035
Tel [598](2)23-60-61 and
afterhours 77-09-50
FAX [598](2)921691
  AMB: Malcolm R. Wilkey
  DCM: John P. Jurecky
  POL: Janet L. Crist
  ECO/COM: John E. Hope
  LAB: Charles W. Evans
  ADM: John M. Salazar
  CON: James P. Walsh
  RSO: Richard A. Shoupe
  IRS: Vincent Gambino (resident in
    Sao Paulo)
  AGR: Marvin Lehrer (resident in
    Buenos Aires)
  PAO: David P. Wagner
  AID: Peter R. Orr
  ODA: Capt. Marshall W. Bronson
    USN
  MAAG: Col. Richard J. Brown
    USAF

VENEZUELA

CARACAS (E), Avenida
Francisco de Miranda and
Avenida Principal de la Floresta
P.O. Box 62291, Caracas 1060-A
or APO Miami 34037
Tel [58](2) 285-3111/2222
Telex 25501 AMEMB VE
FAX [58](2)285-0336
US Agricultural Trade Office:
Centro Plaza, Tower C, Piso 18,
Los Palos Grandes, Caracas
Tel [58](2)283-2353/2521
Telex 29119
USATO VC
  AMB: (Vacant)
  CHG: Kenneth N. Skoug, Jr.

  POL: Donna J. Hrinak
  ECO: Alfred J. White
  COM: Kenneth Moorefield
  LAB: Robert A. Millspaugh
  CON: Daniel R. Welter
  ADM: Michael A. Boorstein
  RSO: K. Scott McGuire
  AGR: Lloyd J. Fleck
  ATO: William Westman
  PAO: Guy Farmer
  IRS: Tom R. Edwards
  ODA: Col. William R. Mainord
    USAF
  MILGP: Col. Jose Muratti USAF
MARACAIBO (C), Edificio
Sofimara, Piso 3, Calle 77 Con
Avenida 13, or APO Miami 34037
Tel [58](61)84-253/4, 52-42-55,
84-054/5
Telex 62213 USCON VE
FAX [58](61)524255
  PO: Jim E. Wagner
  CON: Matthew Kaplan
  ADM: Robert A. Armstrong

WESTERN SAMOA

APIA (E), P.O. Box 3430
Tel (685)21631
Telex (779)275 AMEMB SX
  AMB: Everett E. Bierman (resident
    in Port Moresby)
  CHG: William P. Francisco III
  RSO: David R. Haag (resident in
    Canberra)

YEMEN ARAB REPUBLIC

SANAA (E), P.O. Box 1088
Tel [967](2)271950 through 58
Telex 2697 EMBSAN YE
Workweek: Saturday-Wednesday
Commercial Office Tel
[967](2)272417
USAID Tel [967](2)231213/4/5
  AMB: Charles F. Dunbar
  DCM: Georgia J. Debell
  POL: Bradford E. Hanson
  ECO/COM: Jeffrey J. Baron
  CON: Deborah L. Elliott

ATO: John A. Williams (resident in Jeddah)
ADM: Cornelius M. Keur
RSO: Patrick Moore
AID: Duncan MacInnes
ODA: Ltc. William A. Behrens USA
OMC: Col. Martin C. Frey USA
FBO: W. Lawson Young

YUGOSLAVIA

BELGRADE (E), Kneza Milosa 50
Tel [38](11)645-655
Telex 11529 AMEMBA YU
AMCONGEN (BEG) APO NY 09213
FAX [38](11)645-221
Workweek: Monday-Friday 7:30-4:15
Consular Section 7:30-3:30
AMB: Warren Zimmermann
DCM: Robert Rackmales
POL: Louis D. Sell
ECO: Patrick J. Nichols
COM: David K. Katz
CON: William E. Ryerson
ADM: John M. O'Keefe
RSO: David Tanner
SCI: Robert E. Day, Jr.
AGR: Steve Washenko
PAO: Bruce R. Koch
IRS: Frederick Pablo (resident in Rome)
ODA: Col. Richard L. Whisner USAF

ZAGREB (CG), Brace Kavurica 2
AMCONGEN (ZGB) APO NY 09213
Tel [38](41)444-800
Telex 21180 UY AMCON
FAX [38](41)440-235
CG: M. Michael Einik
POL/ECO/COM: Douglas C. Greene
CON: Lorraine W. Polik
ADM: Frank J. Finver
BPAO: Mark J. Smith

ZAIRE

KINSHASA (E), 310 Avenue des Aviateurs
APO NY 09662
Tel [243](12)25881 thru 6
Telex 21405 US EMB ZR
AMB: William C. Harrop
DCM: Marc A. Bass
POL: Gerald W. Scott
ECO/COM: Ralph E. Bresler
CON: Barbara Hemingway
ADM: Philip D. Gutensohn
RSO: Nanette Krieger
AGR: Richard J. Blabey (resident in Abidjan)
AID: Dennis Chandler
PAO: James J. Hogan
ODA: Ltc. Jerry R. Fry USA
MAAG: Col. Mansfield Latimer USA

LUBUMBASHI (CG), 1029 Blvd. Kamanyola
B.P. 1196
APO NY 09662-0006
Tel [243](011)222324
CG: James H. Yellin
POL: Philip A. Bauso
ECO/COM: Peter H. Barlerin
AID: Bruce Spake
CON: Kimberly A. Daley
ADM: J. Christopher Laycock
BPAO: (Vacant)

ZAMBIA

LUSAKA (E), corner of Independence and United Nation Aves.
P.O. Box 31617
Tel [2601]228-595/6/8, 228-601/2/3, 251-419, USIA 227-993/4, USAID 221-314, 229-327
Telex AMEMB AZ 41970
AMB: Jeffrey Davidow
DCM: Marshall F. McCallie
POL: Philip H. Egger
ECO/COM: Blaine D. Porter

CON: Paul D. Birdsall
LAB: Harry J. O'Hara (resident in Nairobi)
RSO: Kevin M. Barry
ADM: Stanton R. Bigelow
AGR: Susan R. Schayes (resident in Nairobi)
AID: Leslie A. Dean
PAO: Charles L. Bell

ZIMBABWE

HARARE (E), 172 Rhodes Ave., P.O. Box 3340
Tel [263](14)794-521
Commercial Section: 1st Fl., Century House West, 36 Baker Ave.
Tel [263](4)728-957
Telex 24591 USFCS ZW
  AMB: (Vacant)
  CHG: Edward F. Fugit
  POL: Gerard M. Gallucci
  POL/ECO: Paul B. Larsen
  CON: Sally M. Gober
  ADM: Alphonso G. Marquis
  RSO: John P. Gaddis
  LAB: Paul M. Almeida
  AGR: Roger F. Puterbaugh (resident in Pretoria)
  AID: Allison B. Herrick
  PAO: Samir M. Kouttab
  DAO: (Vacant)

Taiwan

Unofficial commercial and other relations with the people of Taiwan are maintained through a private instrumentality, the American Institute in Taiwan, which has offices in Taipei and Kaohsiung. The addresses of these offices are:
AMERICAN INSTITUTE IN TAIWAN (Taipei Office), 7 Lane 134, Hsin Yi Road, Section 3
Tel [886](2)709-2000
Telex 23890 USTRADE

AMERICAN INSTITUTE IN TAIWAN (Kaohsiung Office), 3d Fl., No. 2, Chung Cheng, 3d Rd.
Rel (07)251-2444/7
The Taipei office of the Insitute operates a trade center located at 600 Min Chuan East Road (Tel 713-2571).
For further information, contact the Washington office of the American Institute in Taiwan, 1700 N. Moore St. (17th Fl.), Arlington, VA 22209, (703) 525-8474.

Namibia

Namibia is not an independent country, but a UN trust territory under the administration of South Africa. The U.S. Liaison Office does not perform any commercial or consular services.
Windhoek (USLO), Auspian Building, 14 Lossen St.
P.O. Box 9890, Windhoek 9000, Namibia
Tel [264](61)229-791, 222-675, 222-680
FAX [264](61)229-792
  DIR: Roger A. McGuire
  DAO: Ltc. Doyle L. Raymer
  POL/ECO: Robin Renee Sanders
  PAO: Harvey I. Leifert
  ADM: (Vacant)

DEPARTMENT OF COMMERCE DISTRICT OFFICES

ALABAMA

Birmingham—Suite 302
Berry Bldg.
2015 2d Ave., North
35203
Tel (205) 731-1331

ALASKA
Anchorage—222 West 7th Ave.
P.O. Box 32
99513
Tel (907) 271-5041

ARIZONA
Phoenix—Federal Bldg.
Room 3412
230 N. First Ave.
85025
Tel (602) 261-3285

ARKANSAS
Little Rock—Suite 811
Savers Fed. Bldg.
320 W. Capitol Ave.
72201
Tel (501) 378-5794

CALIFORNIA
San Francisco—Fed Bldg.
Box 36013
450 Golden Gate Ave.
94102
Tel (415) 556-5860

Los Angeles—Rm. 800
11777 San Vicente Blvd.
90049
Tel (213) 209-6707

San Diego—6363 Greenwich Dr.
Suite 260
92122
Tel (619) 557-5395

Santa Ana—116 W. 4th St.
Suite 1
92701
Tel (714) 836-2461

San Jose—111 W. St. John St.
Rm. 424
95113
Tel (408) 291-7648

COLORADO
Denver—1625 Broadway
Suite 600
80202
Tel (303) 844-3246

CONNECTICUT
Hartford—Rm. 610-B
Fed. Off. Bldg.
450 Main St.
06103
Tel (203) 240-3530

FLORIDA
Miami—Suite 224
Fed. Bldg.
51 S.W. First Ave.
33130
Tel (305) 536-5267

Clearwater—128 N. Osceola Ave.
34615
Tel (813) 461-0011

Jacksonville—3100 University
Blvd.
South Suite 200A
32216
Tel (904) 791-2796

Orlando—111 North Orange Ave.
Suite 1439
32802
Tel (407) 648-1608

Tallahassee—Collins Bldg.
Rm. 401
107 W. Gaines St.
32304
Tel (904) 488-6469

GEORGIA
Atlanta—Suite 504
1365 Peachtree St., NE
30309
Tel (404) 347-7000

Savannah—120 Barnard St.
A-107
31401
Tel (912) 944-4204 ext. 204

HAWAII
Honolulu—4106 Fed. Bldg.
P.O. Box 50026
300 Ala Moana Blvd.
96850
Tel (808) 451-1782

IDAHO
Boise (Denver Dist.)—2d Floor
Hall of Mirrors
700 W. State St.
83720
Tel (208) 334-3857

ILLINOIS
Chicago—1406 Mid Continental
Plaza Bldg.
55 E. Monroe St.
60603
Tel (312) 353-4450

Palatine—Algonquin & Roselle
Rd.
60067
Tel (312) 397-3000, ext. 232

Rockford—515 N. Court St.
P.O. Box 1747
61110-0247
Tel (815) 987-8100

INDIANA
Indianapolis—One North Capitol
Suite 520
46204
Tel (317) 226-6214

IOWA
Des Moines—817 Fed. Bldg.
210 Walnut St.
50309
Tel (515) 284-4222

KANSAS
Wichita (Kansas City
Dist.)—River Park Pl.
Suite 580, 727 N. Waco
67203
Tel (316) 269-6160

KENTUCKY
Louisville—601 W. Broadway
Rm. 636B
U.S. Post Office and Court House
Bldg.
40202
Tel (502) 582-5066

LOUISIANA
New Orleans—432 World Trade
Center
No. 2 Canal St.
70130
Tel (504) 589-6546

MAINE
Augusta (Boston Dist.)—77
Sewall St.
04330
Tel (207) 622-8249

MARYLAND
Baltimore—415 U.S.
Customhouse
40 S. Gay St.
21202
Tel (301) 962-3560

Rockville—101 Monroe St.
15th Fl.
20850
Tel (301) 251-2345

MASSACHUSETTS
Boston—World Trade Center
Suite 307
Commonwealth Pier Area
02210
Tel (617) 565-8563

MICHIGAN
Detroit—1140 McNamara Bldg.
477 Michigan Ave
48226
Tel (313) 226-3650

Grand Rapids—300 Monroe NW
Rm. 409
49503
Tel (616) 456-2411

MINNESOTA
Minneapolis—108 Fed. Bldg.
110 S. 4th St.
55401
Tel (612) 348-1638

MISSISSIPPI
Jackson—Jackson Mall Office
Ctr.
Suite 328
300 Woodrow Wilson Blvd.
39213
Tel (601) 965-4388

MISSOURI
St. Louis—7911 Forsyth Blvd.
Suite 610
63105
Tel (314) 425-3302/4

Kansas City—Rm. 635
601 E. 12th St.
64106
Tel (816) 426-3141

NEBRASKA
Omaha—11133 "O" St.
68137
Tel (402) 221-3664

NEVADA
Reno—1755 E. Plumb Lane
Suite 152
89502
Tel (702) 784-5203

NEW JERSEY
Trenton—3131 Princeton Pike
Bldg. #6
Suite 100
08648
Tel (609) 989-2100

NEW MEXICO
Albuquerque—5000 Marble NE
Suite 320
87110
Tel (505) 262-6024

Santa Fe (Dallas, Texas
District)—c/o Economic Devel.
& Tourism Dept.
1100 St. Francis Dr.
87503

NEW YORK
Buffalo—1312 Fed. Bldg.
111 W. Huron St.
14202
Tel (716) 846-4191

Rochester—121 East Ave.
14604
Tel (716) 263-6480

New York—Rm. 3718
Fed. Off. Bldg.
26 Fed. Plaza
Foley Sq.
10278
Tel (212) 264-0634

NORTH CAROLINA
Greensboro—203 Fed. Bldg.
324 W. Market St.
P.O. Box 1950
27402
Tel (919) 333-5345

Raleigh—Dobbs Bldg.
Rm. 294
430 N. Salisbury St.
27611
Tel (919) 755-4687

OHIO
Cincinnati—9504 Fed. Off. Bldg.
550 Main St.
45202
Tel (513) 684-2944

Cleveland—Rm. 600
666 Euclid Ave.
44114
Tel (216) 522-4750

OKLAHOMA
Oklahoma City—6601 Broadway
Extension
73116
Tel (405) 231-5302

Tulsa—Rm. 505
440 S. Houston St.
74127
Tel (918) 581-7650

OREGON
Portland—Rm. 618
1220 SW. 3rd Ave.
97204
Tel (503) 221-3001

PENNSYLVANIA
Philadelphia—475 Allendale Rd.
Suite 202
King of Prussia
19406
Tel (215) 962-4980

Pittsburgh—2002 Fed. Bldg.
1000 Liberty Ave.
15222
Tel (412) 644-2850

PUERTO RICO
San Juan (Hato Rey)—Rm. G-55
Fed. Bldg.
00918
Tel (809) 766-5555

RHODE ISLAND
Providence (Boston Dist.)—7
Jackson Walkway
02903
Tel (401) 528-5104

SOUTH CAROLINA
Columbia—Strom Thurmond
Fed. Bldg.
Suite 172
1835 Assembly St.
29201
Tel (803) 765-5345

Charleston—JC Long Bldg.
Room 128
9 Liberty St.
29424
Tel (803) 724-4361

Greenville—P.O. Box 5823
Station B
29606
Tel (803) 235-5919

TENNESSEE
Nashville—Suite 1114
Parkway Towers
James Robertson Parkway
37219
Tel (615) 736-5161

Memphis—22 N. Front Str.
Falls Bldg.
Suite 200, 38103
Tel (901) 521-4137

TEXAS
Dallas—Rm. 7A5
1100 Commerce St.
75242-0787
Tel (214) 767-0542

Austin—P.O. Box 12728
Capitol Station
78711
Tel (512) 482-5939

Houston—2625 Fed. Courthouse
Bldg.
515 Rusk St.
77002
Tel (713) 229-2578

UTAH
Salt Lake City—U.S. Courthouse
Room 340
350 S. Main St.
84101
Tel (801) 524-5116

VIRGINIA
Richmond—8010 Fed. Bldg.
400 N. 8th St.
23240
Tel (804) 771-2246

WASHINGTON
Seattle—3131 Elliott Ave.
Suite 290
98121
Tel (206) 442-5616

Spokane—P.O. Box 2170
99210
Tel (509) 353-2922

WEST VIRGINIA
Charleston—3402 New Fed. Bldg.
500 Quarrier St. 25301
Tel (304) 347-5123

WISCONSIN
Milwaukee—Fed. Bldg.
U.S. Courthouse
Room 606
517 E. Wisconsin Ave.
53202
Tel (414) 291-3473

Eight Areas of Possible Temporary International Employment

Child/Elder Care and Domestic Work

Advertisements for these positions can be readily found in newspapers. Positions are often live-in, and wages tend to be relatively low. On the positive side, care givers often find themselves travelling to interesting places with the family. It's also common, over time, to build up an extended network of friends through the family. These contacts often lead to other job experiences.

Here are ten agencies that may be helpful in your efforts to locate a child/elder care position:

The Au Pair Company, 50 Avenue Rise, Bushey, Hertshire, England WD2 3AS, tel. 01-950-3125.

Childcare Agency, 40 Uppleby Road, Parkstone, Poole, Dorset, England BH12 3DE, tel. 0202 737171.

Euro-Pair Agency, 28 Derwent Ave., Pinner, Middlesex, England HA5 4QJ, tel. 01-421 2100.

London Au Pair & Nanny Agency, 23 Fitzjohn's Avenue, Hampstead, London, England NW3 5JY, tel. 01-435 3891

Interlingua Centre, Torquay Road, Foxrock, Dublin 18, Ireland, tel. 01-893876.

Okista, Turkenstrasse 4, 1090 Vienna IX, Austria, tel. 23 75 26.

Pro Filia, 14B Ave. du Mail, 1205 Geneva, Switzerland, tel 22 29 84 62.

Relaciones Culturales Internacionales, Calle Ferraz No. 82, Madrid, Spain 28008, tel. 479 64 46.

Relations Internationales, 20 rue de l'Exposition, 75007 Paris, France, tel. 45 50 23 23.

Universal Care, Chester House, 9 Windsor End, Beconsfield, Buckshire HP9 2JJ, tel. 04946 78811

Agriculture

Casual work in this area usually requires stamina and the nerve to approach a farmer in the field. Jobs frequently are not advertised at all. You simply present yourself at a harvest, planting, shearing, etc. If you look strong, you have a good chance of getting a day or two of trial work. If that goes well, you'll be taken on as a regular—often without a handshake or a contract of any kind. Agricultural workers frequently find themselves traveling from harvest to harvest. Earnings for an extended summer of hard work can be substantial.

Bulletin boards in pubs and rural markets are often good places to look for agricultural work.

Teaching English

In many countries, the most direct route to a better paying job is to learn English. The demand for English-speaking tutors is therefore high, and wages are often quite good. For bonafide positions within companies and established language schools, register with the TESOL Job Placement Service, 1118 22nd St. NW, Suite 205, Washington, D.C. 20037. For a subscription fee of $18 you will receive bi-monthly listing of English-teaching jobs around the world. A 1988 book, *Teaching Abroad*, is available from the Institute of International Education, 809 United Nations Plaza, New York, NY 10017. The cost at the time of publication was $22.

More casual positions as an English tutor can be found by watching ads in foreign newspapers or, just as good, placing an ad of your own. If you are willing to provide a bit of child care along with your tutoring, you may find yourself advantageously employed by a family. You will also want to check directly with private language schools, which will probably appraise you much more on the professionalism of your appearance and quality of your speaking than on academic preparation. Bring along a briefcase (that omnipresent symbol of capability) and a neatly typed resume. Especially in Asian countries, carry a business card that you can leave behind. Often your best employment contacts will come from call-backs.

Shops and Selling

Particularly in tourist areas, your ability to speak English and your bright, healthy appearance may land you a casual job in a shop or as an outside salesperson for a manufacturer or distributor. These jobs are found through newspaper ads and by approaching shopkeepers directly. It is not uncommon for these people to offer you a percentage of your total sales during the day. You may want to give yourself a week to see what sort of numbers you're able to achieve on such a commission basis. Your grooming and dress will be a major factor in a shopkeeper's or manufacturer's decision to let you represent his or her products.

Manual Labor

If you don't object to a ten-hour day of grueling and often dirty work, stand around a construction site until the boss takes your interest in work seriously or asks you to leave. Wages, when compared to domestic work or childcare, can be good. But expect to do hard time: wheeling loads of wet concrete up ramps, carrying heavy bricks and construction block to bricklayers, and digging trenches in rocky ground.

You'll often be paid cash for your labor at the end of each day. Be sure to get a reference letter before you leave the job. The letter will make it much easier to get your next manual labor job, and may place you a bit higher in the pecking order of workers.

Military Installations

Throughout the world, the United States maintains military bases that can be a nirvana for those seeking non-permit work. Military employment officers are often willing to bend the rules a bit to accommodate an earnest (and hungry) face from home. It's necessary, however, to obtain a visitor's pass to get past the gate guard. Ask by phone or in person how to get the pass, then present yourself and your story to the officer in charge of casual labor. Be flexible in what you're willing to do. Typical military base jobs include cleaning, kitchen work, gardening, and language tutoring.

Yachts, Cruise Lines, Fishing Boats, and Commercial Shipping

If you have your sea legs (or want them), check harbor areas for opportunities at sea. You may find yourself swabbing decks, preparing meals, cleaning staterooms, baiting hooks, or performing more prestigeous duties. If you have entertainment skills, be sure to mention them and be prepared to demonstrate them. Cruise lines are often looking for night-time dancers and singers who are also willing to do manual work by day.

Resort Work

This broad category includes opportunities for ski instructors, divers, exercise leaders, maintenance workers, security guards, ticket-takers, food servers, and many others. The key to finding such employment seems to hinge on getting past the written job application. You have to meet the person doing the hiring face to face. You then have a minute or two to make your best case. If you can impress him or her with your enthusiasm and presentability, you'll probably get the job. Experience (of almost any kind) can be very helpful in your application. If possible, carry letters of reference with you from previous work experiences.

Useful Books for the International Job Search

Asian Markets: A Guide to Company and Industry Information. Washington Researchers Publishing, 1988.

Careers in International Affiars. Sheehan, G., Georgetown University School of Foreign Service, 1989.

The Career Guide, 1989: Dun's Employment Opportunities Directory. Dun & Bradstreet, 1989.

Directory of American Firms Operating in Foreign Countries. World Trade Academy Press, 1987.

Directory of Executive Recruiters. Kennedy and Kennedy, Inc., 1988.

Directory of Foreign Manufacturers in the United States. Georgia State University College of Business Administration, 1979.

Directory of Jobs and Careers Abroad. Vacation Work Publications, 1989.

Directory of Opportunities in International Law. Stanback, W.A., University of Virginia School of Law, 1988.

Directory of Overseas Summer Jobs. Woodworth, D. Writers Digest, 1988.

The Directory of Work Study in Developing Countries. Leppard, D. Vacation Work Publications, 1987.

Directory of U.S. Based Agencies Involved in International Health Assistance. National Council for International Health, Washington, D.C., 1987.

The Global Market Place. Moskowitz, M. Macmillan, 1987.

International Business Travel and Relocation Directory, 5th ed. Gale Research Co., Detroit, MI, 1988.

The International Business Woman. Rossman, M.L. Greenwood Press, 1986.

The International Consultant. Guttman, P. Cantrell Corporation, 1987.

International Directory of Corporate Affiliations. National Register Publishing Company, 1984.

International Employment Hotline. Cantrell, W. (editor), P.O. Box 3030, Oakton, VA 22124.

International Jobs Bulletin. University Placement Center, Southern Illinois University, Carbondale, Illinois.

The National Ad Search. Box 2083, Milwaukee, Wisconsin.

The National Job Bank 1990. Bob Adams, Inc., 1990.

Major Companies of Europe, 1989. Whiteside, R.M. (ed.). Graham & Trotman, 1989.

O'Dwyer's Directory of Public Relations. J.R. O'Dwyer Co., Inc., 1989.

"Overseas Business Reports." (monthly) U.S. Department of Commerce, Washington, D.C.

Peterson's Guide to Engineering, Science, and Computer Jobs. Peterson's Guides, 1989.

Peterson's Guide to Business and Management Jobs. Peterson's Guides, 1989.

Principal International Businesses, 1990. Dun's Marketing Services, Inc., 1990.

Study and Teaching Opportunities Abroad. McIntyre, P. U.S. Government Printing Office, 1983.

Teach Overseas: The Educator's World-Wide Handbook and Directory to International Teaching Overseas. Maple Tree Publishing Company, 1984.

Ulrich's International Periodicals Directory. Bowker Press, 1989.

Who Owns Whom, 1989. Dun & Bradstreet Ltd., 1989.

The World Directory of Multinational Enterprises. Stopford, J. (ed.). Gale Research Inc., 1983.

Worldwide Chamber of Commerce Directory. Johnson Publishing Company, Inc., 1989.